D0447421

If These WALLS *Could* TALK:

OAKLAND A's

Stories from the
Oakland A's Dugout,
Locker Room, and Press Box

Ken Korach and Susan Slusser

TRIUMPH
B O O K S

Copyright © 2019 by Ken Korach and Susan Slusser

No part of this publication may be reproduced, stored in a retrieval system, or transmitted in any form by any means, electronic, mechanical, photocopying, or otherwise, without the prior written permission of the publisher, Triumph Books LLC, 814 North Franklin Street, Chicago, Illinois 60610.

Library of Congress Cataloging-in-Publication Data

Names: Korach, Ken, author. | Slusser, Susan, author.
Title: Oakland A's : stories from the Oakland A's dugout, locker room, and
   press box / Ken Korach and Susan Slusser.
Description: Chicago, Illinois : Triumph Books LLC, [2018] | Series: If these
   walls could talk
Identifiers: LCCN 2018043423 | ISBN 9781629375809 (paperback)
Subjects: LCSH: Oakland Athletics (Baseball team)—History—Anecdotes. |
   BISAC: SPORTS & RECREATION / Baseball / General. | TRAVEL /
United States / West / Pacific (AK, CA, HI, NV, OR, WA).
Classification: LCC GV875.O24 K67 2018 | DDC 796.357/640979466—dc23
LC record available at https://lccn.loc.gov/2018043423

This book is available in quantity at special discounts for your group or organization. For further information, contact:
   Triumph Books LLC
   814 North Franklin Street
   Chicago, Illinois 60610
   (312) 337–0747
   www.triumphbooks.com

Printed in U.S.A.

ISBN: 978-1-62937-580-9

Design by Amy Carter

Page production by Patricia Frey

*In memory of Frances Korach
and Richard Slusser*

CONTENTS

FOREWORD *by Dennis Eckersley* vii

CHAPTER 1: Ken Korach: "It's Great to Have You with Us" 1

CHAPTER 2: Rickey Henderson: Leadoff (Super)Man. 29

CHAPTER 3: Ken Korach: A Mother's Legacy 41

CHAPTER 4: Susan Slusser: Brought Up with Baseball 57

CHAPTER 5: Dave Kaval: Relentless Ingenuity 67

CHAPTER 6: Ken Korach: So You Want to Be a Broadcaster? 81

CHAPTER 7: David Forst: From Harvard to Hatteberg 103

CHAPTER 8: Susan Slusser: So You Want to Be a Beat Writer? . . . 117

CHAPTER 9: Bob Melvin: Calm, Cool and Collaborative. 133

CHAPTER 10: Cooperstown: Kings and Angells 145

CHAPTER 11: Mickey Morabito: Steinbrenner, Martin
and the A's Real MVP 169

CHAPTER 12: Moneyball: "It's Incredibly Hard". 181

CHAPTER 13: Clay Wood: Groundskeeper's Field of Dreams 195

CHAPTER 14: The Best Games We Ever Saw 207

CHAPTER 15: Keith Lieppman: The Man Behind
the Future Stars 247

CHAPTER 16: Susan Slusser: All the President's Scribes 261

CHAPTER 17: Jonas Rivera: The A's Most Animated Fan 273

CHAPTER 18: Ken Korach: Broadcast Tidbits 283

CHAPTER 19: Allan Pont: The Doctor in the House 291

CHAPTER 20: Baseball Travel: Going, Going, (Always) Gone 301

CHAPTER 21: Steve Vucinich: Half a Century of Inside Dirt 313

CHAPTER 22: An Improbable 2018 321

ACKNOWLEDGMENTS 335

FOREWORD

The focus of this book is the work that the people in and around the A's franchise do, from the front office to the support staff to the media and fans.

That makes Dennis Eckersley—who grew up in Fremont and became the greatest closer of his day—the ideal Oakland great to provide the foreword. He practically invented a job when Tony La Russa began using him only in one-inning save situations—the birth of the modern closer. He's also been a starter, broadcaster, and inventor of the phrase "walk-off." When it comes to working for the A's, the Hall of Famer is the gold standard.

Looking back, the Oakland A's sort of saved my life.

Coming from the Cubs, my time was sort of done there after the 1986 season. I didn't know what my future was, but when Chicago traded me to Oakland, I was like, "Man, this is great, to go back home."

Those nine years were the greatest times in my life, something I will absolutely never forget, and I had no idea that it was coming. Isn't that weird?

Becoming a closer wasn't my plan. It was simply meant to be. Some of the best things in my life have not been planned—such as finding the right job, in the right place.

I sort of walked into it. I was never geared up to do something like closing, although it fit me, it really did. It fit how I went about the game emotionally… demonstratively. That's the perfect job for someone like me. Physically, you have to be in the right place, too. I wasn't physically there, in my thirties, to go more than a couple innings anyway.

To put an exclamation mark on all those great moments during that A's era, I feel fortunate. It could have been somebody else, it just happened to be me.

I don't know if I could have handled closing when I was 20, 21, when I first broke in. I might have been too fired up. I had such better command when I was 32. I was a new-age type of closer too, not a blow-you-away-type closer.

It was a new age because of Tony La Russa and the timing of it all. I don't know if it was the beginning of the ninth-inning closer role as we know it today, but it sure was damn-well close.

The "Moneyball" analytics were just kicking in, that gets overlooked. A lot of that stuff was Sandy Alderson. Little did I know at first what Sandy was—I thought he was just a brainiac—but Sandy was the whole package. I knew there was something special going on above the field. Like a lot of people with that team, Sandy was the right guy for the job at the right time.

When it came to closing, I got to be so superstitious. I used to do this little jog: I'd run over to 66th Avenue and down close to the airport and come back. Then I had a turkey sandwich from the Hofbrau—mustard, lettuce, tomato, no cheese—same sandwich all the time. That was the typical routine. Everything worked out so well that the more the saves piled up, the more stuff I added. I'd wear the same T-shirt every day. It gets crazy after a while. Obviously, you don't touch the rosin bag. You don't touch the lines. I don't want to seem like one of those flaky pitchers because I wasn't. I was just superstitious.

One of the duties that comes along with the job is talking to the media. Writers often bring up the long interview session I did right after the Kirk Gibson homer in the 1988 World Series, but for me, it was like therapy: "I'm going to get through this and take it." I didn't like it, but it's important to turn the page, even though it isn't easy.

That was a skinny little clubhouse at Dodger Stadium and everyone was pissed off because we'd just lost, guys are trying to shower, and reporters just kept coming and coming. I just sucked it up. I was so disturbed, but I knew it was the right thing to do. I'm proud of it. It was one of my worst moments but one of my proudest. I felt that responsibility.

I took tough losses to heart a lot. Tony was good about helping with that. We were at Cleveland once when Jerry Browne hit a two-run game-winner off me on the getaway night. We get to Baltimore at 3:00 AM and I'm grinding. I get my room key—and there's a note with my key. I get back to my room, thinking, "What the hell is this note?" Tony put it there. It said, "Eck, you're the best." That meant everything to me. That's leadership. It's important to have somebody there for you—with a teammate, it's one thing, but the manager of all people!

It makes me want to send people notes. I think that's so classy. I knew he meant it.

Those Oakland teams were so fun to see come together. Everybody had a part in it. The front office knew what the hell they were doing. Dave Stewart, out of nowhere, became a major piece. Jose Canseco and Mark McGwire were turning into stars, then they added Dave Henderson, Walt Weiss got called up, and Carney Lansford's the captain—an angry captain, but the captain. We used to call him "the Angry Man." He was always mad. He played mad.

That pitching staff came together because of Dave Duncan and the front office's strategy. Great starting pitching is the key to all great clubs, and grabbing Bob Welch and Mike Moore, what great moves those were.

We had that home flavor, a lot of guys from Oakland—me and Rickey and Stew. I took so much pride in that. We were bad, man. When we went on the road, we were strutting. Some guys got carried away, but I didn't care.

We were a force, we just should have won more. I took pride playing for the Indians, Red Sox, and Cubs, but it was nothing like the A's. It meant more because I'm from there, and it came at a time in my life when I really could appreciate it. There's nothing like playing on a superstar team in your hometown.

There was a comfort to it. It's like you know the fans. My mom and dad would sit in the stands. How great is that? I would nod at my mom. I feel very fortunate to have had that happen in my life. They didn't miss a game. They were there every night.

I don't know if the crowds were different then. All I know is that the A's were hot in the '70s and nobody really came out. We had it going on for like five years when it came to packing the Coliseum. We had it all covered.

Maybe this is wishful thinking, but the A's have been through so much since then and they've kept themselves on the map throughout. They made runs in 2012 and 2018 when nobody thought they could. Wishful thinking tells me that they're going to get a stadium, and five years from now we're going to be saying, "Isn't this great?"

I want to be there when that happens.

—Dennis Eckersley

CHAPTER 1

KEN KORACH: "IT'S GREAT TO HAVE YOU WITH US"

I can't pinpoint the exact date I began thinking about a career in broadcasting, but I imagine it was around the time the Dodgers moved to Los Angeles and I first heard Vin Scully's voice on the radio.

It was 1958 and the move west proved to be the perfect marriage of baseball, broadcasting, and the new team in town. L.A. didn't have a baseball stadium ready yet, so the Dodgers spent their first four years in the cavernous Memorial Coliseum, where a diamond was fit awkwardly into a football configuration. It seemed like the field was a mile away from the seats, but because so many people brought transistor radios, following the game was easy. It was like a giant speaker system was placed all over the stadium.

It was Vinny who introduced Major League Baseball to a wildly growing population. L.A.'s history with pro baseball went back over a half-century to the early days of the Pacific Coast League. Teams like the Hollywood Stars and L.A. Angels featured players who would go on to become all-time greats and when visiting teams came to town fans got a look at young guys named Williams and DiMaggio.

But this was different. The Dodgers were the first MLB team in town, and Vinny's broadcasts introduced teams and players to a city that had only been exposed to the big leagues from a distance.

It's impossible to overstate the ubiquity of Vinny's voice. People listened in their living rooms, back yards, and at work. And because the Giants were the only other team west of the Central time zone, Vinny's voice during night games from the Midwest and East accompanied another growing reality of life in L.A.—rush-hour traffic. In 1964, Robert Creamer wrote a wonderful profile of Vinny in *Sports Illustrated*:

> "Everybody" probably is not a mathematically precise description of the number of people who listen to Scully's broadcasts, but it is close enough. When a game is on the air, the physical presence of his voice is overwhelming. His pleasantly nasal baritone comes out of radios on the back counters of orange juice stands, from transistors held by people sitting

under trees, in barber shops and bars, and from cars everywhere—parked cars, cars waiting for red lights to turn green, cars passing you at 65 on the freeways, cars edging along next to you in rush-hour traffic jams.

The fact the Dodgers only televised nine games each year abetted my growing fandom. If you wanted to follow the team, Vin's voice was the conduit. In a close game, he had you transfixed. Radio has a way of fueling the imagination, and Vin's colorful descriptions conjured all sorts of images for his audience.

I listened to every word of Sandy Koufax's perfect game against the Cubs in 1965. In the ninth inning, Scully said: "There's 29,000 people in the ballpark and a million butterflies." Even today, I imagine dozens of butterflies churning inside an anxious stomach.

The Lakers moved to L.A. in 1960, and so you had Chick Hearn to fill the fall and winter nights, and if I turned the radio just right at night, I could listen to the captivating broadcasts of a devilish-looking guy from San Francisco named Bill King.

My dad coached baseball and basketball in high school and junior college, so my exposure to sports probably came before I could walk. We spent every weekend going to games. It didn't matter the sport—football, basketball, baseball, track meets—we went to everything.

My sports claim to fame came somewhat vicariously. As seniors at Palisades High, we got on a roll and reached the L.A. City basketball tournament. After winning easily in our first game, we matched up against Jefferson High in the quarterfinals. Jefferson was led by Glenn McDonald, who became a first-round pick of the Celtics out of Long Beach State in 1974. We beat them to advance to the semifinals at Pauley Pavilion, where we beat Reseda High—which featured two players who had already committed to UCLA, Gary Franklin and Greg Lee, who was that year's City Player of the Year. (Lee was the point guard when Bill Walton went 21 of 22 from the floor against Memphis in the NCAA championship game in 1973.) We then lost in the finals to Jordan High.

3

The local NBC affiliate televised the game and there were 8,000 fans in attendance, including my parents, but I was fastened to my usual spot on the bench.

I was the sports editor of our school newspaper, then majored in journalism at San Diego State. When my good friend Steve Karman became editor in chief of the *Daily Aztec*, he asked me to be his sports editor. This was 1972, halcyon days for the Don Coryell–coached Aztec football team. The '72 team, led by Bengals' first-round pick Isaac Curtis, went 10–1.

I transferred to UC Santa Barbara for my last two years and my major was an amalgamation of political science, anthropology, and sociology. Not exactly practical for a career in broadcasting, but a great education nonetheless.

* * *

My first job out of college was at a clothing store near the UCSB campus. One evening, a woman named Jackie Linden came in with her two kids. I left work two hours later wondering what I had gotten myself into.

Jackie ran Santa Barbara Group Homes, a treatment facility for delinquent kids who had been placed in her care by the authorities in Southern California. She had 24 kids living in four homes, with two adults serving as surrogate parents in each home. That night at the store, she asked me if I wanted to be part of a cross-country trip she was planning with the kids. It was a wild idea, but there was nothing in the world that deterred Jackie once she made up her mind, no matter the obstacles.

We took off from Santa Barbara with two dozen kids and five adults in three vans. I have no idea how she got approval from the state agencies, but she did. We covered 33 states and two Canadian provinces with a budget that would make a shoestring seem like a fortune. Three or four kids had issues during the trip and had to be sent home, and two of the adults left halfway through because of fatigue and stress.

To save what little money we had, we spent most of the nights camping at national forest campgrounds because they were free. If we were in an urban area, Jackie called youth organizations to see if she could find a place to stay.

We had a brush with fame in New York. Jackie had a hard time finding accommodations and the only place that would take us was a youth center in Spanish Harlem. That's where we stayed for a night, and we had a great time, but while we were there, word somehow got out that this large group of kids from California was hanging out in Harlem, and the local NBC affiliate sent a crew out to interview us. The legendary Tom Snyder was anchoring the local news and after the piece ran, the phone started ringing and Jackie could have had her choice of several five-star hotels if she had chosen to extend our stay.

After we limped home, I stayed on at SBGH and wound up as assistant director. It was fulfilling but taxing work; I was on call 24 hours a day. But it never felt like a career, and it wasn't long after we returned from the trip that I began thinking it was time to get serious about radio. There was one problem. I had no experience, at least nothing documented on tape.

* * *

My old friends will tell you that I was broadcasting games when I was 10 years old, because I did play-by-play out loud as we were playing pick-up basketball games on the blacktop after school. I was quieter when I went to games with my parents because I called the games in my mind.

My mom was instrumental at home. We set up a card table in my bedroom with a microphone, a recorder, and a scorebook, and I would turn the sound down on the TV and call the games.

I did four or five baseball games for the campus station at San Diego State, but that was the extent of anything that resembled a formal broadcast.

In need of an audition tape, I set out on a tour of California with my cassette recorder. This was in the late '70s, when the Oakland Coliseum was dubbed the Mausoleum at the end of the Finley era and I had whole sections to myself. That's where the baseball segment of my audition tape came from. I'd buy a ticket and sit in a lonely spot down the left-field line where no one would bother me. I learned years later that Giants' voice Jon Miller had done the same thing when he was in high school. Jon's spot was down the right-field line.

I recorded a basketball game at the Sports Arena in L.A. between USC and Utah, but getting a football tape was more of a challenge. I went to Candlestick Park for a 49ers game and sat in the upper deck, but there was a good crowd and I'm sure people around me were thinking, "What in the world is going on here?"

I completed my tape by reading news stories into a cassette player out of the local paper. The news accounts went at the end of the tape, after segments of play-by-play that lasted about five to 10 minutes for the three sports.

I got a huge break when my friend Kelly Wolfe became the head professional at Bennett Valley Golf Club in Santa Rosa, California. Kelly hired me as his first assistant, although I need to make one thing clear: I've always been a pretty good player, but I was never a pro.

Starting a radio career in a big city was going to be next to impossible, so living and working in Sonoma County was the perfect place to be. I sent my tape to several local stations, and to my surprise, I got a response almost immediately from KTOB Radio in Petaluma.

The station's program director, a talented announcer named Bob Nathan, called to say he had no openings in sports, but there was an opportunity on Saturday mornings to play records from 6:00 to 10:00 AM. The pay was $3.35 an hour. It wasn't what I wanted to do, but it was a chance to get started, although I told Bob I had some trepidation because I had no idea how to cue up a record. His response: "We have a very understanding audience."

Sadly, small stations like KTOB have become dinosaurs, but working there was the greatest broadcasting education imaginable. Bob Lipman, KTOB's owner, believed in community involvement, and the station's programming reflected that philosophy. KTOB broadcast city council meetings live, produced comprehensive election coverage and local news shows, allocated two hours each morning for a talk show that focused on current events, and carried as many as a dozen sporting events each week featuring local high schools.

KTOB had a decent daytime signal—1,000 watts—but the power shrunk down to 250 watts at night, so our voices weren't exactly booming all over Northern California. They had two broadcasters, Ron Walters and Kevin Rafferty, who were doing play-by-play when I joined the station. Walters hosted the morning show and was, in many ways, the Bill King of Petaluma because of his myriad interests and talents. He invited me to join him for a football broadcast in the fall of 1980 involving the small Catholic school in town, St. Vincent High. At halftime, Ron asked me if I wanted to do the second half—and that's how I made my professional play-by-play debut.

* * *

It wasn't long before I joined the regular rotation. The station focused on four local schools—Petaluma High, Casa Grande High, St. Vincent, and Rancho Cotate High, which was up the road in Rohnert Park.

My arrival at KTOB coincided with the Angels moving their California League affiliate to Rohnert Park and in 1981, Rafferty worked out a deal for the station to carry 50 games—25 home and 25 road. Kevin traveled for the road broadcasts and he asked if I would like to work with him when the team was home.

It was at about the same time that Bob Nathan offered me a full-time job and I haven't worked in any other profession since. My assignment was to host the 10:00 AM to 2:00 PM slot, co-host the noon news, and then record commercials in the afternoon.

My air shift was a potpourri. I played records and interviewed guests and we took phone calls. The show started with a segment called "Swap Shop," which was kind of a classified ads of the airwaves. Folks could call in and try to sell an old washing machine for $10 or something like that. I interviewed everyone from Barbara Boxer when she ran successfully for the first time for Congress to the lightweight boxing champion Sean O'Grady.

On the diamond, 1981 turned out to be a strike year in the big leagues and a large chunk of the middle of the season was lost. The games continued in the minors and, looking to fill a void, the Angels and Padres invited their California League teams to spend the 4th of July weekend in Southern California. The Pioneers played the Reno Padres at Anaheim Stadium on July 3, then the teams drove down to San Diego for a game the next day.

It was kind of incongruous because we lived so much closer to Dodger Stadium and Scully was the voice of my childhood, but my dad and I became bigger fans of the expansion Angels. Maybe it was an underdog thing or because my dad was never a big fan of Dodgers owner Walter O'Malley, but I was more emotionally invested in the Angels even though we rarely went to games in Anaheim. I had listened to hundreds of games from the Big A and I got a taste of the big leagues when we worked the July 3 game in the Angels' home radio booth.

The Pioneers' pitcher that night was a right-hander named Ron Romanick. Ron went on to start 82 games in his career for the Angels, and 27 years after that Friday night in Anaheim, he joined the A's major league staff as bullpen coach and was elevated to pitching coach in 2011. He allowed three hits in seven innings, but the Padres won the game 2–1.

Ron was the first of several players whose games I broadcast in the minors who later became coaches for the A's. Matt Williams and Mike Aldrete, who are currently part of Bob Melvin's staff, played in Phoenix when I did games there in the mid-'80s. It's fun to reminisce about those early days and how we're still chasing baseball dreams after all these years.

The game in San Diego was a festival. The Padres sold tickets for a dollar, gave away free slices of watermelon in the parking lot, and the lure of postgame fireworks helped draw a crowd of more than 37,000 to Jack Murphy Stadium. The Pioneers earned a split of the two games with a 2–0 win.

The game was a homecoming for the Pioneers' manager, the late Chris Cannizzaro. Chris, who was an original Met, was also an original Padre, and was their first All-Star in 1969.

I had been told that if two players off a Cal League roster made the big leagues, it was better than the average. So for 90 percent of the players on those clubs, that weekend would be their only time playing in a big-league ballpark. It was the same for me. I had no idea if I'd ever work in a major-league press box again.

Life in the minors can be just as uncertain for broadcasters as it is for players, and the Pioneers failed to land a radio deal in '82 and '83. But at least I had my full-time gig at the station.

* * *

I was doing as many three high school games a week. During baseball season, we took a cassette recorder to the high school fields, sat in the bleachers and recorded the games for playback that evening. The challenge was making sure the tape didn't run out in the middle of an inning, especially if something dramatic happened. So if an inning was running long and there was a short break in the action, we'd say, "Now time for this tape-change time out."

ABC television put Petaluma on the map in those days because of the World Wrist Wrestling Championships, which were contested every year at the Veterans Hall downtown and featured on *Wide World of Sports*. We carried the thing live on the radio! I've done a lot of things in my career, but I'm not sure anything prepared me for doing wrist wrestling. "Their hands are locked at the start and it's a stalemate…now, Smith has the advantage, but Jones is hanging on for dear life…now Smith forces

Jones' arm down toward the table…he pins the back of his hand to the table and Smith advances to the next round!"

I came full circle in a way when Ralph Barkey guested on the show in 1982. Ralph was the basketball coach at UCSB when I was a student and he was as sharp as any coach around. Now he had just taken the job as the athletic director at Sonoma State University, which was resurrecting its sports programs at the Division III level. Ralph and I worked out a deal to broadcast the football and basketball games. I sold the advertising and bought air time from Bob Lipman on KTOB. I named my little enterprise Vintage Sports Productions. Ralph even did some color on the home basketball games, and he was as good as anyone. I grew up with a dad who was a great coach and I attended John Wooden's camps when I was a kid, but I learned more basketball from Ralph than anyone.

I spent three years doing Sonoma State's games. Coached by Dick Walker, they reached the NCAA D-III regionals in basketball in 1983, before they moved to D-II the next year.

* * *

I got back into pro baseball in 1984, when a Southern California businessman named Michael Watkins bought the Pioneers. One of his first moves was to upgrade the front office and search for a radio deal. It was a coup for the Pioneers to get KSRO, the big station in Santa Rosa, to carry the games. I used the July 3 game in Anaheim in 1981 as my audition tape and got the job.

Life with the '84 Pioneers was a thrill a minute. The Cal League season was 140 games in 150 days, but their play was like an injection of energy every night.

The Pioneers went 53–17 in the second half and 91–48 for the season. Jose Canseco hit a massive homer for the Modesto A's that sealed their fate in the playoffs, but their legacy was secured when six members of the team—Mark McLemore, Devon White, Jack Howell, Bob Kipper, Carl Nichols, and T.R. Bryden—made it to the majors. We had a backup third baseman named Mike Rizzo, who's had a nice run as general manager of the Washington Nationals. Left-hander Bryan Price joined the team mid-season, and he became Melvin's pitching coach in Seattle and Arizona and managed the Reds. McLemore, one of my favorite people in the game, played his last major-league game for the A's in 2004.

The manager, Tom Kotchman, spent part of his career scouting for the Angels and his son, Casey, turned out to be a solid big-league first baseman. The '84 season was pretty much the last hurrah for the Pioneers. By 1986, the franchise moved to Palm Springs and Rohnert Park Stadium is now an undeveloped tract of land with a Costco behind it.

* * *

My time doing Sonoma State's games ended in 1985 when KCBS in San Francisco acquired the rights to Stanford football. Trying to make inroads in the burgeoning Silicon Valley market, KCBS was also the home of San Jose State football. Now, they had two D-I schools in their stable.

Ted Robinson moved from doing San Jose State's games to Stanford, which opened a spot on the SJSU broadcasts. A mutual friend had told Ted about me, which helped, because there are few things as deflating as the realization that you're nothing more than one of about 100 anonymous tapes sitting on a program director's desk. Barkey, always in my corner when I worked at Sonoma State, called KCBS program director Charlie Seraphin with a recommendation that Charlie said helped separate me from the other candidates.

I was paired with ex-SJSU player Dave Ellis. I've always felt Dave was one of the most underrated analysts in the Bay Area. As a former quarterback, he could see things on the football field I could never see, and he had the anticipation of a football savant. Plus, his glibness transferred perfectly to the airwaves.

11

Lynn Eilefson, the SJSU athletics director, worked out an arrangement with a San Jose station to carry basketball, and I moved to an apartment near the Stanford campus to be about halfway between San Jose and San Francisco, since KCBS was using me to fill in on their morning and afternoon newscasts.

KCBS was owned and operated by CBS. My parents were loyal to Walter Cronkite, which meant we rarely missed the *CBS Evening News*.

I remember the first time I walked into the KCBS studios on the 32nd floor of One Embarcadero Center in San Francisco. Photos of the CBS giants dotted the walls. I had grown up with Cronkite, Rather, Collingwood, Edwards, and Sevareid, and I had the feeling that those legends were looking down on me and whispering, "Kid, we've got pretty high standards over here."

My time with San Jose State was characterized by extreme highs and lows. On the gridiron, the Spartans went to three bowl games in my first six years and wound up ranked in the top 20 in 1990. Fresno State was their archrival and, with two fiery coaches on the sidelines, Claude Gilbert and Jim Sweeney, the Spartans and Bulldogs staged an epic battle in 1986 that was later named the college football game of the year by *Sports Illustrated*. The Spartans came back late to score two touchdowns after trailing 41–31 with 1:15 left to pull out a 45–41 win.

Ellis' words rang out in the aftermath of the game-winning touchdown pass from Mike Perez to Lafo Malauulu in the far corner of the south end zone at Spartan Stadium: "Mike Perez, Mike Perez, in the grasp of a Bulldog!"

* * *

Fortunes were far different on the hardwood. The most bizarre and troubling event of my career took place early in the 1989 season, when 10 players walked out on coach Bill Berry.

Berry was tough guy. He was rigid, and his style took being in your face to the extreme. An Associated Press story mentioned "verbal abuse and mental cruelty." The players played like they were on pins and needles because they were often pulled from a game over the slightest miscue. I was filling in my scorebook before one of my first games in 1985 and approached Berry to ask if he had a starting lineup. He said, "I do." Then he turned and walked away. That was life with Bill Berry.

Even though I empathized with where the players were coming from, there was no way I could condone the walkout. (When Berry was fired after the season, athletic director Randy Hoffman made it clear that the players who left wouldn't be allowed back on the team.)

Berry was undeterred. Recruiting players from intramural leagues and the football team, he put together a new team in two days. There was a 6'9" kid named Craig McPherson who was going to school and had had no intention of continuing his basketball career after transferring from Santa Clara. But he joined the team, and he might have been the best player on both versions of the Spartans that year.

We had a conference game at Fullerton three days after the walkout. Berry forged ahead, refused to talk about the old players, and focused on coaching his team, and although they didn't win a game, they competed. I remember Johnny Johnson, the gifted running back and future Pro Bowler with the Phoenix Cardinals, going toe-to toe with UNLVs' Stacey Augmon and holding his own.

The Spartans II came close to winning, even taking Fullerton into overtime in the return engagement in San Jose, but finished 0–12 after the walkout.

Those losses were tough, but nothing compared to what Berry endured later that year when his son Ricky committed suicide in Sacramento. I always said that Ricky Berry and J.R. Rider, who played at UNLV in the early '90s, were the two most talented players whose games I broadcast. Ricky played for his dad and was drafted in the first round by the Kings in 1988.

Berry was let go after the '89 season and replaced by onetime Cal player and former UOP and USC coach Stan Morrison. Stan was one in a long line of class acts I've been fortunate to work with. His buoyancy, even with an underdog team starting from scratch, set a great example of how to stay positive in the face of adversity.

* * *

I was in the right place at the right time before the 1986 baseball season. The Pioneers lost their radio deal with KSRO after the '84 season and I didn't do minor-league ball in '85. That off-season, I sent tapes and résumés to the teams in the Pacific Coast League. I had no expectations, but things were changing in Phoenix, where Martin Stone had taken over as owner of the Phoenix Giants. He changed the name to the Firebirds and had designs on being positioned if Major League Baseball expanded to the Valley of the Sun.

Part of his plan was to have a big-league style broadcast. That meant two broadcasters for every game, which was rare in the minors. They had MLB broadcast veteran Kent Derdivanis on board and I got the number two job after interviewing with the team's general manager, Jack Singer, at the winter meetings in San Diego.

Kent and I had a great time for two years. Kent had already worked for the Red Sox and Brewers and had done college football and basketball for Arizona and UCLA. He had a lot of talent and far more experience than I did. And he was a pro in every way.

During one of our first road trips, I got off the team bus and was heading to my room when I was stopped in my tracks by the Firebirds' manager, Jim Lefebvre. Jimmy said, "You don't go to your room after a game. This is what we do: We have a couple of beverages and we talk baseball." What an education that was! I learned a ton of baseball from Jimmy, and his stories of his time with the Dodgers were like a trip down memory lane.

He was the second baseman on the Dodgers' all switch-hitting infield of the 1960s. In Vinny voice: "Parker, Lefebvre, Willlllls, and Gilliam."

I've never been around anyone with Lefebvre's energy. Travel in the PCL can leave you dead tired. It wasn't atypical to have a 4:00 AM wake-up call in Tucson, fly to Salt Lake, change planes, fly to Calgary, bus to Edmonton, and go right to the park for a game. But someone as tireless as Lefebvre wouldn't abide any complaining, and it was almost by osmosis that I learned to push the fatigue aside and grind out a broadcast.

It cooks, of course, in Phoenix in the summertime. One night we played a game even though it was too hot for the planes to take off at Sky Harbor Airport, about 116 degrees.

The broadcast booths were terrible. Really, they weren't booths at all—they were two concrete bunkers that sat right above the last row of stands. It was like working in a brick oven or sauna.

Kent and I had an idea for the '87 season. We arranged with a carpenter friend of Kent's to build a platform above the bunkers. The platform was just below the cantilevered roof at Phoenix Municipal Stadium, so there was air circulation from behind. We each chipped in $100 (though we never got a permit from the city of Phoenix) and the carpenter built a wooden ladder to access the platform. We dubbed our new digs "The Catbird Seat," an homage to Red Barber and his booth at Ebbets Field in Brooklyn.

The Catbird Seat was still standing when I joined the A's in 1996 for spring training at Phoenix Muni. Ray Fosse and I deferred to Bill King when it came to where we set up for a broadcast. If it was too windy—and Bill despised the wind—he would opt for the bunkers. If it was a nice day, it was up to The Catbird Seat.

The late Wendell Kim managed the Firebirds in '87, my last season in Phoenix. I was just getting used to the vicissitudes of radio life in the minors when the Firebirds' radio deal shrunk to about 20 games in '88.

* * *

That was my last summer without baseball, but the summer was memorable because Denise Moran and I got married on August 27. We had met while Denise was working for the Spartan Foundation at San Jose State in 1985. She's never failed to understand life with a sports announcer, which began with a honeymoon in Santa Fe that was planned around SJSU's football season opener at New Mexico State.

Another lucky break came my way before the '89 baseball season, when I got a call from Bob Blum, who was overseeing broadcasting for the Las Vegas Stars. Blum had spent most of his career in the Bay Area, where he was a play-by-play pioneer. He was one of the first to do college games when sponsors like Tidewater Oil Company owned the rights to local schools' radio packages. He had helped Franklin Mieuli produce the Giants' broadcasts after the move from New York in 1958. The broadcasters: Russ Hodges and Lon Simmons. The next year, a young guy named King joined the crew and all three of them are now Frick Award recipients from the Hall of Fame. Bob was also the first radio voice of the Raiders, and when the team was looking to hire a new broadcaster for the '66 season, it was Blum who told Al Davis, "Bill King is your guy."

My partner in '89 was a character named Dom Valentino. Dom was in the twilight of a career that had taken him to the NBA with the Cincinnati Royals and New York Nets, the NHL with the Islanders, and the big leagues with the Yankees and A's. He was part of the A's radio team in 1980, the year before Bill and Lon were hired.

Dom and I worked one season together before the Stars hired Rich Waltz in 1990.

We had a bunch of managers over the years, like Steve Smith, Russ Nixon, Jim Riggleman, Pat Kelly, and Tim Flannery. Few people have had the success across as many platforms as Flan. He spent 11 years playing in the big leagues and has three rings from his time coaching with the Giants. His first foray into broadcasting came with the Padres. When he asked me for some advice, I told him, "More than anything, don't let anyone out-prepare you." That's been our calling card. I'd walk onto the field in San Francisco or Oakland before a game and Flan would yell across the diamond: "Don't let anyone out-prepare you!"

* * *

It wasn't long after we got back to the Bay Area after the '91 baseball season that I got a call from Mike Bucek, who had been the assistant general manager of the Firebirds when I worked in Phoenix and had moved on to the White Sox as director of broadcasting.

The Sox made a change to their broadcast team for the '92 season. Wayne Hagin, who had worked in the Bay Area for KCBS and the Giants and A's, wasn't retained by the Sox, who hired Ed Farmer to work with John Rooney.

Ed pitched for eight teams in a playing career that began with the Indians in 1971 and ended with the A's in '83. He was scouting and doing front office work after his playing days, but his radio experience was limited to a few fill-in shots on the Sox broadcasts. Rooney was also busy as the number one voice of CBS Radio Sports, a gig that took him away from baseball during spring training for the NCAA Tournament and then during the regular season for *Sunday Night Baseball*.

The Sox were looking for someone to replace John on Sundays. Mike flew me to Chicago to interview with Sox vice president Rob Gallas and Jim Frank, the news director of the team's 50,000-watt flagship station, WMAQ.

A tug of war ensued. Mike and Gallas made it clear that I was their choice, but the station was dead set against me. Jim Frank said it was nothing against me, but there was no way he would hire someone from the minor leagues. The stalemate became protracted. Bucek's strategy: "Wait 'em out," he said, and it worked.

My assignment was to broadcast 20 regular season Sunday games, beginning with the first week of the season and ending around Labor Day, when CBS Radio switched its Sunday programming to the NFL. In addition, I was responsible for any games John missed for the NCAA Tournament or any other CBS assignment. It turned out to be about 22 straight weekends of commuting from Vegas to wherever the Sox were playing, including the last week or two of spring training.

The Las Vegas Stars used John Sandler, the current voice of UNLV basketball, to do all their games, but Don Logan, the team's general manager, kept me around to work the weekday home games. In addition, the Stars aired a package of telecasts. We traveled to about a half-dozen games in the PCL with an array of analysts who lived in Vegas and had deep ties to the big leagues, like Marty Barrett, Dick Williams, and Jerry Reuss.

Working and traveling with Dick Williams was a baseball education and was especially valuable later when I was hired by the A's. It was Dick, of course, who piloted the A's to the first two of their three straight World Championships. He was a lot like Jimmy Lefebvre in that there was always a little detour to the bar after a game. Talking baseball with Williams was like listening to an oral history of the game.

Williams and Blum were close friends and were mainstays of a Thursday baseball lunch group that still gets together in Vegas almost every week. There was pure jubilation amongst the regulars in 2008 when Dick got a long-awaited call from the Hall of Fame.

My first taste of big-league ball came when I flew to Florida for spring training in 1992. Then, 13 years after I sat in the stands recording games into a cassette recorder, I did my first regular-season major-league broadcast at the Oakland Coliseum, on Sunday, April 12. The Sox won the game 6–4, despite two home runs by Mark McGwire and a solo shot by Jose Canseco.

* * *

I hope I've been clear about the debt I owe to so many people for their support over the last four decades. Ed Farmer is right at the top of the list.

Ed was my tour guide around the American League. The Coliseum was the only American League ballpark I had visited in the previous 11 years. I was a stranger in a strange land, but Ed eased what could have been a difficult and intimidating situation. I had no idea where the press boxes or clubhouses were located and hardly knew anybody, but Ed, being a prince of baseball, showed me around and introduced me to everyone. I was the guy coming up from the minors every weekend but he never "big-leagued" me.

I was still trying to shed the overly analytical ways from my time at San Jose State, but Ed never took anything too seriously and that was the perfect recipe for me.

I'm sure Ed's positive attitude was a huge factor in his winning battle against kidney disease. Kidney failure had taken Ed's mom when he was 17, and his illness became so acute that he almost died before he received one of his brother's kidneys in 1991.

Mistakes can be a boon if we learn from them. And one reason I had some success in Chicago was the memory of a miserable first year doing San Jose State football on KCBS. I was tied up in knots that year trying to sound like a "major market" announcer. It was a prescription for failure. I didn't have enough confidence in myself to be me. It was as if I was trying a different approach every game. Then I got stuck in a cycle of listening to tapes until I drove myself silly. It sounds so simple, but it was a tough lesson to learn that the only person you can sound like is yourself. Or, like Red Barber's warning to Vin Scully about spending too much time listening to other announcers: "You don't want to water your wine."

Being in the big leagues was exciting enough, but I also had the good fortune to broadcast for a team with a bunch of rising stars. The opening day lineup in '92 featured guys like Frank Thomas, Robin Ventura, Tim Raines, George Bell, and Ozzie Guillen, with "Black" Jack McDowell on the mound. They finished the year with 86 wins, made the playoffs in 1993, and were locked in a battle for Central Division supremacy with the Indians when the work stoppage hit in '94.

Virtually every game I did for four years was either on a weekend or Opening Day, and so I never had to grind through a Tuesday night game somewhere with only a few thousand fans in the stands.

Plus, I became kind of a good luck charm. Broadcasters will tell you a time-honored axiom in our business: Nobody ever says "good broadcast" after a loss. The Sox were victorious the first seven Sundays of the season. The front office started keeping tabs on my record and my arrival at the park was usually greeted with comments like, "Well, it's a guaranteed win today."

I had nothing to do with it of course, and, honestly, some of those broadcasts were probably not so hot. But it's a lot easier to be liked when you're delivering good news.

* * *

The news coming from Major League Baseball was disconcerting as the 1994 season unfolded and the threat of a work stoppage hovered. There were conflicted feelings everywhere, especially in Chicago and Cleveland, where both teams had their sights set on a postseason berth.

I arrived in Cleveland on July 23 for a game between the White Sox and Indians the next day. The Sox were 20 games over .500 and one game ahead of the Indians. Sunday dawned warm and clear downtown, and as I walked to Jacobs Field, I was thinking that I was about to call one of the most important games of my career. But I was also thinking that the game probably wouldn't mean a thing. There were almost 42,000 fans at Jacobs Field to watch the Sox, behind Alex Fernandez, beat the Indians 4–2. It was a strange feeling and, sadly, the season ended August 10, after a game between the Sox and A's in Oakland.

The Sox didn't make the playoffs until 2000, and in Montreal, baseball never recovered. So many people associated with the game, from taxi drivers to hotel operators, to ticket takers and concessionaires, were deeply affected.

The '95 season started late—my first game was at Fenway Park on April 30—and the regular season was preceded by a bizarre episode known as "replacement ball." I don't think anyone really wanted to do those spring-training games, but we had a job to do. I remember going to Al Lang Stadium in St. Petersburg for a game between the Sox and Cards. Jack Buck, who was nearing his 70th birthday, ambled his way

Denise, Emilee, and Ken Korach, 1992.

up the stands to the Cards' broadcast booth next door, strapped on his microphone and opened his broadcast. I was thinking, "If Jack Buck can do this game, then you sure as heck can do it, too."

The White Sox clubhouse was generally subdued but professional. Robin Ventura was a go-to guy for me, and I was lucky to call Frank Thomas' games for the Sox and A's. He resurrected his career and burnished his Hall-of-Fame résumé when he joined Oakland in 2006, but Frank was at the peak of his powers during my time with the White Sox. I was amazed at the numbers he put up, even though there were games in which he only got two or three good pitches to hit.

* * *

My Sox schedule fit perfectly with the college-football schedule, but I had a new employer when the 1992 football season rolled around.

The 1991–92 basketball season had been the last year of Jerry Tarkanian's run in Vegas. The Rebels went 26–2 but had nowhere to go because of NCAA sanctions. With a new athletic director, Jim Weaver, on board, and the Tarkanian era ending, UNLV decided to take its broadcasts in-house. I left San Jose State to broadcast UNLV football and basketball and because it was a three-quarters time staff position in the athletic department, Denise and I were entitled to health care and a pension plan.

I got to call two NCAA Tournament games, in 1998 and 2000. The Rebels played Princeton in the regionals in Hartford in '98 and then matched up against Tulsa in Nashville in 2000. Both appearances were one-and-done but, still, the magic of being part of the Big Dance was a career highlight. Some of the most fun came the day before those games when my broadcast partner, the late Glen Gondrezick and I, spent all day at the arena watching the tournament teams practice.

Gondo was a tremendous partner. His legendary status in Vegas dated back to his playing days and especially to 1977 when UNLV reached the Final Four for the first time. He played a central role on a team nicknamed the Hardway Eight. They averaged more than 100 points a game before the season came to a heartbreaking end against North Carolina, when Gondo fouled out late and the Rebels lost 84–83.

Gondo's playing days were characterized by an all-out hustling style that saw him spending considerable time diving on the floor or crashing into the scorer's table. His huge heart endeared him forever with fans of the Rebels. But the big guy with the big heart succumbed to heart failure after a heart transplant in 2009. He was only 53. I flew back to Vegas from Texas where the A's were playing and was honored to be asked to speak at Gondo's memorial, which was fittingly held at the Thomas & Mack Center.

I've been asked to speak at three memorials—for Gondo, Bob Blum, and Bill King—and it doesn't get any easier with experience.

I quit doing football after I was hired by the A's in November of 1995 because of the overlapping schedules, but I continued to do basketball for another nine years.

I did my last home game on March 6, 2004. UNLV was playing BYU and Tina Kunzer-Murphy, who was my boss for ESPN Regional, surprised me during a time out in the second half. She yanked me out of my courtside chair and escorted me out onto the court. Twelve years was a long time doing UNLV's games and there were as many lows as highs and more controversies than tournament appearances. I've always tried to understand that although my paycheck has come from the teams I've worked for, the reality is: We work for the fans. You hope to make an impact but most of the time, you're never sure. That day in Vegas, 15,000 fans rose to a standing ovation. Denise and my daughter, Emilee, were in the crowd. I'll never forget that moment and if I could have thanked every fan in person I would have.

* * *

The story of how I got hired by the A's began when I was in San Jose for a UNLV-SJSU football game. There was a story in the *Mercury News* about how Lon Simmons wouldn't be returning to the broadcast team for the 1996 season.

Until then, Lon not coming back was the last thing on my mind, especially since he was one of my idols and the King-Simmons team had reached exalted status in the Bay Area.

After the empty Coliseum days of the late '70s, things had changed dramatically for the A's in 1980 when the Haas family purchased the team from Charlie Finley. It helped that the new owners retained the popular and mercurial Billy Martin as manager, but everything else was new, especially in the front office, where a talented and innovative staff was being assembled.

Vin Scully and Ken at the Coliseum, 1997.

But the move that sent shock waves throughout Northern California proved to be the most brilliant personnel decision in the history of baseball broadcasting.

It was almost inconceivable that Bill King and Lon Simmons could be paired, but that's what happened. Very few people remembered that Bill had worked as the third man in the booth with Simmons and Hodges from 1959–1962; after that it was strictly football and basketball for Bill. Simmons and Hodges worked together until Russ retired in 1970, but Lon was let go when the Giants changed radio stations after the 1978 season.

In my research for my book about Bill, the sentiment was unanimous from former A's front office folks I interviewed: Matching up Bill and Lon on the radio was the most important decision the A's made to establish credibility and build a fan base.

Still, people were in disbelief when the decision was announced. Lon was so closely identified with the Giants that a move across the Bay was unexpected. And Bill? He was doing the Warriors and Raiders full-time and had reached such iconic status with those teams that baseball was that last thing anyone thought of when they pictured him behind a microphone.

As A's equipment manager and team historian Steve Vucinich told me: "It was like a merger of CBS and NBC."

I loved listening to Lon and he had a profound influence on my approach. Much of the time when I worked at Bennett Valley, I lived in a remote area without television. I spent many days and nights listening to Bill and Lon. I was very familiar with Bill's work in basketball and football, but my exposure to Lon had been limited to earlier visits to the Bay Area when he was working for the Giants.

Lon's voice was rich and as golden as the California hills during the summertime. Maybe the greatest baseball voice of all time—or, at least I'd put him right up there with Ernie Harwell and Scully. He had a low-key style and a dry sense of humor that was the perfect juxtaposition to Bill's more rapid rhythm and intensity.

The main thing I learned while listening to Lon was that there was no need to be in a hurry. He was never in a rush and he never tried to pry extra words into an inning just to impress people with how much he knew. I don't think anybody wants to be bombarded by verbiage on a broadcast and Lon's voice and tempo were soothing and the perfect baseball company.

I admit there were a few times when those guys left me in the dark because some of their jokes were of the inside variety. I learned quickly after working with Bill what Lon meant when he would say—after Bill indulged in an a particularly satisfying snack—something like: "I spent all those years in the National League working with Russ, but now that I'm working with you I didn't realize that they built every ballpark in the American League next to a sulfur factory."

After reading about Lon's departure, I applied for the job and the process was as smooth as possible. Mike Bucek and Don Logan called A's execs Alan Ledford and Ken Pries on my behalf, and Bob Blum, without me knowing, put in a good word with Bill. How do you thank someone for what Blum did? He called Bill and said, "Korach's your guy. He's one of us."

Having worked previously in the Bay Area didn't hurt. I had a small "in" with the organization since John Trinidad, the longtime studio producer of the A's broadcasts, was our remote engineer during the San Jose State football days.

It was a stroke of good fortune that the audition tape I sent featured the A's in a game against the White Sox in 1995. Jay Alves, the A's PR director, had had some interesting insights into starting pitcher Ariel Prieto's defection from Cuba, and I was able to use that story in the first inning when Prieto faced the Sox at Comiskey Park. I included a couple of highlights, probably from the Big Hurt and Ventura, to open the tape and included the top and bottom of the first.

I flew up to Oakland in November of '95 to interview with Ledford and Pries and it wasn't long after that I got the job.

* * *

I learned I had been hired the day Denise and I had planned on having dinner with my aunt Charlotte, who was in Vegas on vacation. It was Charlotte who took me to my first World Series game—Game 3 between the Dodgers and the Yankees in 1963, when Don Drysdale threw a three-hit shutout.

Charlotte was my grandmother's youngest sister and she and my mom were very close. She took my mom's passing when I was 21 as hard if not harder than anyone. Just the mention of my mom had her shaking her bowed head in disbelief, and I think in expressing the pride she felt after hearing the news that I had been hired by the A's, there was some of my mom's voice in hers.

I never talked to Bill King during the hiring process, but we made up for that in a hurry. I didn't really know Bill at that point. We had spoken briefly a couple of times before games, but that was it. Denise likes to remind me of how our phone bill grew before the '96 season. Bill and I talked several times on the phone and when I hung up, Denise would usually ask if I knew how long we had talked. I was so enthralled that I had no idea. Denise remembers some of the calls lasting well over an hour. After all, one of the voices of my youth was now coming out of our phone.

Between then and the time he died, I never tired of hearing that voice.

CHAPTER 2
RICKEY HENDERSON: LEADOFF (SUPER)MAN

Rickey Henderson, an Oakland native, is the all-time stolen base leader and a first-ballot member of the Baseball Hall of Fame. Henderson serves as a part-time instructor with the team and he often returns to work with the big-league players, as well as traveling to affiliates to teach A's minor-leaguers the finer points of baserunning and outfield defense. He regularly attends team reunions and other functions at the Coliseum, where his No. 24 is retired and where the A's play their games on Rickey Henderson Field. He sat down with Ken Korach and Susan Slusser for a conversation in May 2018.

Part of the job of a living legend is to interact with fans, and you're so gracious. How did you learn this skill?

When I was a kid, Reggie Jackson was tough for me, real tough. Reggie made me so mad because he never gave me an autograph, but most of all, he always got me punished at the house because I waited so long for him at the ballpark that I got in trouble. I stayed out here for him, and he still just messed me up. I used to go, "Wow, man."

My first year in the major leagues when we got an opportunity to play the Yankees, I think I got dressed so fast that people were wondering, "Why are you wearing your uniform to the stadium?" I just took off and ran to the ballpark.

Reggie was in the cage hitting. I sat back by the cage looking at him. He had a few minutes to get out of the cage and let somebody hit, then he was going back in, so I grabbed him and said, "Mr. Jackson, Mr. Jackson. I'm that little kid who used to always be outside waiting on you to get an autograph. I finally made it to the big leagues!"

He said, "I want to give you some advice. When I come up to the plate, I would like for you to move way back because I hit the ball a long ways."

Wow, what kind of advice is that? You don't even know what type of player I am, but you're giving me advice on what *you* are doing, not how to stay in the big leagues. You're telling me to back up because you're coming up to hit?

Rickey Henderson celebrates and raises third base after setting the all-time stolen base record on May 1, 1991. (AP Photo/Eric Risberg, File)

I said, "You don't know me. You haven't read up on me when I was coming through the minor leagues. I'm a real fast guy. I can run the ball down, run real fast and steal a base."

Reggie said, "Move back because I hit the ball a long way," and I said, "Okay, I'm going to move *in*."

When he came up, I thought, "I'm messing with the man."

Now batting, Reggie Jackson.

I start sprinting in. He steps out of the batter's box, waves at me to move back, and I go, "No, no, no, I'm staying right here."

He ended up getting a 3-2 count and hitting a ball to left-center, a good shot to left-center, and I ended up catching it, just barely. When he got to second base, he tipped his hat toward me. And he still didn't give me an autograph.

It took him until I broke the American League record for stolen bases, it took him that long. When he got traded to the Angels, he sent a bat over for me to sign for him.... So I kept the bat—*You ain't getting that bat back!*

He was an idol for me coming up as a kid because of the things he did on the baseball field, and I was just trying to learn the game of baseball.

Now we're really close. Over the years, as I ended up getting to talk to him, he was complaining about the pressure. There was so much on him and so much he had to do. Now, I can feel you because I know about that.

Still, he didn't have to be the way he was. I thought, "I was a kid, I wasn't a grown man trying to follow you around. I was a little boy. I would go home and get in trouble, and you didn't even care."

When I told him about that, he laughed. As he got older, I think he wished he hadn't had to do the things he had to do at that time.

At first, it was all bad, but then when you see the other side to it and what ballplayers have to go through at certain times, as popular as he was, you can sometimes understand it.

When I was a kid and Reggie was playing, I learned that we're playing for these fans, so I always paid more attention to the fans. They might holler, they might wave, and I took the time to recognize what they were doing out there. I accepted it.

If I'm out there and the game was slow, I wanted somebody in the stands to talk to me, just to keep me into the game. I remember there were a lot of times Dwayne Murphy used to say, "Did you see that pitch? You were over there talking to the man in the stands during that pitch."

I said, "When I hear the crack of the bat, I go and get the ball."

Some of the time, I didn't see some of the pitches, and I jumped to, "What happened?"

I was always into the fans. They gave me a lift. They gave me a boost in energy. I wanted to go out there and do something for them.

How did you approach playing in your hometown? Some players believe it can be a mixed blessing to play where you grew up.

That was one of the best feelings of all, just to be an Oakland A, because I came out of the back yard and was surrounded by the A's players... and I used to sneak into the ballpark just to see them play! To get an opportunity to play in Oakland was a dream come true. My schoolmates, my mom, my brothers, and everybody who knew me in Oakland got a chance to see me play. That was a great feeling to know I had somebody backing me.

Most of all, I used to hear my mother in the stands, and she would be getting all over me all the time. I was wondering who was up there yelling, and it was my mom!

"What are you doing? I'm trying!"

"Well you're not doing it, son. I need you to get with it."

She kept boosting me, she wouldn't let no one else talk about me, but she would talk about me. She yelled at me when I wasn't hitting, she'd yell I'm not playing hard, I'm not running. "What are you doing? You're looking at balls. Can you see? Do you need glasses?"

I think wanting to do something for all of them, for her, it gave me a boost, a chance to go out there and do well.

You always show up at all the events the A's have for the 1980s and '90s teams and other honors, such as the 50 top Oakland players as voted on by fans in 2018. What are those like as a participant?

It's nice to hear what you accomplished. I don't get in the habit of thinking about what I accomplished, because when I played the game it wasn't about what you were doing, it was going out there and trying to help the team win and give it your best. At the end, you hear a lot about what you achieved.

When I was playing, I had no clue what I was doing. I was just having fun and playing the game. You always, in a way, want to make yourself better every day, sometimes you go 0-for and you try to improve and get better the next day.

What was the key to your success as a major-league player? What went into it behind the scenes that fans might not know about?

I kept my body in shape. I kept my body sharp, because when we were coming up, they always said that if you get hurt, you might lose your job. So you wouldn't go to the training room at all. If you had a nagging injury, you would stay away from the training room.

My thing was staying in tip-top shape. I did a lot of sit-ups, push-ups, stretching at the hotel before I went to bed.

I learned that if you stretch before you go to bed, the next day your body is much looser than it is when you don't stretch. I was walking up with my legs tight, then I started to stretch, and when I got up, I didn't have to go out there and stretch. I was pretty much loose. It kept me that way.

I did a lot of yoga, meditation, stuff you do with your body, your mind, and your muscles. I did dumbbells in my room. Nothing was better for me than to go out there and be on the field. When I was a kid, my mom used to say if I didn't get dirty, I wasn't playing the game, so I always wanted to be out there and to try to get dirty.

It was a passion that I learned, because I really was a football player. When I got into baseball, I started concentrating. I started talking to ex-ball players, what they went through, what it took for them to go out there and play the game the right way.

I got a lot of information that way. I think now the players don't interact with the older guys to try to figure out what they would do in situations. I think now they "know it all" more. But we *never* know what the game is all about. Every day I wanted to learn something about the game. When one of the players that played the game came around, we would just talk to them about what they were doing. I think it helps you.

What were the biggest challenges of the job?

Trying to figure out how to get out of slumps. "What was a slump? Why wasn't I getting a hit every day?"

I had to make adjustments. I think a lot of the younger generation, they don't understand that baseball is a failure game, they're trying to be perfect. But you just have to go out there and have success with one or two hits, or three hits out of ten here and there. When you get on a streak, then you get more hits, then you learn about the highs and the lows.

When I was hitting the ball really well, I would get so hyped up that I was so great, then when I was in a slump, I had my head between my legs and tried to hide from everyone. I learned that in Double-A. I was in a bad slump, hitting .187 or something like that. I couldn't understand it. This game hadn't changed or what I was doing, but I'm not getting a hit.

I had a general manager who was giving me rides home. One night was miserable. I told him to stop the car. He said, "What do you mean stop the car?" I said, "Stop the car, I've got to get something off my mind."

I got out of the car, and I just screamed.

Dick Williams and Ken at the Coliseum on Opening Day, April 1, 2008, the day Rickey Henderson Field was dedicated at Rickey's alma mater, Oakland Tech High School. The A's also honored Williams that day for his upcoming induction into the Hall of Fame. (Michael Zagaris)

He said, "What's wrong with you?" I said, "I'm fine now. It's good."

With the ups and downs, you've just got to let it go. Each and every day, you've just got to give it your best.

What are the top misperceptions about you?

One of them was John Olerud and his batting helmet; people thought I didn't remember he wore that in the field. John and I got together and said it ain't true. I knew why he was wearing it. It just caught everybody's attention, and they just stuck with it. [Olerud had had a brain aneurysm while in college; he and Henderson were teammates in Toronto and then again with the New York Mets, where legend has it Rickey told Olerud, "You know, when I played in Toronto, we had a guy who wore a helmet.")

The Billy Beane story was true. [Beane was sent to the minors for a month and when he was finally recalled, Henderson, who lockered nearby, said, "Hey, man, where have you been?"] It's got to be true because every time I see Billy at a lunch or gathering, he brings it up. It was true because I was focused on getting to the ballpark and just playing, I really wasn't worried about what everybody else was doing. I knew my job, what I had to come out and do. I had to get myself prepared. I came out here and worked at it. I didn't see who was playing and who wasn't playing.

The bench guys, they didn't play every day. Billy, he wasn't playing at that time. When he was sent out, I thought he got hurt or he was sick. Every day, I would come in and he wasn't there. When he came back, I asked him where he had been, and he said. "They sent me down."

I was coming in to do a job, not see what everybody else was doing, who was playing, who wasn't playing. I tried to stay out of the training room. If someone was in the training room hurt, I didn't know he was in the training room hurt because I didn't go in the training room.

You've spoken about the need to give back to the sport, to help the next generation. Why do you feel that way?

There's a responsibility as far as giving something back, trying to help the young kids who come up, because that's what I learned from the veteran guys. They helped us, they gave us knowledge. There was always someone willing to talk to you, tell you, "This is what we see," or, "You're doing this." It seemed like we were always willing to help one another.

That's sometimes something I don't see here. I don't see it around the league. I think sometimes we give them all the information, so we don't give them a chance to go out there and *think* about, "What really is he doing to you?"

Now we tell them so much that I think they get in trouble by relying on that instead of saying, "Okay, I know these are the pitches he has. I have to make adjustments to how he is coming at me."

If we were all relying on the chart, I think we would all be messed up. It all depends on how the pitcher feels that day, how you feel that day. How he is approaching you? I think that's what we were good at, watching one another to see how the pitcher was pitching you that day.

Do you enjoy working with prospects?

I love it. They're trying to get to the big leagues. They're trying to learn. They're young kids who come out of high school or college and now they're in a different level.

I don't think people are focused enough. People thought I talked to myself. I looked at a clip last night that somebody showed me, and I could see that what I was doing was reminding myself what was going on at that time: I know that pitcher is throwing a slider, and I'm trying to tell myself to stay on that pitch. I never went into a game without reminding myself of what I was trying to do or what was going on. That's what made me successful.

I like what I'm doing now. I tried coaching in the majors; it's a big responsibility. I think players don't give coaches as much credit as they deserve in being out here each and every day to help you. I think some don't realize what they go through. It's a tough job. I tried it as the first-base coach with the Mets, and I thought I was going to have fun. I would get to the ballpark at 1:00 PM and leave the ballpark at midnight. This is not what I wanted to do.

Jose Reyes was the guy they wanted me to work with. He was the leadoff hitter and he could run and steal bases. All of a sudden, he went in a little slump. I said, "Every time I look at you at the plate, we need you on because we need you to create something. You're swinging at everything. You're looking at me every time you swing. Let's go out to the cage, and I'm going to work with you on being patient and what pitch I think you should be swinging at."

I got in trouble because I wasn't the hitting coach. I really didn't understand that. I thought we were all there to help. I thought, "Y'all are telling me to help him, but he ain't getting on base for me to help him. Whatever you were doing with him wasn't working."

Had the hitting coach came out and said, "Rickey, what are you saying to him?" I would have said, "This is what we discussed." Instead, they're saying I can't take him out to the cage again. That was enough for me. This ain't the game for me that you're saying we can't help. I thought I was *here* for that. That hurt me.

They weren't understanding how I was trying to help out. It was a bummer. I said, "I don't need to be a coach."

You look at the great players who played the game. You wonder why they aren't coaches. I see why.

What are players' responsibilities to the fans?

My mom would get mad at me. I played hard and did so much, then I had a whole parking lot of people waiting for me to sign. She would wait 30 minutes on me and say, "I'm going to go and let you sign autographs." That was a big part of the job.

Nowadays, I tell you what I look at a lot. A pitcher, he can go out there and be tremendous or he can go out there and he can get hit. When he walks off the mound, in my day, all the pitchers, the fans are clapping and giving you love. Then they come back out and tip their cap and say, "Thank you." I don't see that anymore.

To me, you have to acknowledge the fans when you have a good game; instead, guys just walk off. I really don't like that. I think you should acknowledge the people because they're the ones coming to see you. They're happy for you. Don't just walk off, head down.

That's one of the things I see in the game that's so different than what we were all about, what was keeping us going. We weren't playing for the stats. We were out here to have fun and entertain the fans who were coming out here to see us play. We were entertainers.

Sometimes I think if the players ever really acknowledge the fans and play for them, they might relax more. They won't put so much pressure on themselves. Good or bad, they're behind you. Acknowledge them, then you won't feel so bad.

If I ever had a bad day, and someone was cheering me on and trying to help me up, then I wanted to acknowledge that. I didn't want to think about what had happened, I wanted to think about the love that they gave me or appreciation they showed me.

CHAPTER 3
KEN KORACH: A MOTHER'S LEGACY

It was as close as I've ever come to losing it on the air. I suppose people would have forgiven me, considering the Hollywood nature of what had just happened, but, still, I've always tried to keep at least a slight detachment, so I can do my job—which, ultimately, is to give a clear description of what I'm seeing.

The problem was, my eyes weren't clear at all.

Dallas Braden had just thrown the 19th perfect game in Major League history, which would have been momentous enough, but he did it on Mother's Day, on May 9, 2010, nine years after he had lost his mom to cancer and with his grandmother, who was his guiding light, in the stands. Now, a minute after Tampa Bay's Gabe Kapler grounded to short and after his teammates exploded out of the dugout in pure jubilation, Dallas' grandmother was escorted onto the field.

The moment Dallas and Peggy Lindsey embraced is frozen in time, its evocation reflecting a confluence of sports and real life and a culmination of a journey they had taken together against long odds.

Hours earlier, the day had dawned gray and overcast, which seemed fitting for me since Mother's Day had never been a joyous occasion. My mom took her own life when I was 21. And although I hadn't talked specifically about Mother's Day to Dallas, it seemed appropriate to speculate in the bottom of the eighth inning that he might have similar conflicted feelings about the holiday.

The top of the ninth took exactly three minutes and 26 seconds to complete. That's how much Braden was in command, at least until the end of the Kapler at-bat, when the pitcher lost track of the count and came perilously close to a base on balls.

Then Braden threw a fastball that Kapler hit in the direction of shortstop Cliff Pennington, and I had the privilege of calling history:

"Taken there, Pennington's got it... he throws... a perfect game! Dallas Braden has thrown a perfect game! The kid from Stockton has done it for the A's!"

I didn't say anything for the next 30 seconds. There wasn't much that needed to be said since the pandemonium on the field spoke for itself.

Dallas Braden hugs his grandmother, Peggy Lindsey, after Braden's perfect game against the Tampa Bay Rays on Mother's Day 2010. (AP Photo/Marcio Jose Sanchez)

Then, like so many at the Coliseum, I spotted Dallas and Peggy between home plate and the A's dugout. Describing that scene and the tears they shared, trying to explain how much they had meant to each other and how Peggy had kept Dallas from falling off the tracks—that's when my emotions took over. I was fighting back tears and working hard to hold it together.

* * *

The memory of what I was feeling is lasting and always brings a smile to my face when I think about Mother's Day. But it wasn't always like that.

My mother, Frances Korach, committed suicide in 1973, when I was starting my third year of college at San Diego State University.

I knew she was depressed and dealing with a back injury, but I had no idea of the depths she had fallen. Looking back now, I think there were two battles that she was fighting—physical and emotional.

First, she had had a very complicated relationship with her mother. My grandmother Pearl was part of a large Jewish family that immigrated from Russia to New York not long after the turn of the 20th century. It wasn't unusual in those days for families to become fragmented, but this was an extreme case. Pearl, as the oldest of the siblings, came over first with her father. Initially, the rest of the family, including my great-grandmother, stayed behind. She was next to arrive, along with my Aunt Esther, who was one of triplets, the other two of whom didn't make it over until after World War I. Because money was scarce, my grandmother had to work, and her formal education ended in her early teens. Her first job was cleaning chickens and selling them to markets and restaurants.

Slowly, the rest of the family trickled over and, looking for greener pastures, settled in Los Angeles. There were 10 in the immediate family; Pearl had six sisters and a brother. I always felt badly for my Uncle Izzy because he was so severely outnumbered.

My grandmother became like a second mother to those kids, and she went to exhausting lengths to try to keep the family together. Those were tough times, and she forfeited what we would consider a normal adolescence because of her expanding responsibilities at home.

Eventually, in 1923, my grandmother married a wonderful man named Louis Groper. My grandfather was quiet, wise, and dignified in an understated way. For a brief period, my grandparents owned a restaurant, but for most of his adult life, my grandfather got up at 2:30 in the morning and drove a bread truck.

* * *

My mom was born in 1924, and, with time, my grandmother's life became a great paradox. She had taken on the role of matriarch of what was becoming a larger extended family, but, ironically, she looked out for everyone's best interests except those of her daughter.

Feeling overextended, my grandmother sent my mom several miles away to live with my great grandparents and my Aunt Charlotte, who was my grandmother's youngest sister.

My dad remembers that my mom was around 10 at the time. Charlotte tried her best, but her parents spoke little English, so communication with them was difficult. And instead of living in a nice home in a good neighborhood, my mom had been sent to a crowded home in a tough part of town away from her friends. It was an untenable situation.

My mom felt discarded and isolated. She put on a tremendous amount of weight, which, I suppose was the manifestation of the issues she was dealing with. My dad told me it was the only time that her schoolwork suffered. She was a straight-A student all the way through high school, but in that period away from home, she got Ds and Fs and her behavior was downgraded by her teachers as well.

Thankfully, the arrangement didn't last forever and when she went back in her early teens to live with her parents, a comeback began. She

Frances and Simon Korach on their wedding day in Los Angeles. (courtesy Ken Korach)

lost weight, and as her grades improved, she set her sights on attending UCLA.

Frances became the first member of her family to graduate from college and that was a huge source of pride for all of them. And it wasn't just that she graduated—she did so Phi Beta Kappa in less than four years.

She was their shining light, and she was almost literally so in photos of my parents' wedding in 1947. My mom was barely five feet tall. In fact, her nickname was "Tiny." (My dad and others called her "Tine.") In those photos, she is vivacious and radiant.

My mother's career took her to Orthopedic Hospital in downtown L.A., where she worked as a psychiatric social worker counseling terminally ill kids and their parents. It was tough work. She would come home with gut-wrenching stories of kids who were dying and parents who were agonizing along with them. I'm sure it was a good release for my mom to share her experiences, but I admit, there were times the stories were so intense that I told her to stop.

* * *

My mom deftly balanced her career with being a mother. My dad was a high school (and later junior college) baseball and basketball coach and he stayed after school many days for practice or games and it wasn't unusual for him to spend an hour fighting L.A. traffic driving home from work. My mom worked things out with the hospital to leave early so she could get dinner ready and spend time with me.

She didn't have a lot of rules for me at home, but I was limited to two hours of television per night and there was no way I could even think about watching TV until my homework was finished.

My dad always lamented that my mom never went back to school to get an advanced degree so that she would be more qualified for an administrative position at the hospital or even become a doctor. But she was okay with what she was doing. She died young, of course, but I've always felt that her impact on those families lasted long after she died.

My mom and dad were a wonderful couple. My dad has always been a charming, handsome guy. They were very active and went out dancing quite a bit. They also loved tennis and became a formidable mixed-doubles team. I remember watching them play and they had great chemistry on the court. My cousin Susie remembers seeing my mom, dressed in her tennis attire, looking athletic and full of vitality, and has no doubt that being an athlete was ingrained in her identity, which speaks to the second thing that impacted my mom as she reached her mid-forties.

I don't remember the exact year, but early in my college days she began feeling the painful manifestation of a back condition known as spondylolysis. Daily tasks were becoming increasingly difficult, and running, which she loved to do on the tennis court, was next to impossible. Even today, back surgery is an inexact science, but as her pain increased, my mom felt that fusion surgery was her only option. I spent most of my time back then, including the summers, in San Diego, and I wasn't fully aware of how much pain she was in.

Her physical issues coincided with my grandfather being diagnosed with cancer. My mom adored her dad. He was a sweet man who never had an unkind word for anyone. My grandmother was the effusive, domineering mother out of central casting, and thus my mom never blamed my grandfather for that time when she had been sent away from home.

I was very close to my grandparents. It was part of our weekly routine on Fridays to take a 30-minute drive down to their house, which was close to L.A. landmarks like the Farmers Market and Gilmore Field. Gilmore was a legendary old ballpark where the Hollywood Stars of the Pacific Coast League used to play before the Dodgers moved west; it was later leveled to make way for a complex of studios known as CBS Television City.

Even though English was his adopted language, my grandfather had a huge thirst for reading, especially politics. I remember my dad brought him used copies of *Time* and *Newsweek* every time we visited.

* * *

My mom's condition became crystalized the day of a huge party to commemorate my grandparents' 50th wedding anniversary.

This was a big deal. They rented a ballroom at an L.A. hotel and hundreds of people RSVP'd.

All our family and my grandparents' friends were planning on attending, as were members of the community who had shared in their charity efforts.

My grandmother lived a lifetime of service. She volunteered for decades at the City of Hope, a sprawling hospital northeast of Los Angeles, and she never took a dime. She also spearheaded a group of

Ken, Frances, and Simon Korach in Los Angeles, 1970. (courtesy Ken Korach)

women called The Pioneers, who raised thousands of dollars for the hospital. I have a scrapbook full of letters of commendation she received from celebrities and politicians.

Late in 2017, my wife, Denise, spent several days at the City of Hope with friends of ours and their young daughter, who had been stricken with cancer. One day, Denise made an emotional trip to the hospital's synagogue and found a plaque honoring Pearl and Louis.

I drove home from San Diego for the party and found my mom depressed and in great pain. The surgery was unsuccessful, and she was spending most of her time bedridden. She was adamant that she wasn't going to the party, saying that she couldn't face anyone, especially her parents, in the condition she was in.

I don't recall the details of the conversation I had with my mom that afternoon, except that it was basically one-way. She resisted my entreaties for quite some time and it got emotional.

But she went. She sucked it up and got through it and looked beautiful.

My grandparents made a grand entrance. They walked out from behind a door to the stage—my grandmother with my dad, and my mom with her father. My mom was holding her dad's arm as they walked in. She wore a white dress with a pink carnation and I was so proud of how she persevered that night.

No doubt, her appearance masked her physical and emotional pain. And then there was her father, who was fighting a terminal illness. I'm an amateur at this, but I don't think she felt she had the strength to see her father slip away. And the scars and the feelings of resentment and bitterness toward her mom, which had been dormant for years, had no doubt resurfaced with the erosion of her physical and emotional strength.

A short time later she was gone.

She walked downstairs to our pool, took some pills and drowned herself. My dad came back from work and found her at the bottom of the pool.

My Aunt Margaret, my dad's only sister, called me with the news. There wasn't much small talk or preliminaries. She got right to the point that it was suicide.

I drove home and found my dad in our kitchen. My dad, who was always the picture of composure, was distraught, as you might imagine. We shared an embrace and then he handed me a note. My mom didn't say much, but there were a couple of lines about how if I had any questions, I should contact her shrink.

I decided that I was going to speak at my mom's funeral, even though one could characterize my own emotions at the time as muted. I was going through a period in my life when I wasn't much of a feeling person.

* * *

By the fall of 1972, I had become disillusioned with school at San Diego State and had already contemplated quitting. I suppose, like a lot of kids that age, I was searching for answers about love and life in general. Those were the days of Vietnam and protests and the assassinations of the Kennedys and Martin Luther King and I was also dwelling way too much on the breakup of my first serious relationship. As my self-esteem lagged, being in touch with my emotions was kind of a distant concept.

My cousin Susie, the youngest of Margaret's three children, was taking a graduate class at Cal in crisis intervention at the time. My mom was a huge role model for Susie and a big reason why she chose a career in social work. A section of the class focused on the stages of grief, and Susie was concerned that in trying to be strong, I was underreacting emotionally.

I spoke at the service about the need for our family to find the strength to stay together. Dealing with the death of someone as beloved and as young as my mom would have been hard no matter the circumstances, but the fact she took her own life only added to my family's despair. In addition, I wanted to celebrate my mom's life and focus on the way she lived and not the way she died.

The service was brutal. There was a family area behind curtains to my left and as I was speaking, my grandmother was shrieking. It was awful. She was screaming: "How could she do this? How could this happen? Why? Why? Why?"

My grandfather passed away shortly thereafter. I spent time with my grandmother whenever I was in town, and although she hung on for a few more years, for all intents and purposes, it was over for her the moment my mom died.

I headed back to San Diego, and it wasn't long before I quit school. This was a blow to my dad—kind of a piling on in a way. I took about eight months off from school and resurfaced at UC Santa Barbara, which was one on the best decisions I've ever made.

Jackson Browne, in "Running on Empty," sings about how he used to "look to my friends to pull me through." He could have written those lyrics about me, except my friends are still pulling me through.

I moved to Santa Barbara with my great friend and roommate from San Diego, Craig Burger, and it wasn't long before many more of our friends joined us. They became my family, and the support we've given each other over the years has been something I've treasured and never taken for granted. I can count on every one of them.

Forty-seven years after we first met, I asked Craig and two of my other closest friends, Marty Lurie and Dr. Allan Pont, if they would be presenters at the induction ceremonies for the Jewish Sports Hall of Fame of Northern California. Thinking of all those years and the miles we've traveled, I was close to tears when I asked Craig.

As for my dad? He's a tough guy and, as a child of the Great Depression and a veteran of World War II, very little has ever deterred him. He's dealt with the inevitable feeling of remorse that he could have done more, but long ago came to grips with the reality that he can't change the past. He became focused on moving on after a long period of healing and he and his wife, Janet, have been happily married for more than 40 years. He's 100 years old and writing this chapter has given us a platform to talk more about the period before my mom's death. He's been a good role model, as always. We've talked about how I wish I was more in touch with how my mom was feeling, but, as he noted, you can't dwell on it.

* * *

The memory of seeing Braden hug his grandmother in the immediate aftermath of his perfect game still brings emotions to the surface for me. And, I think one of the things about that experience, and fighting back tears on the air, is that I was present in the moment. That's a great memory, too—the fact that there were no barriers separating me from feeling it.

I don't think that would have been the case for many years after my mom's death. Here's what I was thinking after she died: I wasn't going to let my mom's suicide become an excuse or a crutch if I encountered difficulties in my life.

While that might have been a noble notion—to take responsibility—it was totally unrealistic and a prime example of denial. How in the world are you not going to be affected by something like that?

It's been a long process to allow those feelings to come to the surface and now I think it's healthy to concede there have been some rough patches. I really miss my mom and I probably miss her now more than ever. That doesn't imply that I didn't miss her before, it's just that I'm more in touch with it now. Those feelings come to the surface most when I think of our daughter, Emilee, and how my mom never knew that she had a granddaughter.

My mom left that note telling me to contact her psychiatrist if I had any questions, but I never called and that's on me. I regret that now.

Suicide is uncomfortable for people to talk about. I've been part of hundreds of conversations over the years about parents. When the conversation comes around to me and I mention that my mom took her own life—I'd say 90 percent of the time silence or a quick "I'm sorry" follows and it ends right there.

That's one of the great tragedies of suicide. It's hard to talk about, and if people were more open and willing to talk and/or seek help, especially those suffering from depression, the odds of prevention would rise. It's a two-way street and involves friends and family being willing to fight through the feeling of being a little queasy so they can enable those conversations.

It's not a sign of weakness for someone with depression to come forward. To me, it's a sign of strength to admit being vulnerable, although in a world like baseball, for instance, sometimes empathy is hard to find. I have a good friend who had a great playing career who scoffs at the notion of a ballplayer being depressed. "How can that happen when he makes all the money in the world?" That's shallow but not isolated thinking.

Communication is the key to so many things in life. In work, in life, in everything. It breaks my heart to hear stories of kids—I mean kids eight or nine years old—killing themselves after bullying incidents in school.

The latest statistics from the Centers for Disease Control list suicide as the second leading cause of death of people 15–24. "Even more disturbing," the Centers' website states, "is that suicide is the fourth leading cause of death for children between the ages 10 and 14."

We all have an obligation to set good examples in everything we do, especially in the times we live in, where the divide in our politics has stretched the boundaries of civility beyond anything I've seen in my lifetime. We have leaders who, rather than elevating the national discourse, would rather browbeat those in opposition. Being strong and tough is a component of leadership—but those qualities don't need to conflict with humility and grace.

* * *

Causes of Teen Suicide (From the Centers for Disease Control Website)

There are several different factors that may lead a teenager to take his or her life, but the most common is depression. Feelings of hopelessness and anxiety, along with feelings of being trapped in a life that one can't handle, are very real contributors to teen suicide. In some cases, teenagers believe that suicide is the only way to solve their problems. The pressures of life seem too much to cope with, and some teenagers look at suicide as a welcome escape.

Other factors that may contribute to teen suicide include:

- Divorce of parents
- Violence in the home
- Inability to find success at school
- Feelings of worthlessness
- Rejection by friends or peers
- Substance abuse
- Death of someone close to the teenager
- The suicide of a friend or someone he or she "knows" online

* * *

Suicide is a lonely act—maybe the ultimate lonely act, and it strikes me that my mom has been lonely in death.

Part of what helps us deal with losing someone is to celebrate their life. That hasn't happened too often with my mom because suicide is still a tenebrous place for people to go.

Even though she died in her forties, she made a significant contribution. She fought through a lot as a kid. Susie and I think that time away from her parents may have given rise to an independent streak that characterized her life. She wasn't a pioneer, of course; there were other women doing what she did. But still, in the early 1950s, it was far from the norm for a woman to graduate with honors from college in less than four years, pursue a career that required intense commitment and balance that with being a wife and mother. Doing it all and having it all with verve. This might seem contradictory, but the fact she was so strong-willed and such an independent thinker may have led to her decision. We'll never know for sure, but the hopelessness of her physical condition may have led her down those steps to the pool. She didn't want to live that way, and perhaps she felt suicide was her only way out.

Her academic accomplishments and work ethic set a great example. Susie carries that inspiration with her today and she credits my mom for changing her life and impacting her decision to choose a career in social work in public education in the Bay Area. She and her husband, Al, raised three fantastic kids. I'm sure those kids would have adored my mom.

I think of my mom all the time, of course, and especially in the current political climate. She encouraged me to be open to different points of view and there were no subjects that were off limits.

I want to keep those memories alive, and Braden's perfect game has helped facilitate that. I think of her almost every time I think about that game, and that's been a wonderful thing.

For Dallas and me, Mother's Day had become an occasion for both celebration and mourning. But on a day when he was perfect, it was an occasion to remember that our imperfections are what make us human. They can be beautiful, too.

CHAPTER 4

SUSAN SLUSSER: BROUGHT UP WITH BASEBALL

When I was six, my dad flipped on the TV one day to the ALCS between the A's and the Tigers.

That was unusual. There wasn't much TV time in my house, unless it was PBS or Carol Burnett; I had to sneak over to friends' houses to watch *The Brady Bunch* or *Batman*. I probably would have been hooked by baseball no matter what, but the rarity of sitting down to watch anything with my dad made me extra curious.

My dad, Richard, a Navy meteorologist and former pilot who was born in Kalamazoo, Michigan, and grew up a Tigers fan, explained the game clearly and thoroughly, despite the fact he was talking to a second grader. He dove right into the importance of the count, how each pitch affected the one before and after it. That psychological battle between pitcher and hitter fascinated me from the get-go—and it didn't hurt that the A's were wildly watchable. My dad wasn't so tied to the team of his youth that he was immune to Oakland's charms, either: We both loved Rollie Fingers and Campy Campaneris and Dick Green and Vida Blue—and, especially, Sal Bando.

The A's went on to win that ALCS of course, and then the World Series... and the next... and the next. For a little girl living on the naval base in Alameda, a 20-minute drive to the Coliseum, it seemed as this must be the natural order of business. Oakland wins the World Series every year!

My green-and-gold bubble burst in 1975, when the Red Sox beat the A's in the ALCS. I was devastated, but I was nine; I figured I would root for Boston in the World Series, reasoning at least then the A's would be the second-best team.

That 1975 World Series was so sensational, so gripping, that I turned into a rabid Red Sox fan, which is how almost everyone I grew up with recalls me. Shortly after that Series ended, my dad handed me Roger Angell's World Series recap and I became obsessed with the *New Yorker*'s baseball writer, reading every word he's written on the subject before and since.

Susan riding Charlie O the mule at a birthday party in Alameda, California, 1975.

The A's always remained No. 2 on my list, and unable to see Red Sox games unless they happened to be the Game of the Week, I watched every Oakland game that was televised (not many were in those days) and, more important, listened to every game that wasn't on TV.

Age 10, I decided I wanted to be a baseball play-by-play announcer. I was lucky enough to attend a summer camp at Stevenson High School in Pebble Beach when I was 12, and the school had a radio station, so the station director, Hamish Tyler, took me and several other campers over to broadcast Salinas Spurs' minor-league games. While attending

Stevenson as a high schooler, I did play-by-play for all the football games while also playing basketball, softball, and a little lacrosse (there was no girls' team, so I played with the boys). In college, I continued on, doing color announcing for Stanford football games as well as play-by-play for some basketball games and for all of Stanford's baseball games, along with my friend and co-announcer, David Fisher.

In 1987, Stanford won the College World Series, and David and I called it—I was on the mic for Paul Carey's dramatic, game-winning grand slam off LSU's Ben McDonald in the semis—and because Palo Alto's cable service didn't get ESPN, most of the campus and town listened to KZSU, our little campus station. We got loads of enthusiastic feedback; I still occasionally hear from people who remember those broadcasts.

While playing lacrosse and double-majoring in English and History, I also worked at the campus paper, the *Daily*, which I loved every bit as much as I did KZSU, despite many late nights and early mornings—or maybe because of them. Few things are as much fun as putting out a student newspaper, and things get a little loopy at 2:00 AM. We often performed a ridiculous "hurry up" dance next to particularly slow writers to try to propel things along. I occasionally wish to do that to pokey colleagues (and husband) to this day.

I still dreamed of doing baseball play-by-play, and I interned for Ted Robinson at KCBS radio station in San Francisco in the summer of 1986 and at KPIX-TV in 1987–88, when the legendary Channel 5 crew included Dave McElhatton, Kate Kelly, and Wayne Walker, plus one of the great sports producers of all time, Art Dlugach (and my current Chronicle colleague Steve Kroner, Art's right-hand man). Then, after graduation in 1988, I interned at the *Sacramento Bee*, which had an amazing staff featuring Scott Price (now S.L. Price of *Sports Illustrated*), Tim Keown (now of *ESPN the Magazine*) and news columnist and author Pete Dexter.

My college play-by-play partner, David, was off working in the minors, at Quad Cities, Iowa, doing numerous jobs, including broadcasting, for next to nothing, and when the *Bee* offered me a full-time job, I took it. I figured there were no women doing baseball play-by-play, I wasn't sure I wanted to go to the lowest levels of the minor leagues, and I was happy in Sacramento. I decided being a baseball writer would be pretty great, too.

It still took some time. I worked at the *Bee* for six years and was the primary backup baseball writer for much of that stretch, but while I absolutely loved my time there and my co-workers, I was never offered a full-time baseball job. When A's writer Ron Kroichick asked to come off the beat and I asked to go on, the paper's editors wouldn't make the switch—I was "too delicate to travel full time," one editor told me, "not aggressive enough," another said.

These descriptions make people who know me laugh out loud.

I left at the first chance I got after that, going to cover the Orlando Magic for the *Orlando Sentinel*. I enjoyed everything about the job—the paper was sensational and the Magic were a blast. They went to the NBA Finals the season I was there, 1994–95, with Shaquille O'Neal and Penny Hardaway and Horace Grant. All the players were wonderful—Shaq was a hoot, Penny a sweetheart, and Horace just super cool. The supporting cast was fantastic, too. Dennis Scott was hilarious, Donald Royal smart and full of gossip, Brian Shaw friendly and thoughtful. Brian Hill, the coach, was tremendous to deal with, honest and funny and with a little bit of a New Jersey edge that kept everyone on their toes. It was an embarrassment of riches.

I was convinced that Shaq didn't know my name—he often called me "Selena," because Selena Roberts had covered the team the year before, and he called me "man," "dude," and "bro," all of which always made me laugh. He also did something that would endear him to any beat writer: During the season, the *Sentinel* was the only paper that traveled with the Magic full time, but once the playoffs started, there were suddenly dozens of reporters and broadcasters around. Any time I got boxed out of a scrum with Shaq, he'd say, "Where's our beat writer? Get Susan in here before I start, she's been with us all year!" That's when I learned he *did* know my name. He just liked to tease people.

I still wanted to cover baseball, though, so when I got an offer from the *Dallas Morning News* to cover the Rangers in 1995, I moved on to cover another delightful bunch—especially the 1996 Rangers, the first playoff team in club history. I knew Will Clark from covering the Giants with the *Bee*, and of course there was Pudge Rodriguez, just turning into a star, and fearsome slugger Juan Gonzalez. Mark McLemore, Kevin Elster, and Darren Oliver were among a handful of Californians on the team, so I always leaned on them. My favorite ever, though, was the late Darryl Hamilton, who was a media darling: smooth, great for a sound bite, warm, and genuine. (Stephen Vogt might be the A's closest approximation in recent years.) The Rangers manager, the late Johnny Oates, could be guarded but he treated everyone fairly, and he had a sneaky sense of humor. He loved to just sit and talk about baseball, and I learned so much from him and his staff.

Many Californians have misperceptions about Texas, but I thought Dallas was a fantastic place to live. It's vibrant, with great restaurants and museums and nightlife, and my neighborhood, Oak Lawn, is very diverse and includes the gay section of town, so it reminded me a lot of the Bay Area. Coming from the humidity of Orlando, the heat wasn't even that bad—most of the time.

The *Morning News* had the best sports section in the country at that time, winning countless awards and sending dozens of writers to big events. They hadn't had a ton of women sportswriters, though—none covering baseball, as was often pointed out to me. When I walked into the building on my first day of work, the sports editor yelled across the crowded newsroom, "Hey, Susan, my golf pro wants to know what I'm doing hiring a woman to cover baseball!" I apologized for not having the correct chromosome.

The same time I was hired, my boyfriend (now husband) Dan Brown, turned down a job at the *Morning News* in order to go to the *San Jose Mercury News*, so after the 1996 baseball season, I went home to the Bay Area and began working at the *San Francisco Chronicle*—the newspaper I grew up reading every day at the breakfast table. When I was 10,

I once wrote the *Chronicle* sports section a letter asking why one of my favorite Red Sox (Denny Doyle—shut up, I was 10) wasn't playing and got back a lovely note from now-colleague Bruce Jenkins explaining that Doyle had a sprained ankle and telling me if I ever had any other questions, to contact him. I try to make a point of asking Bruce any and all baseball questions possible now.

* * *

I spent two years as the backup baseball writer at the *Chronicle* and have covered the A's for 20 years full time, but one year into the job, there was a twist: Dan became the *Mercury News'* Giants writer and he covered them for the next three years.

That, of course, meant that we did not see each other much during baseball season for the first three years of our marriage. The Giants are on the road when the A's are home, and vice versa. We lived together at spring training, we saw each other during interleague play, and otherwise, it was little or nothing.

Often, one of us would drop the car off in short-term parking and the other would fly in and pick it up an hour or two later. Once, we met in romantic Columbus, Ohio, for lunch when the A's were playing in Cleveland and the Giants in Cincinnati.

Fortunately, as much as Dan loves baseball, he dislikes traveling, so he was relieved to be switched onto the 49ers after the 2002 season. He's now a columnist and a features writer, so there's a new problem: He occasionally writes about the A's, and we work for rival newspapers, a situation which really came to the fore during the 2017 winter meetings. Dan wrote about it for the *Mercury News* a few months later:

> Sometimes, because of the nature of our jobs at competing Bay Area outlets, we are forced to wage war against each other. It's husband vs. wife, mano-a-womano, vying for the same news. It makes for terrible date nights.

Leo Durocher, the long-ago Giants manager, once said: "If I were playing third base and my mother were rounding third with the run that was going to beat us, I'd trip her. Oh, I'd pick her up and brush her off and say, 'Sorry, Mom.' But nobody beats me."

I am married to Leo Durocher.

Except she wouldn't say "sorry."

Being married to a fellow sportswriter is ideal, though—you understand each other's bizarre schedules, which include working nights and weekends and missing holidays and family events. It's common in the industry; at one point in the early 2000s, five *Chronicle* sportswriters were either married to or dating people at the *Mercury News* or the *Contra Costa Times*.

Naturally, Dan and I met at a sporting event. I was covering UC Davis for the *Bee*, and he was working for the student paper, the *Aggie*. He came up to chitchat to me at the end of UC Davis' first football game in 1990, and I turned on my heel and walked off without saying a word. Charming! He finally got me to talk to him three or four games into the season, and many years later, when he proposed, he did so at Buck Shaw Stadium in Santa Clara—the very place I'd snubbed him.

He wrote about this when the stadium was renovated in 2008.

Quarterback Jeff Bridewell threw for 402 yards, UC Davis beat Santa Clara 31–19, and I made the greatest catch in the history of Buck Shaw Stadium. It happened near the corner of the end zone in the waning minutes of the fourth quarter, while waiting to conduct postgame interviews. That was when I said the first words to the woman who would become my wife.

Granted, those words were, "Bridewell had a good game," and granted, her response was to turn and walk away, but the moment remains nonetheless historic. It was the first play of what would turn out to be an all-time upset: a girl like that with a guy like me. The Miracle on Eyes.

He's so corny. And punny. Very, very punny.

* * *

Even though my dad is the one who set me on my baseball path, my mother, Joyce Fay Slusser, was the one who wound up being an A's obsessive.

A great athlete herself growing up in San Francisco—Ice Capades skater, ski instructor, champion golfer—my mom started off following the team just to read my articles, then began watching some games... and then every game.

Her favorites over the years included Miguel Tejada, Barry Zito, Kurt Suzuki, and, most of all, ex-catcher-turned-broadcaster Ray Fosse. She had such a crush on Fosse, which I always thought was cute and funny until she'd tell me how much she learned about baseball from Ray on the A's telecasts. "Sheesh, Mom," I'd say, "I cover the team, too!"

Toward the end of her life, A's broadcasts were what my mom looked forward to most every day—the team really kept her going, especially during that magical 2012 season. She was 85 and in poor health, and that club gave her so much joy, for which I am ever thankful.

CHAPTER 5
DAVE KAVAL: RELENTLESS INGENUITY

Before the 2017 season, Dave Kaval was named the seventh president in Oakland A's history. Kaval, a Cleveland native who attended Stanford and the Stanford Graduate School of Business, was tasked with leading the team's search for a new stadium. While president of the San Jose Earthquakes MLS team from 2010 to '16, Kaval spearheaded the development of the team's award-winning Avaya Stadium. In 2003 he founded the independent Golden Baseball League. He met with Ken and Susan in his office at the Coliseum in June 2018.

How did you become interested in becoming a sports executive?

For me, it was more like I wanted to start my own business and run my own business. The entrepreneurship was the driving force. We chose minor-league baseball because it was a passion. I've always loved baseball. I grew up in Cleveland going to Municipal Stadium, seeing the Indians, going to Browns games, seeing what sports could do to create community in all these different cities, bringing people together across socioeconomic lines to really have a shared experience around sports. I love that. That was a cool thing.

That was the one thing that made sports so neat, the players and the storylines and different narratives. When I could be a part of starting a league from scratch and put teams in places like Chico, California, and Yuma, Arizona, and St. George, Utah, bringing baseball to those communities, that was really powerful. I didn't go into it thinking I just want to be a sports executive. I went into it like I want to build something. I've always been a builder in my life with whatever I've done—the Golden League, the Earthquakes, or here with the A's. That was the biggest draw for me when I got started.

My dad started his own real-estate business, so I think I always saw the success that he had. That was a big thing for me. He had gone to Stanford Business School back in the '60s. The whole notion of working for yourself and being your own boss and being able to wake up every day and decide what you're going to tackle and attack was the way he lived his life and that was appealing for me.

What are the primary challenges with your position?

It's lonely at the top. You really have to make these impulse decisions alone, but by the same token, you do get to chart the course of the organization. You get to be the leader. You get to not only set that vision but deal with the setbacks and the accountability when things don't go well. You have to be adept at dealing with both those things. That was something I always wanted to do and I think seeing my dad and the success that he had in business, it was something that made a lot of sense for me.

Are there misperceptions about the team president job?

There's a lot of confusion. The first question I always get is: Do you travel with the team? If I travelled with the team, I would probably be divorced. I'm already at home games. If I went to away games too, it would be kind of a lot. The reality is there is a lot of work that goes on beyond the games. We're doing planning for the next season, whether it's sponsorship or community relations or, in my case, with the ballpark development. A lot is going on beyond the scenes. I have an amazing team of people who work for me who make that stuff happen day-to-day. I'm involved in the bigger decisions. I think that's the number one misconception, like old-school baseball, traveling on trains or something like that, playing cards on the train. That's not exactly the way it works.

Do you find that people assume you're involved in player decisions and transactions?

Not as much because we have Billy Beane, and Billy has such an amazing background and expertise and reputation. I think people know that Billy is doing all of that. I think there is confusion about the day-to-day things I'm dealing with. I interface with a lot of fans. I'm on Twitter or I'm meeting people at office hours. I'm always trying to keep the pulse of the fan base and what's going on.

How difficult is it to navigate the best course for an organization when you have to try to keep fans, employees, ownership and other local interests happy?

Everybody has their own agenda. That's not to say that they're bad agendas. People have different points of view and things they're trying to accomplish. When you're at the top, you're looking out for the best of the entire organization, for all the stakeholders, players, front office staff, fans. Sometimes you have to weigh difficult decisions, determine who wins out in different scenarios.

Sometimes there are people who are upset with the decisions I make. Sometimes the decisions I make are wrong. That happens all the time. I'm not infallible. I'm trying to hit .300 and make the Hall of Fame. There are a lot of mistakes that are made in business, and I think it's most important to learn from that and have a culture where the people around you understand that none of us are perfect. We're all trying as best we can to pursue the goals we have. We just want to do it in an authentic way.

What sort of atmosphere are you trying to create, particularly with new offices and so many new hires?

All the places I've ever worked, I've wanted to have a culture that was collegial, innovative—a place where people are risk-taking and have a growth mindset and are open to learning. I think you have to invest in that and you have to hire other people who believe in those things. If you have any people who are divergent, who don't have that shared goal or alignment, it can really be the one apple that spoils the bunch.

As the leader of an organization, you have to make sure that you are constantly understanding the culture and seeing where people are going astray or need reinforcing. Say somebody tried something and it was a big failure. That's okay. We needed to try something new and it didn't work. The hard thing is sometimes it means you lose money or, in the short term, have a setback. You have to have the longer-term view to deal with those short-term setbacks and persevere. That can be super hard if you don't have people who are resilient. I always look for people who have grit, people who have been through challenging situations in the past. That is a good indication if they are going to fit in the culture here.

How much to do you stay on top of business trends or find new approaches to problems?

I'm a really prolific reader. I just read tons of books. I read Peter Thiel's *Zero to One* the other day and I'm reading *How to Think* by Alan Jacobs. It's really interesting. I read the book on Billy Martin, *Flawed Genius*, the other day. It's a fantastic read. Sometimes when you're a genius, you're right on the edge of almost insanity. That was a really powerful lesson on leadership from Martin, who was so associated with Oakland and the A's.

I do like to study other leaders and people who have been successful or look to see who had failures, to learn from that. I talk to CEOs and other people in leadership positions, whether it's me and Billy talking or checking in with friends who are running businesses to understand the way they look at the world and what's working. I don't have it all figured out.

You're famously active and enthusiastic. Do those traits help in leadership?

I've always been a high-energy person. I think a lot of times people like working with me because I am high energy and positive. Even when things are pretty tough, I always try to see the glass half full, even if it's empty. I think it's important, especially in a long season, in a business where there are so many opportunities to get discouraged, to build people up. Even when things are hard, focus on the positives. You have to do that.

It is a really long season. You can't try to sprint through it. The other thing about baseball, which works for me because I really love baseball, is you can't fake it. If you're head honcho of one of these NFL teams, it's eight games. Here, it's 162 games. You really have to like what's going on. When we're on the road, I'm listening to it on the radio or I'm watching on TV. If I have something else going on, I'm reading beat writers' tweets.

I'm so into it. That part is really important. If that's something that's not for you, I think this sport can be a bad choice. I talk about this when I talk about career choices with younger people. Know what you want. Be introspective and self-aware of what makes you tick. Understand if this is a good fit. If not, that's when it can really grind people out. Maybe it's a different sport or different job that's better for them.

Can it be tricky running an organization that includes an ownership group?

Since I started the baseball league, I've never had a boss, per se. I've always reported to a board or ownership. For me, that's a very common state of nature. I think it's a pretty good fit for my skill set. I wake up and I have all sorts of ideas about what needs to get done that day and how to prioritize all of the input, whether it's a call from the league about a grievance or a call from a partner about something that's not working about the sponsorship and they want to pull out. There are all these crises that come up. Being able to understand what to spend time on is critical. That only comes with experience, like the years in Golden League or with the Earthquakes, knowing I should have spent a little more time finding a new jersey partner or understanding our player-acquisition efforts. It's important to weigh those things.

When I think about ownership, it's great because you report back when you need to, but I'm intrinsically motivated. I have a clear set of convictions about where we need to go. I mobilize the resources and the team and the folks who are working for me to go in that direction.

It's not like I'm working for a different set of owners when I spent the last six or seven years working for the Quakes, the sister organization. It was an easy situation since the situation in San Jose went very well. We built this very nice privately financed stadium. The team really grew in revenue and we sold out the stadium for three years and a number of great events.

It was logical to pursue a similar strategy here in Oakland. Oakland itself is a great asset. We *are* rooted in Oakland. From Day One when I was introduced, that was the focus. That's something that I believe in very strongly, that 50 years in this city, even though the Warriors and Raiders are leaving, this can be our great asset. I think that's something that has come through with the communications, as well as our actions.

You seem to relate to fans so well, how much does that have to do with your own background?

I think the biggest thing when I started was people just wanted someone in authority to care. They cared so much for this team and what it meant for the community and their life and their relationship with their family members. They wanted someone in an authority position to care, too. I think what they saw in me was that. It was a perfect time to come in with that perspective. I've always been a fan myself, growing up in Cleveland and seeing the Indians, seeing the Browns. I'm still a fan at heart, so I know that feeling.

The decisions I made out of the gate, whether it was holding office hours or a meeting with fans or honoring our history again—which was a thing that had kind of been lost—those were obvious ones to me. It was like, "Of course we're going to do that." I think for the fans, that connection and that authenticity really went a long way. I think being so accessible has been really important for the fans. Even though I don't have all the answers, I'm trying and we're trying to figure it out together. I think people are willing to go on a journey with you if they feel that it makes sense, that we're actually moving in the right direction.

How much of what you've implemented has come out of talks with fans?

This was the second time this exact thing has happened. When I took over the Earthquakes, the team did not have a spokesperson, a face of the team. I saw the power of that. Some of the same things I did early on there, and some of them I didn't do all that well, but then when I came here we had already done this one time. Miguel Duarte came over with me as my chief of staff, and he was like, "Remember how we had that early Q&A and people loved it? Let's do office hours." In the first month, we had 80 people show up. It was on television, it was a big event. We learned from what we had done in the past. It ended up being a great way to connect to fans and get the pulse of the fan base.

Someone came into the office and said, "It would be cool to name the field Rickey Henderson Field," and we did it. Someone said, "I really want to move Fan Fest to Jack London Square," and we did it. People have gotten jobs. Taj Tashombe, who came to my first office hours, is now our VP of external affairs. This has changed people's lives. It really isn't just lip service. It's the way we're conducting and running the organization. I think it's unusual, and another reason for people to appreciate what we have here and hopefully be a part of it.

What are the most innovative things the organization has done during your tenure?

I think the free game is up there. I remember being in the senior management meeting and people were like, "How can we honor 50 years?" I said, "Well, let's do a free game," and everyone was quiet. "Oh boy, Kaval is crazy."

People were like, "How are we going to do it operationally? It's never been done." The league is calling like, "What's your plan? This has never been done."

I convinced people that it was going to be a great thing and the fans were going to react in a positive way. And they did. It was a huge success. I think it was as positive a fan experience as I've ever seen at the Coliseum in coming here for 25 years.

People were having so much fun. It was like a block party. Even though we had so many people here, they were very respectful. They were just happy.

I think that was something that was a little different. I think some of the fun stuff we've done with the Giants and amplifying the rivalry is

Mascots resembling Dennis Eckersley and Rollie Fingers entertain fans prior to the A's "Free Baseball" night against the White Sox on Tuesday, April 17, 2018, to celebrate the A's first game in Oakland, which was held exactly 50 years ago against the Baltimore Orioles. (AP Photo/Ben Margot)

something that's important for baseball, whether it's the McCovey Cove takeover or the hat buy-back. Those are important things when we think about making sure that 1) we maintain that rivalry and 2) we get our mojo back as an organization

I think for a long time with the Giants' success, we've kind of played second fiddle. Hey, we have nine world championships and we have some of the greatest players in the history of the game. We have an innovative spirit and history with Charlie Finley and Connie Mack and all the different people who have been here. We have to play into that. We have to remind people that's who we are and educate the next generation. It's gone back to the elephant, the Giants, and the Philadelphia A's. This is the kind of thing that casual fans can pick up on and be interested.

What are the main obstacles in finding a stadium site?

Obviously, building anything in California is challenging. I did this one other time, and it was super challenging then. It's super challenging here, but by the same token, it's something that's so worth it. It can have such an impact on the A's as an organization, our ability to win a world championship, plus the impact on the city of Oakland. This is something that could create a renaissance not only around the ballpark but also the district around it in terms of job and economic development and quality of life.

It's a hard task, but it's very worthwhile and it's something I'm very passionate about. For someone who travelled to all 30 ballparks in 38 days and wrote a book about it, to be able to design and develop and open a new ballpark that could be at the cutting edge of ballpark design, that is a complete dream come true. I feel like my life arc has brought me to this position at a perfect time with the right skill set and this great opportunity, this great fan base and great community, to make it a reality.

What was your reaction when the college district board of directors suddenly ended talks about the first stadium site the team settled on, near Laney College, in 2017?

When I got the call at 6:30 in the morning from Jowel Laguerre, who is the chancellor, I was shocked. It really was like getting hit by a two-by-four. We were not expecting it at all.

It was a very difficult blow. It was not only difficult for me, personally, but also for the staff. We were second-guessed in the community. We made the wrong decisions.

At the end of the day, nothing ventured, nothing gained. We felt like that was the Goldilocks site, that it could be perfect in a lot of ways, but it's a decision we needed to make together with the community. If they weren't comfortable with it, then we have to find a different place.

At some point after we had sulked over it for a little bit, we had to pick ourselves up by the bootstraps and attack these other sites, the Coliseum and Howard Terminal, and ensure that we pursue the best option. That's why we're exploring those on a parallel track, because of that experience of losing at Peralta.

It's important to acknowledge that it was a setback and a loss. We can't sugarcoat it. We're on to the next thing. It's frustrating that we spent all that time and it didn't work out, but that happens. Sometimes you strike out.

There were some hard lessons with that, but the most important thing is we persevere and focus on the goal.

How do you view the future on the field, particularly with the young core in place?

I think we have this really nice timing going on between baseball operations and the business side where we have a really good young team that can mature as we open a new ballpark. It's something that Billy has talked about like the Cleveland Indians model in the '90s, which I'm very familiar with. I think it was 455 consecutive sellouts the Indians had when they opened that new building.

If we can get the support of the community and get them excited about the core group of six or seven or eight key players who are going to be here seven, eight, nine, 10, 11 years, players who can compete and contend for world championships, that's something that people can rally around.

People know that Billy and David Forst have put together great teams. The challenge has been keeping them together. That's where the ballpark and additional revenue streams come in. We're going to be able to sign these players and pay them the bigger amounts in arbitration years and beyond that. It's lining up nicely with how the team is developing and the timing of opening the stadium in 2023.

What is the state of the team's relationship with the city and the fan base after so many strong efforts to win back support?

I think it started with repairing bridges. I think for a long time we had turned our back on a lot of them. There was a lot of damage done from that, centering stadium searches on Fremont and San Jose. The first year I was here, we focused a lot on "Rooted in Oakland" as more than a slogan. The elephant mural downtown, events downtown, the *Black Panther* screening, really connecting to the community and being an important pillar of Oakland, connecting to the business community, whether it was Kaiser or Clorox or smaller companies, like 1-2-3-4 Go! Records, reaching out to all of these different organizations to make sure we were in the fabric of Oakland.

That took some time, but now when I'm out there and we're getting exclusive negotiation agreements on the Coliseum and Howard Terminal, we have the relationships and also the bona fides and the credibility to ask for these things. People are like, "Yeah, the A's, they're an upstanding part of the community."

When we went to Port Commission, we had 20 people speak and they talked about what we had done locally. A guy from Ocho Candy said, "I made these candy bars and they sell them at the Coliseum. This is a great thing. I'm employing people. Dave did a deal with us, and this is fantastic." Those are the kinds of things that have made a big difference. It's really down to talking to people. Going to Acts Full Gospel Church and addressing the congregation or having office hours at Everett and Jones Barbeque or going to community events in West Oakland, you connect with people in real ways. The word of mouth that comes out of that is invaluable. It's not just building support, but I learn a lot about what people really thinking about. What are their concerns, whether it's gentrification, homelessness, jobs? How can baseball be a place to bring folks together? Instead of division, unify people around something. In this day and age with Twitter and all the negativity, I think sports is one of the last things in our society that can bring people together. I think we actually have a responsibility to do that. That's the vision I have.

It's empowering and it's energizing when I walk down the concourse and talk to people or when I walk in downtown Oakland and people come up to me. Even today, I was in Jack London Square and a guy came up to me and gave me a high five and said, "Thank you."

People are grateful for what we are doing here. It's like a family member, and people just want to see it do well. I think it's a very powerful thing.

CHAPTER 6

KEN KORACH: SO YOU WANT TO BE A BROADCASTER?

I have a love-hate relationship with the clock. If you can't budget your time, there is no way to survive 162 baseball games in 180 days. I actually find the regimen oddly attractive. The key is to submit to the rhythm of the season. My wife, Denise, says I'm useless from April to October, and there is a lot of truth in what she says. If it's a night game at home, I'm normally up around 6:30 AM and by 1:30 PM I'm in the shower and the ETA at the Coliseum is usually around 2:45. I get home around 11:00 at night and then the whole thing starts again the next day.

Not that I relish the 3:00 AM arrivals and the 55,000 miles we fly each season, or the stretches of 20 games in 20 days in six different cities, but I get to call a ballpark my office and I'm still living a kid's dream.

My great friend Debbie Gallas, aka, "The Fixer," who retired from the A's after the 2017 season after a career of keeping things together for people like me, once had a tough time with the grind. I told her that you can't fight it. There are days in which fatigue sets in and you feel like you'll never be rested again. But two or three days later everything usually defaults back to normal, or at least as normal as it can be during the baseball season.

There's more freedom on the road. Home is where the clock becomes more of a factor since real life responsibilities need to be wedged into the day. Bill King used to hate the intrusion and he would joke that the time would come when he would only do the road games. He was much more relaxed on the road where he could lead his kind of "civilized" life. This might include a glass of wine or two at a favorite lunch spot, a nap and then he was ready to go. None of that happened at home, especially because the act of driving was anathema to Bill. His commute to the park could take more than an hour.

It's not all work, let's be clear about that. Once the weather warms up in the Bay Area, I try to play golf once a week, sometimes on the morning of a night game and other times when our coaches organize a round after a day game. In June and July, you can play until 9:00 PM.

The season requires almost total immersion, and it's important to find separation, even for a few hours. Golf helps, and so do art museums and other activities on the road. My routine starts with about 90 minutes of homework each morning in the hotel and then I try to pick a diversion for another 90 minutes or so that gets me that separation. It's hard to beat spending a summer day in the cities we visit. Then it's a bite to eat and a workout in the hotel gym or a walk and time to head to the park.

Cabs or hotel shuttles are options in many of the cities and we can walk to the park in places like Cleveland and Minnesota. Mickey Morabito, the A's Hall-of-Fame worthy director of team travel, schedules two busses to the park. If it's a night game, for instance, the first bus usually leaves at 2:00 and the second bus—which is often dubbed "the broadcasters' bus"—leaves for the park at 3:30.

I do much of my prep work at the Coliseum when we're home since I'm at the park so early. One thing I never have to worry about is the quality of the production and technical aspects of the broadcasts. Our home engineer, Mike Baird, is as talented and knowledgeable as anyone in the business. He mixes a game exactly as it should be. You shouldn't have to fight the crowd noise to hear the play-by-play, but you should always hear the crowd. His ability to walk that fine line, especially in the big moments where the fans are going nuts, is a source of huge comfort for me. Mike and I have done almost 2,000 games together and I've never questioned him.

Our control center is at our studios in San Francisco. For years our producer was John Trinidad, who was known as kind of a guru to the other producers and engineers in the Bay Area. That's how highly regarded he is. John's fought health issues in recent years and has passed the baton to Robert Costa, who does most of the games, and Scott Pastorino, who spells Robert on Sundays. I've always envisioned the studio looking like the cockpit of a 747. Those guys need to be on their toes, because they're playing commercials, editing interviews, searching for highlights of other games, producing pregame vignettes, cutting and organizing the postgame highlights, and running our network.

We've come a long way since John was our remote engineer for San Jose State football and he would pile dozens of cassette tapes on top of a recorder for playback during the highlight segments. Everything is done digitally now, and I have no idea how it happens.

My pregame responsibility is to record the *Bob Melvin Show*, and the time can vary from around 3:30 to 4:30 if it's a night game at home and it can be as late as 5:30 on the road.

Melvin's superstitions are well known around baseball circles, although he hedges a little if you ask him about it. "I'm not superstitious," he says. "But, just in case..." The time and place for his show depends on the outcome of the previous game. If the A's lose and we did the show before he met the media that day, then you can be certain we'll do the show after he meets the media the next day. And we might shift locations from the dugout to his office.

Melvin is not alone with his quirks, of course. Years ago, A's manager Art Howe tried to break a losing streak by hiking deep into the right-field stands at Fenway Park to tape a show with Bill King from the red-covered seat that marks where Ted Williams' massive, 502-foot home run against the Tigers landed on June 9, 1946.

Trying to break a similar curse in Detroit, Ken Macha and Bill ventured down the right-field line and did the show in the cramped, subterranean bullpen at Tiger Stadium.

I've recorded the show sitting down, standing up, in the dugout, in Melvin's office, behind home plate and down the left-field line. If the A's win and I'm sitting to his left, then I'm sitting to his left next time. Sometimes I'm on the couch and he's at his desk in his office. There are times when we'll debate whether the statute of limitations has run out on a location. Do you want to change after a loss that follows a winning streak or hang in there one more day to give what's been working another shot?

All of this adds some levity during the season and among the Bay Area media, the feeling is pretty much unanimous among that BoMel embodies everything you'd want in a manager. He's a tough competitor who burns badly to win, but he's also gracious and accommodating with the press and communicates with a rookie reporter as he would with a veteran player. And not that he needs the validation, but he's one of a select group to win the Manager of the Year Award in both leagues. The others are Bobby Cox, Tony La Russa, Lou Piniella, Jim Leyland, Dave Johnson, and Joe Maddon.

Spending time with Melvin is a big part of the pregame routine for the press, and Bob normally schedules his session around the time the A's take the field to get ready for batting practice. The home team hits first—usually at around 4:15. On the road, he'll usually meet the press at around 5:15, which makes the prep time a little more condensed.

I'm a creature of habit in the first two innings of a broadcast. In fact, I think our listeners can probably predict where I'm going once the game begins.

My broadcast partner, Vince Cotroneo, does the lineups and then throws it to me for the first pitch. I'll set the defenses in the top and bottom half of the first and then there are some bookkeeping items, like the time and temperature at first pitch and the umpires. If we're on the road, I'll mention the dimensions of the outfield, especially in some of the quirkier places like Houston and Fenway. I'll run through the American League West standings and review the action of the West teams from the day before. I'll profile the starting pitchers and, if it's the first game of a series, talk about what the other team has been doing recently.

Time permitting, and often beginning in the second inning, it's fun and informative to rehash situations that need clarifying from the game before. This is one of the areas where Melvin is helpful since he's so forthcoming when it comes to his decisions. Among many other things, Vince is on top of this aspect of what we do. He's diligent about asking questions of players and coaches, and the insights add a nice layer to the broadcasts. Taking our listeners inside the game is something that baseball's pace affords. As Vince says, "Baseball is a talking sport."

* * *

There are many fine lines in what we do, especially when it comes to getting information into a broadcast. No matter how much information you have, the game always comes first, and there have been thousands of times over the years when I've harkened back to conversations with the legendary Tigers broadcaster Ernie Harwell.

Ernie usually had simple answers to my questions, but those answers provided sage advice. And whenever I asked him something that pertained to our jobs, he responded with an answer that was so clear, it could have gone into a baseball-broadcasting textbook.

One time in 2003, when the Tigers were in the middle of a 119-loss season, I asked Ernie how he stayed motivated. Ernie: "Every game is its own chapter." The same season, Charlie Steiner, the radio voice of the Dodgers, asked Ernie how he stayed so positive. "Charlie," Ernie said in his Georgia drawl, "you can either look at life through the windshield or the rear-view mirror."

Another time, when the Tigers were looking at a five-hour flight to the East Coast after a night game in Oakland, I asked him how he handled the travel after all the years. Ernie: "I've got a good book and I have nothing better to do." The message: Don't hassle the things you can't control and make the best of every minute.

I loved Ernie and I could have listened to him read the phone book for four hours and enjoyed every second. To me, he had one of the greatest voices of all time—the perfect blend of Southern mellow and a seasoned timbre that came from a lifetime on the air. He had this almost musical rhythm, keeping the perfect tempo but never over-talking it.

Baseball announcers come in all shapes and sizes and voices. I'm probably the last person to ask about my own voice. People seem to generally like it and that's been a good thing for my career, but as I've gotten older and more comfortable in my own shoes, I don't compare how I sound to others.

Most of my vocal training came from trial and error. I didn't study broadcasting in school, but I took a short class that focused on diction and enunciation from a broadcasting school in Los Angeles when I was in my mid–20s. I still use some of the exercises, like reading as quickly as possible backward with an emphasis on trying to pronounce the words as clearly as possible.

A baseball announcer doesn't need a voice as resonant as Lon Simmons' to be successful. Certainly, it doesn't hurt and there's no doubt that there are voices that aren't suited to broadcasting work, but the way a broadcaster uses his or her voice is more important than sounding like James Earl Jones. Bill King, for instance, always felt his voice was inferior to Lon's, saying that Lon could cut through the sound of a roaring crowd, while Bill felt his own voice was thin. But Bill had a musician's sense of tonality that was distinctively and pleasantly his own.

Sometimes when I'm on the air, I'll imagine someone driving through the vineyards in Napa and try to set a nice, comfortable, mellow experience and a pastoral vibe for the drive through the countryside.

Baseball announcers need to wear well over time. The great ones like Ernie have the gift of being conversational but knowing when and how to punch things up when the situation warrants. He used his voice as an instrument and conveyed the big moments without going over the top. There are lots of ways to do this. Bill, for instance, quickened his tempo, which was his way of bringing the action into focus. Bill, Ernie, Scully, Simmons and all the masters had the ability—like the great dramatic actors—to move their listeners emotionally without screaming at them.

I asked Ernie once about his philosophy for doing a game: "You call the game, but that would be boring if that's all you did, so you mix in a little color," he said.

I've repeated those words many times to aspiring broadcasters. You focus on the game—that's always the most important thing. Then you augment the play-by-play with your information. How much you use depends on the flow of the game.

One thing I've stressed is the need to find your own style. What might work for one person might not work for someone else. This was a long and tough lesson for me to learn. I got to a major market (San Francisco) after only three years in the business and when I got there, I was tied up in knots trying to sound like the people I idolized. There is only one person you can sound like and that's yourself. Until that happens, you've got no chance.

I was lucky to survive that period because I was a mess for a couple of years. I figured I was ready for the move to KCBS, supposing my work in Sonoma County was good enough or I wouldn't have been hired. But the move to San Francisco revealed insecurities that had been hidden in a smaller market. Kent Derdivanis, my PCL broadcast partner in Phoenix, used to talk about how it was a blessing and a curse to grow up in California. What a gift it was to be influenced by King, Simmons, Scully, Enberg, and Co., but how would you ever be as good as those guys?

I look back at those early KCBS days as a dizzying cycle of doing a game and then over-analyzing it, listening to tapes until I felt I needed to try something different the next time.

It took a couple of years to find my footing, and getting to Phoenix in the summertime and the daily routine of doing 140 minor league games got me away from dissecting everything and into enjoying the experience. I started to think, "If I'm not having any fun, how could I expect listeners to have any?"

* * *

There is no formula or prescription for finding success in our business, but, with play-by-play, it starts with the fundamentals. I try to visualize that a broadcast is built from the field to the booth. It doesn't start with us in the booth and then down to the field. I've listened to announcers who are so obsessed with forcing their information into a broadcast, it's as if they are doing a talk show and the game is going on in the background. As Dick Enberg said, "Don't get in the way of the game."

Enberg, as he began his first season with the Angels in 1969, learned an important lesson from the team's general manager, Fred Haney. Haney, who managed the Braves to the world title in 1957, also had a background in broadcasting. He told Enberg: "When all else fails and you've run out of things to say, remember your first responsibility is to broadcast the ball." That's a pretty good way to cut right to the basics—broadcast the ball.

The score, the count, does the hitter bat left or right? Where are the fielders playing and, especially, if there's a runner at third and less than two outs, is the infield in? Is the third baseman in on grass and is the pitcher working from the third-base side of the slab? You can't give the score too often.

We're very fortunate in that we start every broadcast with a blank canvas and then we try to fill in the colors. Bill, for instance, was fascinated with clouds. He was an artist who would literally paint clouds when he ventured out into the countryside in Marin County and he also painted them in word pictures on the air. There are all kinds of things that can add to a listener's ability to visualize the scene. What does the ballpark look like and how does the hitter look in the box? The effect of the wind and the color of the uniforms. Have the lights taken effect?

* * *

I have no idea how saying "the lights have taken full effect" started for me—it may have come from Scully. When I was working in the California League in 1984, it was my way of saying that it was fully dark outside. The press box at Rohnert Park Stadium, where the Redwood Pioneers played, was tiny and we were all cramped together so that everyone in there could hear everything I said. It got to the point where as soon as I said, "The ..." everyone would chime in with: "... lights have taken full effect."

Fast forward to opening day 2018 and I got a text from the Pioneers general manger that year, Eric Schulz. The A's had just finished a four-hour game with the Angels: "It was great to hear you," Eric wrote. "Had me wondering if the lights were on but had not yet taken effect."

I guess we all must be known for something. For decades, I never had a home run call. Fans and writers would ask me about this all the time, but the simple answer was that I never thought about it much and I didn't want to stay up nights thinking of something that would sound contrived. After I had spent 10 or 11 years with the A's, I said, on a home run, that the outfielder "will watch it fly!" Again, I have no idea where it came from, but it seemed kind of natural and I used it a few times. I didn't think much about it until I was doing book signings for *Holy Toledo*. Fans would ask me to write "watch it fly" along with my signature. You need to be careful, though. You can't be so obsessed with getting your home-run call on the air that you fail to describe what happens.

Kevin Cremin, the longtime producer/engineer of the Mariners' radio broadcasts, who retired in 2017, had a pet peeve about home- run calls. He hates it when an announcer doesn't describe where the ball landed. Is it 10 rows back in the bleachers or did it land in the bullpen? This speaks to being as descriptive as possible.

Just recently I mentioned that A's third baseman Matt Chapman made a "fantastic play" on a bunt. But I never said what he did. Did he barehand the ball or did he field the bunt in his glove and transfer to his hand for the throw? Was it a cross-the-body throw? Just saying he made a fantastic play isn't enough.

Another phrase I've used is: "Ring him up, strike three called!" Again, I have no idea of the origin.

I've tried, with some of these phrases, to pay homage to some of my friends and broadcasters I admire. John Rooney, the voice of the White Sox when I worked in Chicago, always followed the first out of a game by saying, "That's the way our ballgame begins."

What words does one use to describe the balletic pick and throw that is Matt Chapman fielding a slow roller? (AP Photo/David Zalubowski)

Mike Patrick, one of the mainstays on ESPN for decades, would say: "It's great to have you with us" while doing his opening stand-up. Mike was a guest on a talk show I was doing about 25 years ago, and he was so gracious that I thought I would use "great to have you with us" as a small tribute and because it seemed like a warm way to engage the audience.

It's all in good fun. One time, after coming back from station identification on an A's radio broadcast, I failed to say: "It's great to have you with us." I got a message from a concerned fan who said, "When you came back from the ID, you didn't say 'It's great to have you with us.' As fans, we're worried. Are you mad at us?"

* * *

Learning the language helps amplify the calls. There is nothing worse that searching for the correct word or phrase to describe what you're seeing and not being able to find it. It's no coincidence that the announcers I've mentioned had a great command of and love for the language. Ernie was a songwriter, Vin was a voracious reader whose on-air analogies took his listeners back decades and sometimes centuries. "Watching the Dodgers play today reminds me of a story from 17th century French literature...." Bill's command of the language was unparalleled.

One of the most gratifying moments during the 2017 season came at an A's function when a young blind woman approached me to say how much our broadcasts kept her engaged with baseball. Hearing something like that makes it all worthwhile.

Another thing that tied my broadcast heroes together was their class. Every one of them—Scully, King, Enberg, Harwell, Simmons, Hearn— were as gracious as could be.

A brief Chick Hearn story speaks to this. In the Rebels' heyday, Chick moonlighted by broadcasting a package of UNLV basketball games on TV back to L.A. I was doing San Jose State basketball and I was a one-man band. I lugged the radio equipment around, engineered and did the games by myself. To get a break, I recorded a halftime interview before tip-off. On this night, I approached Chick, whom I had never met although he was one of my all-time heroes. Chick obliged and did something I've never forgotten. He took a moment to write my name in his scorebook, so that when he answered my questions he referred to me by name. "Well Ken..." I was a complete nobody, but that simple gesture by Chick elevated me in a way. Chick made it sound like we were old friends. That's class.

* * *

With the understanding that everything starts with the fundamentals, there is no doubt that things change when your team is struggling. In a tough year, you need to be more creative in finding things to talk about. Or, as Vince says, "diversionary tactics."

When the team is good, especially when the calendar turns to the pennant-race months of August and September, the games almost broadcast themselves. So much more is riding on every at-bat because the path of a season can turn on a bad pitch or two. The crowd can take you along for a ride and it's easy to pause and let the energy in the park tell some of the story.

That's harder to do in September when your team is 20 games out. You need to dig a little deeper, especially with a young team.

One time we were down in L.A. while the A's were mired in a very tough year. I was in Scully's booth while the A's were on the field stretching, when Vinny turned to me and said, "Just remember, don't get too caught up with what is going on down there. You've got a job to do up here."

Those thoughts were echoed by my friend Hank Greenwald, who waged a great battle against a variety of ailments before he died at 83 on October 22, 2018. Hank broadcast more than his share of bad games with the Giants, and he said if you get down when your team is struggling, you're going to sound as flat as the team is playing and you can't let that happen.

Bill used to say that no matter the circumstances—even if it was a 10–2 game in the sixth inning—you need to keep your energy up. It sounds so simple and automatic, but early in my career, I had to learn another tough lesson that related to the energy of a broadcast.

I was doing San Jose State football for KCBS Radio in 1985. The station also had the rights to the Stanford games, which led to an unusual arrangement since they had advertising clients to satisfy from both teams.

The Stanford crew did the game live and we followed on tape-delay. It was six straight hours of the same game. Stanford won the game in a blowout and my performance was awful. I got called on the carpet by the station's general manager, Ray Barnett. Barnett, a broadcasting legend, summoned me to his office and chastised me for delivering a boring, uninspiring broadcast—and he was dead right. He asked me why I hadn't shown some emotion, especially because SJSU had played so poorly against one of its rivals. I told him that because I was new on the job, I had decided to focus on the play-by-play and didn't feel comfortable offering any opinions. That's when Barnett delivered some firm advice.

"We hired you to do a job," Barnett said, "which means we trust your judgment. The broadcast had no life, and it doesn't mean you're taking unnecessary shots if you show some frustration. Why not turn to Dave [Ellis, my broadcast partner] and talk about it? Dissect the game. Show some emotion. The fans are feeling it and you should, too. When you do this, it adds life to the broadcast, plus you get it out of your system, which would probably loosen you up, so you don't sound so dead."

There was nothing I could say. It took some time, but it was a lesson well-learned. Later, while working with Bill, I was struck by how well he could blend his criticism of the team with his responsibility as the team's voice. As unvarnished as Bill could be, he told me that he always tried to leave the listener with something positive to remember. Finding context was another reason Bill was so respected within the organization. As Billy Beane told me when I asked him how he felt when Bill criticized the team: "When Bill said it, we probably deserved it."

Even if the A's are 20 games out in August, I try to start every game with the idea that we're going to tell the story of the game that day. But there's also the realization that it's harder to hold an audience during that kind of a season, so finding interesting things to talk about is even more important. This is especially true these days, with the increasingly languid pace of play.

You're nothing in our business without credibility. I asked Scully for his definition of the essence of a baseball broadcast. "That you're believable," Vinny told me. "If you say that everything is great for your team, it won't matter when something really good happens."

I mentioned a story involving former A's centerfielder Dwayne Murphy in my book about Bill and it bears repeating. One time, Murph was miffed when he heard an excited home-run call of Bill's for the opposition. "Bill," Murph said, "I heard your call and it sounded just like one of ours." To which Bill replied, "Murph, you just paid me a big compliment."

It used to drive Bill nuts when he heard a big play by the opponent called by the home-team announcer in a restrained voice as if it was a mundane grounder to short. Bill understood that part of our job is to sell tickets, and there is no doubt he was emotionally invested in the A's wins and losses. But describing the action is what we do and appreciating the great plays—no matter who's making them—is a big part of selling the game. How do you sell anything without credibility?

We've been fortunate in the Bay Area to have a tradition of playing things down the middle. You're never going to hear anyone refer to their team as "we." As I wrote earlier, there are many fine lines in what we do. Getting excited and showing emotion on the big calls for your team is a vital part of the job. But when the call crosses the line into rooting, it peels away the audience's trust.

Not long ago, I had a conversation with an executive from our flagship station in San Francisco. He was telling me how much he enjoyed hearing one of his favorite television announcers rooting nonstop for fly balls to leave the park. He didn't come right out and say it, but I took it as kind of an oblique suggestion. Now, certain styles work in certain markets and an approach like that might be accepted or even encouraged somewhere else. In this case, he was taken aback when I replied, "You're never going to hear that on one of our broadcasts."

I hate it when I hear my call of Miguel Tejada's homer that capped the A's 18th game of the winning streak in 2002. I think it's over the top, but I've taken solace in two things: One, it was what I was feeling at that moment and I suppose if you're going to lose your mind on the air, Tejada's heroics that day would qualify. The other is what Greenwald told me after the game: "The reason that call works is because you don't get excited over every little thing that happens."

* * *

Being crisp and accurate on the calls is something every announcer strives for. Again, there is no formula for how to get there, but I've been trying to reach the kind of relaxed intensity athletes talk about. It's kind of a Zen thing, I guess, since I'm looking for the "no-mind" state that Shawn Green writes about in his insightful book, *The Way of Baseball, Finding Stillness at 95 MPH*. The book has meant the world to me. It's the greatest lesson for life and, in my case, broadcasting, that I've found.

Shawn's journey to become one of the great ballplayers of his time led him away from his ego and the stifling pursuit of what others expected him to be. That was me in my earlier days when I would listen to those tapes over and over.

John Wooden used to preach, "Be quick but don't hurry." It's dangerous on the air if you anticipate and get ahead of yourself. Having just a slight delay is optimal, and this allows for plays to almost happen in slow motion. That's when great athletes feel they have mastery over their sport.

When it comes to making calls, I'm trying to find the uncluttered state that Shawn writes about, so that it's just the game and me with no barriers in between.

Looking back on his 1998 season with the Blue Jays, when he hit 35 home runs and drove in 100, Shawn wrote, "I'd step into the box and, through my rhythmic routines, became aware of my body. Released from my mind's interference, my awareness was now free to connect to the pitcher. By the time the ball left his hand, I was fully alert in the moment, so that the pitcher was now my partner in the moment rather than the opponent."

Part of my pregame routine is filling out my scorebook with lineups, batting averages, and assorted notes on the two teams. I used to also make up a defensive chart. Many announcers write the names of the players with their corresponding defensive positions in their scorebooks or use a separate sheet of paper.

I stopped using a chart about 15 years ago. Again, there is no right or wrong way—the key is getting the calls correct and it doesn't matter how to get there. For me, I found that using a chart takes my eyes off the field, so memorizing the names is part of the pregame routine. I'm not married to this, though. I'll use a chart in spring training and if the A's are playing an unfamiliar team in interleague play, especially in a National League park where double switches are likely.

I'm not sure any plan or philosophy is perfect. When Dallas Braden was beginning the top of the ninth inning of his perfect game, I took my notes and media guides and put them behind me. I didn't want to be tempted by anything that might divert attention from the history unfolding. My focus was as sharp as it's ever been—butterflies were churning in my stomach—and I'm happy with the call of the final out. But it might have been nice to have framed it with some context about how this was the 19th perfect game in baseball history and the A's first since Catfish Hunter in 1968. You can't think of everything, and I suppose scripting a coda to the call might have made it sound contrived.

The Jeter Flip during Game 3 of the 2001 ALDS turned out to be one of the most famous plays of all time. The play had many layers, with action all over the field.

The Yankees were leading 1–0 with two outs in the bottom of the seventh inning and 55,000 fans had squirmed to the edges of their seats at the Coliseum. The A's had a 2–0 lead in the series and all the momentum, but Mike Mussina was pitching a gem and there was the specter of Mariano Rivera looming in the bullpen if the A's didn't tie it up.

Jeremy Giambi was on first for the A's when Terrence Long lashed a line drive down the right-field line. Giambi headed to second as Shane Spencer dug the ball out of the corner. Giambi went to third as the throw came in, but the ball air-mailed a double cut-off alignment of Alfonso Soriano and Tino Martinez.

Now Giambi was at third, with A's third base coach Ron Washington waving him home. At this point, I came a split-second from blowing the call. As the ball was rolling past the first-base line into foul territory, I almost scored Giambi, and that would have been a disaster. And maybe nine times out of 10 he would have scored, but this wasn't an ordinary play. With one eye on Giambi, I saw a figure flashing before my eyes to my right. Now, I don't memorize numbers like I did in football, but even then, Jeter's No. 2 was iconic, and that was a lucky break. Jeter fielded the ball with his momentum headed toward the Yankee dugout as Giambi neared home plate. Jeter flipped the ball backhanded, Giambi didn't slide, Kerwin Danley made the call and Giambi was out. And for all intents and purposes, the series was over, even though the A's were only down by a run. All the air was sucked out of the Coliseum, as well as the A's momentum. They lost the next three games and The Jeter Flip will go down along with Kirk Gibson's home run in the 1988 World Series as the two most devastating plays in A's history.

I'm okay with the call. I did the best I could with it. I wish I had said "flip" by Jeter instead of "pitch," but I'll take it. In life and in work, you hope you've learned some lessons along the way. I imagine the instinct that kept me from scoring Giambi came from doing thousands of games in ballparks from the low minors to the big leagues. Every game is a chance to get better.

Thom Brennaman was doing the national telecast that night. You hear his call most of the time, and for good reason: Thom absolutely nailed it—it was perfection—and he deserves all the kudos in the world for rising to such an important moment.

* * *

I've messed up plenty of calls, and one that stands out is Mark McGwire's prodigious homer in Cleveland on April 30, 1997. I don't know where my head was at, but it wasn't in the moment when McGwire hit a ball that crashed off the scoreboard above the bleachers at Jacobs Field. I stumbled through the call without the needed description and sense of wonder at the majesty of the ball's flight.

Being in the right frame of mind can be a byproduct of preparation. There are many quotations that apply. John Wooden, borrowing from Benjamin Franklin: "Failing to prepare is preparing to fail." Jack Nicklaus: "My confidence was developed through preparation."

Ken Korach in the Bill King Radio Booth at the Coliseum, 2018. (Michael Zagaris)

I've been so fortunate to observe my heroes first hand. Once before a game, I noticed Enberg walking down the hallway to his booth. I was struck by the look of total confidence on his face. He had just come out of an office or the press room and I was thinking that he had probably just finished his preparation and now he was ready to go. I hate the feeling of being harried before a game. If I'm confident that I have everything organized, then it's a lot easier to relax and get into the flow of the game.

Part of my pregame routine involves watching batting practice from the booth to get used to tracking fly balls, especially on the road before the first game of a series. Each ballpark presents unique challenges from the outfield dimensions to lighting and the way the ball carries. The broadcast booths and vantage points vary from park to park, which can affect depth perception. Fenway Park is especially tough. Our booth is very high on top of the roof and almost right over home plate looking down the left-field line at the Green Monster. It's a tough place to judge fly balls. The monster is 37 feet high and I've watched plenty of balls I thought were going out crash into the wall and vice versa.

I started watching BP from the booth over 30 years ago when I was broadcasting for the Pioneers. Devon White, who became a great major-league player, was just a kid back then, but he was the best centerfielder I had ever seen. Devo was incredibly diligent during BP, especially on the road, the way he read balls off the bat as if it was a game situation. This was a part of his training, and four years later, he won the first of his seven Gold Gloves. None of the accolades came by accident, and I owe a tip of the hat to him for setting a very impressive example.

One of the great things about coming up broadcasting baseball in the minor leagues is learning to fend for yourself. The best stories are still the ones you get at the park—from around the batting cage or in the clubhouse or in the press room where the scouts normally hang out before a game.

When I worked in the Cal League, we were lucky to get a one-page printout of statistics, and that was it. There weren't game notes or public relations departments, but that was a blessing in disguise. If you didn't develop good work habits in the minor leagues, you wouldn't have much to talk about.

Going into the 2018 season, for example, I knew I had to spend even more time on the field, knowing that with a very young team, helping our audience learn more about the players would go a long way toward rekindling interest in the team. Like Enberg said, give the listener a reason to care.

There's also information available everywhere you look on the internet, and doing research at home or in hotels goes hand-in-hand with the prep work at the park. Open a computer and a million things spill out. You need to know when to stop.

I usually start with the local papers and MLB.com. It's no different from any other job. You get out of it what you put in. I'll begin looking for basic information on the teams and players and other items specific to the game that day.

The A's and all the teams do a great job of providing game notes with pages of information, and so much of my preparation involves looking for things that go beyond numbers. It sometimes drifts toward kind of a random bit of free association. I might think of a player on the other team who might remind me of a story, and it might remind me of a player who played in the 1920s. You might be searching for the guy on Baseball Reference (an invaluable resource) and maybe just by chance, he's from the Bay Area and now you have a story that, as Scully's says, "knits it all together."

It's also very important to mention that whenever broadcasters use information from newspapers or an online site, they should give credit, unless it's something that's common knowledge or said in a scrum with the manager or players.

I've mentioned idols like Scully, Bill, and Enberg quite a bit because they set such high standards, and one of the many things that separated them was their desire to make every broadcast special. Anyone can regurgitate statistics or game notes, but they went the extra yard searching for interesting stories to draw the audience in.

My last lengthy conversation with Enberg, who died in 2017, came before a game between the A's and the Padres on Father's Day in 2012. I stopped by his booth with some trepidation, because I knew how much he got locked in before a game. He welcomed me in and began telling me about his father. Dick had had a difficult relationship with his dad, a steely man whose personality mirrored the harsh conditions of the upper Midwest winters of his youth. He never praised his son, but left him with words that molded Dick's diligence: "The day you think you're so good that you can't improve, just remember you can only go one way—down."

Their relationship improved when Enberg's dad came west to live with Dick and his wife, Barbara, near the end of his life. Now Enberg was writing an ode to his dad that he would voiceover for the opening of the Father's Day telecast. I could feel the emotion. I'd known he was great for decades, but times like that reinforced that you can't fake authenticity. And that's a common thread among the voices of my youth.

CHAPTER 7
DAVID FORST:
FROM HARVARD
TO HATTEBERG

David Forst began working in the A's front office in 2000, spent 12 years as the team's assistant general manager and became Oakland's general manager in 2015. A graduate of Harvard, where as a senior shortstop he set a team record with 67 hits, Forst has turned down numerous opportunities to run other teams in order to stay with the A's. He's long been seen as Billy Beane's heir apparent. Forst sat down with Ken and Susan for a conversation in his Coliseum office in June 2018.

When did you decide you wanted to work in a major-league front office?

The short story is there was nothing else I wanted to do when I was done playing other than to try to work in baseball. The landscape was different 20 years ago. There were no books or movies about front offices.

I wanted to play in the big leagues. I didn't want to work here, I wanted to play here. There wasn't the publicity about executives; I knew who the Dodgers' GM was but mostly because my dad worked for his brother-in-law, or something like that. You might know who the GMs were, but you didn't know much about scouting or the rest of the front office.

When I figured out I couldn't play here, the next best thing was working here. I knew who Paul DePodesta was because we had friends in common. He moved over here the year that I was playing independent ball and I had heard what he was doing here.

I sent a résumé, and Paul called and said, "We're hiring for a full-time entry-level baseball ops job, would you be interested in interviewing?" I heard from a couple other teams. Josh Byrnes was with the Indians at the time, Kevin Morgan with the Mets, a few others. The A's brought me in for an interview in October 1999.

It was really just Billy and Paul at that time. There was really nobody else in baseball ops. In November, they offered me the job and I started on January 1. I had to learn the business, fill in the gaps. I started out doing elementary spreadsheets for the coaching staff, keeping Excel stats. I did advance reports off of video, and I created my own PowerPoint template.

Paul just said, "Follow along and see where you can add stuff." Rick Peterson was the pitching coach and he wanted first-pitch swing percentage—we didn't have a database of the most elementary stuff. Our database was whatever games I watched on videotape and charted. Dan Feinstein would send me home with three or four videotapes a night and I would chart as many games as I could to create a database of stats.

When I first started, they had a couple of arbitration cases. I sat in on those because there was nobody else to help out. Paul put together the Ariel Prieto arbitration case by himself, and he needed the most basic stuff.

It was a very speedy learning curve. Now, when you have a dozen people in the front office, these younger guys don't get to do that stuff until their third or fourth year.

How much has the technology involved changed?

I charted every game on the same laptop until the middle of 2003. The program we used, Bats, only ran on the software company's laptop, so I had this huge laptop that I had to take home and back. Paul had brought it with him from Cleveland, and the only data you put into that software was what you created. When Bryn Alderson got here, I turned the laptop over to him. It wasn't until 2004 or 2005 that there were companies that provided us with all of the charted data.

Now, the young analysts sit up in a nice suite and watch the game. When I was young, I was sitting in the video room for four hours a night, charting every pitch. It was the only way we had pitch counts. Billy would run in from the weight room: "How many pitches has this guy thrown?" They didn't have it on the broadcast. The pitching coach had it in the dugout, but otherwise we didn't have pitch counts.

It sounds like it was 100 years ago. It wasn't that long ago.

Did you have a sense when you arrived that the team might be on the verge of a long run of playoff appearances?

Having lived in Boston for six years, I didn't follow the A's. I didn't know a lot about it. When I started, Billy and Paul basically said, "We think we're going to be good."

The team in 1999 got better as the season went along. I never imagined we'd win in 2000, my first year. And then to win in the first four years, I didn't know any differently.

I didn't realize how hard that really is. It just seemed like, "Billy is pretty smart, and I'm sure we're going to do this every year." It wasn't until 2007, 2008 that I really looked back and said, "We're pretty lucky."

Moneyball came out in 2003. What impact did that have on the game and how did it affect the A's?

We saw the practices of other teams change pretty quickly after the book was published. It was only a matter of time anyway, but it maybe sped up the process a little bit. I was new enough and competitive enough in 2002 that I didn't really understand why Billy was letting Michael Lewis be here in the front office. In retrospect, it was great for the organization and the game as a whole, but I think Michael signed my copy of the book "to the one guy who was suspicious of me the whole time."

Moneyball definitely changed things. I didn't expect that 15 years later Billy would be still making speeches about it. I thought the book was going to reveal some of our secrets and speed up the way people did things similar to how we do them. I didn't think it was going to change the sports industry the way it has.

It would be hard to say it didn't have an impact. You look at the demographics in front offices now compared to when I started in 2000… Theo Epstein getting the Boston job, Paul getting the LA job, those were huge moments in how people viewed who could be a general manager. It was a combination of things, but I don't think Paul gets the LA job without [owner] Frank McCourt having read Moneyball. Theo was hired a little bit ahead of the publication of the book.

How has your job evolved in recent years?

What I do now is manage people. I manage [director of player development] Keith Lieppman and [scouting director] Eric Kubota, the scouting department and the minor-league guys. Obviously Billy is still very hands on with the major-league club, and he and I manage Bob Melvin on a daily basis, but the nice thing is that I do have a whole baseball operations department to do all the underlying work. I'm not here poring through stats and going over Statcast stuff, but I am managing the implementation of all of that on a daily basis. [Assistant GM] Dan Feinstein handles the international stuff, but I work with him on that, too. Everything that goes into baseball ops is what I manage on a daily basis.

What's the biggest misconception about your job?

When people see quotes from a GM, they think it's all about playing fantasy baseball. It's not. This is about managing an organization. There are hundreds of people who work for you and you're responsible for them. You also have to manage up to ownership. This is a business.

The most public part of the job is: Who are you trading, who are you signing, who is going up and down? That's the part people see on a daily basis. During the six months of the season, it's a huge part of our job, but all year, and certainly during the off-season, the bigger part is managing your personnel.

The great thing about having Keith and Eric in place is that they've been here forever, longer than I have, and we don't have to reinforce our philosophy on a daily or weekly basis because they know it. They know what kind of players we want, what we're looking for.

Obviously, not much has changed. We're still looking for high on-base guys, guys who understand the strike zone. Pitchers who throw strikes. [Minor-league pitching instructor] Gil Patterson is the same way. Gil has been here for a long time. We just understand what we're looking for.

How do you know when players are ready to move up in the minors?

It's more art than science. Keith and the minor-league coaches are the guys who are around the players and know when they are emotionally and mentally ready. We see the box score every day. We read the game report, which gives some insight into how things are actually happening. It's a joint thing.

I'm more aggressive than Keith by nature in terms of moving guys up. We want guys here. That's ultimately the end game. He wants guys to develop and be ready and learn everything they need to so we don't yell at him once they get here.

Typically, Billy or I will say, "Let's talk about moving this guy up, he's performing and doesn't have anything left to do at that level." Then I check in with Keith, ask, "Is he really as good as his numbers say?"

I can look at exit velocities all the way up the minor leagues as opposed to 10 years ago when I just had to assume if a guy was hitting .300 that it was legitimate.

How much do you have to travel to see your minor-league teams?

I won't do it until after the draft. All my travel in April or May is draft-related. Stockton is easy. I'll try to get everywhere else for three or four days in the summer, partly to see our own guys but also to be around the staffs. Those guys are sort of out there on an island and I think it's important that those of us in the office get out and spend time with them, make sure we're keeping track of what they're doing.

We have the minor-league award ceremony every spring. Billy and I go over to the minor-league complex, and part of the speech we give every year is: "You guys may be in Vermont or you may be in Midland, but trust me, we know as it's happening what you guys are doing. We're either watching on milb.com or we're getting text updates from the trainers over there." The more those guys know that they're connected to us here, the easier time they have with their own development there.

Outside of spring training, I probably make a dozen trips a year. I don't travel with the big-league team; technology makes it so we don't have to. I talk to Bob three or four times a day. Obviously, in the off-season we have the GM meetings and the Winter Meetings. I try to get to the Dominican complex once a year. Dan goes six or seven times a year. It's as much about seeing our own guys as spending time with [director of Latin American operations] Raymond Abreu and our scouts down there, managing our personnel.

David Forst (right) and Texas Rangers GM Jon Daniels talk during the 2016 GM meetings in Scottsdale, Arizona. (Mark J. Rebilas-USA TODAY Sports)

Your first pick in this year's draft was very unusual. You took Kyler Murray, Oklahoma's quarterback, who will go back to play football in the fall before switching to pro baseball full time. How did that come about?

It started in March. Eric Kubota saw Kyler very early on and raved about him, said, "He is an athlete unlike any other guy who is out there." The baseball skills were coming at a quick pace considering how much he played. Eric identified Kyler as someone he really wanted us to spend time on. I went to see him, so did Dan Feinstein and [assistant GM] Dan Kantrovitz. It's not something we would have otherwise done because he wasn't a top 30, 40 guy coming into the year. Eric did a really good job identifying him early on.

We all kind of saw the same thing. As the week goes along in the draft room, you start putting the board up and you see what the possibilities are. Everybody has their warts, whether it's medical or signability. Kyler kept moving up and up the board. He was not in the top nine when we started that week but as the conversation went along, he went up and up.

What are the most important attributes in your job?

People skills are important, because your outward personality to the press and the fans is how people see you and also defines how you lead your group from within.

Just like any leader or head of any group or company, you need to be able to manage people. It helps to know players and know stats, but by the time you get to this seat, you've hopefully been in the game long enough that you've done that stuff, you're well-versed in that. It's not super important for me to dissect Statcast data in this chair. I have to have a good enough relationship with my analysts that they want to bring it to me and then be able to implement it.

You have to be the stereotypical Malcolm Gladwell connector. You have to bring this stuff to guys in the clubhouse and you have to work with the manager the same way you work with scouts. You have to be able to interface with a lot of different kinds of people.

How has your relationship been with the team's managers?

I came in during the middle of Art Howe's tenure and Art's relationship with Billy was tenuous and because of that, I was never really close with Art. I was sort of nobody while Art was here. My relationship with Ken Macha developed differently over those five years. When Macha started, I was still an assistant, but over the course of time, because I moved into the assistant GM chair, there was a power struggle, and I think that's natural. I had more oversight over him than I did when he started. I was close personally with Bob Geren. Those relationships are sort of like any employee-manager relationship, where there's a personal side of it but you have to maintain some distance, similar to with the players.

What's the most difficult part of the job?

I've had some very hard conversations with players, either when trading them or sending them down. We've had different managers who are more or less adept at doing that stuff. Bob is fantastic—whether it's sending guys down at spring training or trading guys, he has a relationship with players that takes a lot of the heat off.

Those are hard conversations to have. Obviously the release conversations are the most difficult, and we don't do that very often up here, which is nice. Keith Lieppman has a lot of tough ones in the minor leagues because when you're released by Keith, it's not really clear where you go from there.

I can think of some specific conversations that were hard over the years. I think we try and keep a healthy distance, but there are players over the years who you're still emotionally tied to. I can count on one hand the Barry Zitos and Mark Kotsays and Mark Ellises of the world. All those guys left here at some point, and that was hard. Luckily, we've been able to bring most of them back in one form or another. You spend a lot of time around these guys. We're obviously in the clubhouse a lot. We're at spring training for six weeks. You do find guys you really like.

The A's typically are active at the trade deadline. How do you prepare for it and when do you decide whether you're buyers or sellers?

Where we are now in June 2018 is a great example. We're right at .500. We're seven games back and there are some really good teams ahead of us. There's always a chance we get into a better part of the schedule and we get hot. If we're close in the middle of July, those opportunities are precious. You can't just say, "We weren't planning on competing. Let's not do it." You have to be ready. At the same time, I have scouts looking at other systems in case we're in the same position we've been the last few years where we might pick up some prospects at the deadline.

I spend a lot of time thinking about both contingencies. Every night, when we win or lose and our record changes, I think it changes your perspective. Some nights, you think, "I can't possibly see us competing." Then we win seven out of eight and you think, "We're pretty good." It really changes on a nightly basis. You have to go with the flow of the season.

What's been the most satisfying season for the front office?

The 2012 season to me was absolutely the most memorable. We had come off of five straight years where we were bad. This job was not a lot of fun from 2007 to 2011. There were times where I was like, "How are we ever going to turn this thing around?" I hadn't been through a period like that.

We started the 2012 season having traded away a bunch of guys. We traded Trevor Cahill and Gio Gonzalez. The fact that we did a full 180 over the course of those six months was pretty remarkable. Winning on the last day of the season, that was the best feeling I've had in my 18-plus years.

So much is made of some of the major deals Oakland made involving the 2012–14 playoff teams. How do you look at those now?

Trading Josh Donaldson we knew was a huge thing. It was not an easy decision. We knew the impact it would have on the organization. This has been talked to death, but I wouldn't take back the Yoenis Cespedes trade for a second. I think our process was really good. We absolutely needed Jon Lester. We don't get to that wild-card game without him. We don't have the lead in the seventh inning of that game without him, either. You knew the impact that he had had in a short time.

That morning, I woke Yoenis up with a 7:30 call, and I knew as I was making the call it was going to be a big deal. You know in the moment deals like that will have a huge impact in the clubhouse, on the fan base, all those things.

The other impact is years later you look back and say when we traded for Josh Donaldson, I had no idea what kind of impact that would have. When we were trading Rich Harden, that was devastating for a lot of reasons, but looking back, we would never have had Josh Donaldson. So there are two ways to look at that.

How do you evaluate the current rebuild?

This period is different from that period leading up to 2012. We've been very proactive over the last few years, making trades, trying to get younger players, making sure there's hope going forward. The last time, we hung on too long in 2006 and 2007 and cost ourselves a few years. We were obviously proactive after 2014. As we struggled in 2015 and 2016, it never felt like we were bottoming out or hopeless. We were trying to work toward the next window. I think you just need to keep working and changing things and stick with what has worked before in terms of bringing players into the system.

It was hard in the case of [dismantling] the 2014 team. It was hard—and it wasn't. We saw how that team played in the second half of the season. Without Jeff Samardzija and Lester and all the Band-Aids we put on, we don't even get to the wild-card game. We knew that team was trending down.

From an intellectual standpoint, it was absolutely the right thing to do, to try to restart so we didn't have five years of playing really bad baseball. Emotionally, that was hard coming off three straight playoff appearances. You don't really want to tell your fans it's time to take a step back.

I'll give Billy credit. He was the one who was adamant at the end of 2014 when we lost that game in Kansas City that we can't just run this thing back out there. It's not going to work. He was right. None of those guys really performed the same way. We would have been in really big trouble. We wouldn't be sitting here in the middle of 2018 feeling as optimistic as we do about the future of this team.

It's a fun group. It's a talented group. We have a way to go. We need to stay healthier than we are. There are a lot of teams out there in a lot worse positions than we are right now.

There are at least names on a board somewhere. There's Lazarito Armenteros and James Kaprielian and Daulton Jefferies and A.J. Puk—if we get them all together, they pair really well with Matt Chapman and Matt Olson and Dustin Fowler. There is a perfect scenario out there where it all comes together. We've got the right pieces, then guys get hurt or don't perform and it all changes. You just have to change along with it.

How does the search for a new stadium impact front-office plans?

It's still pretty far out. We have a five-year plan in terms of where we hope our payroll is going, but you don't implement it until you have a site and shovel and a brick. We have an idea, but until there is something more definitive, we're not going to chance anything.

There is a paper somewhere in here that says 2023, here's what we would like our payroll to be, but it's based on a lot of contingencies about what goes into that building.

I've been looking forward to it literally since my interview with Billy in 1999. In that interview, I asked Billy, "How's the stadium thing coming along?" We're coming up on 20 years. It has been out there as long as we've all been around.

I would love to be here for that and see the day we actually do open a new park, but we've been talking about it for a long time.

Do you have any pet peeves?

I try not to complain. As hard as losses are and as grumpy as I can be at times, we know how lucky we are. We have 162 nights every year where we get to compete and you get to win or lose or be a part of something. Those are pretty special things. I've tried to get better about handling the losses over the years. Family gives you perspective. Other things in life give you perspective, which is nice.

I wouldn't say I have a pet peeve. That's another thing Billy has taught me about the big picture and recognizing the things that are important. We work hard. I don't have to prove that we work hard by staying here until two in the morning. We need to do other things and nobody is ever going to doubt that we're committed and passionate about this.

What's the best part about your job?

It's a little bit of everything. It's been working with Billy, it's living in the Bay Area. I always had a sense that being at a place like this with good people and being happy is more important than being "the guy."

Even now, I have the GM title but everybody knows that Billy and I do this together. I could have been the GM by myself a lot of other places. It always seemed like there's no rush and I'm happy here. Why mess with that?

My dad basically worked in the same industry for 40 years. He never had to worry about stability and income. I have two kids who I want to take care of and I'm not looking to move them around the country or have my job be at risk. Anytime you're in this job, there's a chance it's not going to work out, but there's been so much stability here.

Ownership has always treated me very well. People stay here for decades for a reason. It's a great environment. Even when we have bad times, people have the freedom to do their jobs and also to have a life outside their jobs.

How would you describe your relationship with Billy?

I don't even know what words to use. He's like a father figure, he's a brother. He is responsible for me being here. He hired me. Not only did he hire me, but as soon as I walked through the door, he and Paul were completely open to me doing anything and everything. There are so many places you go in baseball that you have to spend years and years before you get access to the important stuff. Because of the way Billy ran and still runs this place, that was never the case. I had access right away to everybody.

I went in the clubhouse, down on the field that first spring training having never played above independent ball, and had instant credibility because Billy vouched for me. That was incredibly impactful. He trusted me enough when Paul left to make me assistant GM. I was 27 years old. There will never be enough words to explain my relationship with Billy and how grateful I am.

CHAPTER 8

SUSAN SLUSSER: SO YOU WANT TO BE A BEAT WRITER?

I won't fib: the life of a baseball beat writer isn't all that arduous. Sure, we love to complain about deadlines and travel and difficult interview subjects, but when you get down to it, we get to watch the world's best sport for thousands of hours a year.

I absolutely love my job. I can't imagine doing anything else, and at this point, 30 years in, I don't think I'd be qualified for anything else. But there are a lot of misperceptions about baseball beat writing.

For instance: Being a beat writer for a local outlet is different than being a sports columnist. Many people confuse the two and wonder why beat writers don't rip general managers for bad moves or owners for not spending money. That's not what reporters do, that's the job of columnists, who write opinion pieces. (Conversely, columnists are constantly bashed on social media and online forums with things like "Stick to the facts!" Well, no: They're paid to write their opinions.)

Occasionally, fans will complain that beat writers just give the team's side of things or the general manager's side. Why, yes, that's literally the job: covering the beat. The team or front office does something, and the beat writers ask them about it and the decision-makers then provide their reasoning. Fans (and columnists!) often might not like the resulting quotes, which is fine. But that's what a beat writer is going to report— who else is going to explain why the A's traded Josh Donaldson except for Billy Beane? The columnists then weigh in on whether the move was good or bad.

In a similar vein, readers sometimes say, "Why don't you ask the tough questions?" Of course reporters always ask every angle possible, but often it's in a one-on-one setting, which is where the most honest dialogs happen. Group settings and press conferences, which are all the general public ever sees, are not where the most sensitive questions get asked—because you're usually not going to get anything usable. Every team official and player knows how to duck a tough question in a group setting. When TV cameras are on, interview subjects are especially careful and bland, which is why the growing trend toward making every interview session a press conference is a poor one. Unless it's Steve Kerr or a handful of other coaches or players across sports, you're seldom going to have as natural an interaction in a press conference as you would in a less formal group setting.

Sometimes reporters won't get a decent answer even one-on-one—we don't have the ability to impel answers, we don't have subpoena power. But if it's a touchy subject or concerns ongoing business, often the answer is off the record or on background only. Why is a team using this player rather than that one? To which area of the team might they add? Who's on the trading block? Readers might not realize the questions have been asked or know where the information is coming from, but they're often getting the answer in their daily coverage, anyway.

Not that sources are infallible or always on the same page—and things change, stories evolve. The team might be firmly set against making a trade and say so. Weeks later, given a better offer or with a different assessment of the upcoming season, a deal might go through. Some clubs have a quicker trigger finger with decisions than others—a general manager who loves a player one week might have soured on the same guy the next week.

Sports, like politics, involve lots of off-the-record sourcing, for any number of reasons. Teams don't want to mess up negotiations. Club officials might want to send a message to a player. Scouts like to trade information about players but they're barred from on-the-record evaluations because they're working for competing entities. A lower-ranking official or employee might not feel comfortable providing on-the-record information without permission from above.

The trust between source and reporter goes both ways, of course, and sometimes, writers get burned. I had an agent once tell me the A's had interest in a free agent one winter, and I tried for hours to get the information confirmed. The agent was so persuasive, though, I put up a speculative blog post, only to get an irate phone call from a club official hours later—there were no talks at all with the agent or player. Luckily, it was just online at that point, so I took it down and provided immediate mea culpas on social media.

The ethics of dealing with some agents' agendas is another topic—but I'd rather not have a scoop than have one that's wrong.

* * *

I'm often asked my favorite players to cover over the years—there are so many, it's really hard to single them out. I mentioned Darryl Hamilton in an earlier chapter; he was in a class of his own. Josh Donaldson, Eric Chavez, Huston Street, Sean Doolittle, Dallas Braden, Eric Byrnes, Scott Hatteberg, Kurt Suzuki, Frank Thomas, Mark Kotsay, Mark Ellis, Jason Kendall, Jose Guillen, Octavio Dotel, Dan Otero, Sam Fuld, Yoenis Cespedes, Stephen Vogt... the list goes on and on, there are many, many more. Those of us who cover the A's have been fortunate, the teams are generally media-friendly and colorful.

The current group might not have as many big personalities, although as he gets more comfortable, Matt Chapman is starting to show his leadership qualities and sense of humor, and Mark Canha has a fun, quirky side. It's a calm, professional bunch that takes after the solid double-play combo of Marcus Semien and Jed Lowrie: hard-working and methodical. That's one reason, I believe, the 2018 team wildly exceeded expectations.

Reporters never should get too close to those they cover, of course, in order to retain journalistic objectivity; a friendship is more appropriate once they've left the team or retired. In days gone by, and in some cases not-so-gone-by, beat writers would get beers with players and (more often) coaches after games. That's much less common now. It's important to keep that distance—friendly but not friends—because there will come a time when a reporter will have to write something less than glowing about a player. I recall mentioning the late Tony Phillips' declining defensive skills once, and I thought I was being fairly diplomatic; I said something to the effect that his glove was no longer his strongest asset. The next day he told me, "That really irks my ass!" and he didn't talk to me for weeks, but he was then and still is one of my all-time favorites.

Everyone around the A's misses his sassiness, his big smile and his infectious cackle of a laugh. He had a snappy comeback for everything.

I once wrote something Nick Swisher didn't care for—in the wake of Esteban Loaiza's DUI, I looked at teams' responsibilities when it came to making sure their players behave responsibly, and some A's coaches mentioned their concerns about Swisher repeatedly breaking curfew. Swisher cooperated for the story, but when it came out, he took some heat from the front office and didn't speak to me for most of the rest of the year. That was astonishing—Swisher not talking! We were back to being fine the next year and still are—he's always a delight to chat with, funny as hell, and talk about big personalities.

As Ken mentioned, most teams and players understand that for a writer or broadcaster to have credibility, they have to include the bad with the good. If you don't report the down times and issues, if coverage is glowing even under trying circumstances, the successes, when they come, don't mean as much. Fans know when a team is struggling. Players know when they're not performing well. Pretending otherwise helps no one.

One reason I'm apprehensive to answer when asked about the best players to cover is that reporters aren't supposed to show favoritism—obviously. Repeatedly calling players by their nicknames, fist-bumping, back slapping, high-fiving, even just taking photos with people you cover can look unprofessional because of the detachment required. There's quite a bit of gray area though—when someone sticks out their hand, it's tough to leave them hanging. When running into someone you haven't seen in a while, it's hard to avoid hugs. Some guys prefer their nicknames (Bob Melvin likes "BoMel," but I just can't bring myself to use it) and some nicknames are so universal, they're impossible to avoid. Who called him "Eric" and *not* "Chavvy?"

Everyone has their biases, much as we'd like to pretend otherwise. Reporters naturally gravitate to players and coaches who are great quotes or more friendly than most and pay less attention to those who aren't interested in talking. The A's have had a few of those over the years, and

Bob Melvin and Susan Slusser, Oakland Coliseum, 2013. (Paul Schraub)

I always tried my best with the less-than cooperative, but some guys are just quiet or shy and that's totally fine. Freedom of speech includes the freedom not to speak.

Newspaper reporters aren't fans. We have to provide impartial observations, plus it's a full-time job—there's just no room for rooting. On a practical level, sure, it's better for a media outlet when a local team is doing well, there's no doubt about it. There's more interest from everyone: fans, advertisers, columnists, editors. Covering a last-place team can be a little on the lonely side; the press box is emptier, the stories wind up inside the section. (I'll always remember one of my favorite Ray Ratto stories from one of the A's down years began, "Meanwhile, back here among the tire ads....") So in that sense, everyone likes a successful team.

When it comes to rooting interests, though, I root for two things: an interesting game to write about and making deadline.

* * *

Twitter could be a chapter on its own. The social-media platform dramatically changed the way sportswriters work, turning our jobs into essentially a 24-7 on-call situation. Any news can be dispersed instantly, without even turning on a laptop or involving any editors (not always ideal).

I've whined about Twitter—everyone has to put up with rude and stupid comments (and, to be fair, we've all made our own share of stupid comments and mistakes on Twitter, too). It can be a massive time drag and, often, depressing.

So what I'm going to say might surprise you: Even with its many faults, I like Twitter. Many women sportswriters, and women, period, have difficulty with offensive morons on Twitter; I count myself lucky because I've experienced very little of that except when the A's wind up in on-field skirmishes with opponents—in one of those kill-the-messenger scenarios, the beat guys get the brunt of some nastiness, too. (For about a year, I liked to joke my hobby was muting Royals fans.)

My interactions with followers are generally delightful. Through Twitter and other social media platforms, for the first time in decades as a sportswriter, I know oodles of fans well, and I've wound up with some legitimately close friends. I met my pal Shelly Robinson when she was mocking me on radio host Rick Tittles' Facebook page—she was so hilarious, I couldn't help but laugh.

My husband wound up in a heated discussion on my Twitter timeline with A's fan James Deitrich, who'd asked me about the mention of a San Carlos running trail in Dan's 49ers book. As a result, Dan has a top-notch bunch of running partners and a huge group of local friends because Jimmy is the unofficial social director of the mid-Peninsula.

Being connected to fans through Twitter and sites such as Athletics Nation is incredibly helpful for a beat writer. It's easy to lose perspective when at the ballpark every day; sometimes things that appear obvious if you're right in the middle of them aren't all that clear to an outside observer. Plus, many perceptive fans follow the team closely and they'll discuss topics or ask questions that might not have occurred to even the most longstanding of reporters. I'm not too proud to get ideas anywhere. Bring it on Twitter peeps, email correspondents and Athletics Nation denizens!

I've learned a lot from Twitter follows and followers—important information about other cultures, correct terminology, and racial sensitivity, fun things about music and cats and TV shows, and some downright silly things, too.

That said, I do have my pet peeves. I'll block anyone who uses bad language or who mocks (or worse, celebrates) players' injuries or who rips one of my colleagues. The relentlessly negative tweeters go on mute—there's enough of that in the world. Also, if you do tweet at me to rip people, at least spell their names right. It really defeats the sting of criticism if you're commenting on Billy Bean's personnel decisions, since Billy Bean is Major League Baseball's vice president of inclusion, not Billy Beane, the A's vice president of baseball operations.

I'm happy to answer any questions that aren't addressed in recent coverage, but if it's something that I've written or tweeted about that week, I'll provide a link. And if I get a question that's addressed to several beat writers at the same time, I'll usually ignore it. Pick one, don't ask all of us at once. (Remember, too, we're all competitors, working for different outlets.) Likewise, if it's something easily Googled... Google it.

I forget how I used to spend all the hours of the day I now spend on Twitter, but on balance, for a baseball writer, Twitter is a good thing. Now, if you'll excuse me, I need to go check my timeline.

* * *

A baseball writer's day begins in the morning with a quick check of Twitter, then going through the local baseball coverage, returning emails and calls, and checking in with team officials or sources or scouts.

The clubhouse typically opens about 3½ hours before the game, and there is work to do in the press box even before then—setting up electronic folders and files (most reporters now do much of the production aspect that editors used to handle, including adding metadata and photos to articles) and checking in with editors about that night's plans and upcoming stories.

During clubhouse access, reporters are looking for notebook fodder: checking in on injured players, talking to players who are on good or bad streaks, chatting with the next day's starter or a player who was involved in a big moment from the previous game.

That's followed by the manager's interview session, which takes place in the dugout while the team is stretching. Injuries and current team trends dominate the pregame questions for the manager.

The A's beat corps is lucky to have Bob Melvin, who really understands what reporters need and who has unending patience with off-the-wall questions or ones he's heard a million times. He always tries to provide something usable, no matter the topic. It's not the easiest task, and many managers who are otherwise superb at their jobs have struggled to handle media duties. That's tough for everyone; beat writers and broadcasters need the manager's help more than any other person affiliated with the team. Writers speak to the manager both before and after the game. If the sessions aren't informative, coverage suffers; if the sessions are awkward, it makes for poor TV.

After the manager's session, writers produce a notebook with tidbits and updates, sometimes two stories, if news warrants. Then it's time for a quick meal in the press dining area when there is time. On the road, there often is not—the visiting team takes batting practice second, and it can be a race to get a notebook finished before the game starts. Some reporters bring food with them in case they miss the opportunity to get dinner. I don't eat meat, so I have to plan ahead in some cities that are light on vegetarian options; the addition of the food trucks at the Coliseum helps in that regard. All the media, local and visiting, love the food trucks!

During the game, writers keep score, of course, but we're also working on at least one story, more if something significant happens during the game, such as an injury or a particularly unusual play. We're also tweeting, which is an enormous distraction; some reporters greatly limit their tweets during the game, which is probably wise. I have thought about cutting back to focus on games, but the moment anything happens, I find myself tweeting. Shrug emoji.

Everyone files an initial story the moment the game ends, and while the beauty of baseball is how unpredictable it is, a game with a lot of late changes is a killer for writers. There are often two, three, four rewrites of a story, and a walkoff means a hastily slapped-together story thrown online minutes after the game is decided. Those usually aren't pretty.

We race downstairs to the postgame interview sessions; the manager is first, 10 minutes or so after the game, then the clubhouse is open. This is all nuts-and-bolts stuff, questions about the whys and wherefores of the game. Feature questions for upcoming profiles or big-picture questions are frowned upon—those are for times when the bulk of reporters aren't on deadline and players aren't rushing to get home.

After wins, the mood is light and quotes tend to flow easily. About the only challenge is hearing players talk above the music blaring in the clubhouse. But after a tough loss, the sessions can be challenging. It gets eerily quiet, and tough questions can require a level of diplomacy, especially if a reliever had a terrible outing or if a player has made an error that cost the team the game.

When players are clearly upset, reporters try to ease into questions, but there's just no right way to go about it. Basically, the real only question is: "What happened?" and variations thereof. There's no graceful way to put that, no real soft-pedaling. Reliever Ryan Madson once told me he'd feel better after giving up a game-winning hit if reporters just said, "How the f— did you screw that up?" "Everyone always tries to be so nice, it makes me feel worse," he said. "I know when I didn't do my job."

The majority of players, relievers most of all, understand it's part of the job to deal with reporters asking them why they failed 15 minutes after a rough night of work. Dennis Eckersley is revered in media circles for his professionalism in spending 30 minutes answering the same questions about Kirk Gibson's homer over and over. Players who are "stand-up guys" and can handle the media on a bad night are respected by their teammates—everyone in the clubhouse knows who messed up. If a player absorbs the responsibility and doesn't point fingers, his teammates will recognize that. These are often the players who go on to become coaches, managers, executives, and broadcasters.

There are a few fellows who either refuse to talk or who snap at reporters. ("You saw it. You write it," is a classic. Another is a heavily sarcastic, "Yeah, I was really *trying* to throw it there.") They are doing their teammates a disservice, because then writers must troop over to someone else, most likely the catcher, to ask what happened. Don't make your teammates answer for you. That gets noticed.

I'm always okay with a no comment, though, if a player really doesn't feel like talking. A polite "not tonight" is fine. I have an issue when someone is a jerk about it. One player, after a game-winning pinch hit of all things, rolled his eyes and waved the media away without a word. Worse, he'd made us all wait for half an hour while getting treatment from the trainer and taking a shower. If you're not going to talk, let the group or the team PR guy know promptly, and be a pro. Why be rude to the media? Beat reporters aren't going to hold it against a player, we're expected to be objective, but we're also there every day, doing our jobs, traveling to all the same places, over the same long season. At least be respectful of that.

Some guys really get it. Mark Kotsay was one of the most clued-in players I've ever known when it came to media interactions and everything else going on in the clubhouse. He was also smart enough to know that once reporters get what they need, they'll leave—so the sooner people talk, the better for everyone, because then the players get their clubhouse back. Once, in Detroit, we were waiting for catcher Damian Miller, who'd had a big game. Kotsay wandered by and asked who we needed, and when told, Kotsay said, "He's in the whirlpool. Give me a tape recorder."

Kotsay took the recorder, went to the training room and asked Miller several hilariously clichéd questions, brought the recorder back and sent us on our way. It made for an even better story.

Once the postgame sessions are done, writers dash back to the press box, throw in some quotes, and depending on deadlines, try to gussy up their stories a bit before filing. With the internet, some will stay much later—several outlets allow for much more time than do newspapers—and a few will add lengthy postgame blogs.

Leaving the ballpark at 11:30 PM is ordinary. If there's a day game the next day or a morning flight, the turnaround can be rough.

* * *

Some of the best advice I've received from writers:

1) Someone once told me not to write about the starting pitcher unless absolutely necessary, because you could wind up writing about the starter every day, it's always the easy way to go. It's better to mix it up, or the coverage just winds up being about the rotation. There are days the starter is the must-do story, but when possible, I try to branch out.

2) Tim Brown of Yahoo.com told me, "Don't ever be too proud to follow up someone else's scoop. You might wind up with something even better, but even if you don't, your readers deserve to get the news. It's not about you—it's about the readers." No one wants to get scooped, it's a bad feeling, and some writers pretend as if competitors' scoops never happened and ignore the news altogether. But Tim's right—if you make some calls, you can add to the story and advance it, or sometimes even find out that the original report wasn't entirely accurate.

Susan Slusser and Dan Brown after the A's clinched a playoff spot at the Coliseum in 2013. (Janie McCauley/AP)

Beat writers are competitors, which can make for a complicated dynamic. Some beats remain relatively friendly, despite the rivalries. On other beats, enmity reigns. The Knicks beat in New York was a legendary battleground. When I worked in Dallas, there was such an intense newspaper war going on that some writers at the *Morning News* didn't even talk to reporters from the *Fort Worth Star-Telegram*. I was chided for being friendly with fellow Rangers beat writer T.R. Sullivan, and I thought, "I'm not supposed to talk to a guy who sits right next to me all spring and all season? The heck with that." T.R. and I remain friends. One of my closest friends was once a fierce rival: Howard Bryant, the ESPN columnist and author, covered the A's for the *San Jose Mercury News* in the late '90s and early 2000s and we butted heads often, but usually by the next day, we were back to being pals.

The beat during those Art Howe–Jason Giambi years was especially fun, with Howard, Brian Murphy of the *San Francisco Examiner*, Mark Saxon of the *Oakland Tribune*, Gary Washburn of the *Contra Costa Times*, Gregg Bell of the *Sacramento Bee*, and Jeff Fletcher of the *Santa Rosa Press Democrat*. We were all about the same age, and we spent a lot of time going to dinner or drinks after games, where things often devolved into arguments over college sports (Murph and Saxon) or music (me, Howard, Gary) or very specifically, George Gervin or Terence Trent D'Arby (Gary vs. everyone).

The media landscape has changed so dramatically that most beats outside of New York and Boston are now much smaller. At one point in the '80s, as many as nine papers covered the A's regularly. Now, there are two: the *Chronicle* and the *Bay Area News Group*, which provides the coverage for the *San Jose Mercury News* and *East Bay Times*.

Websites have stepped into the gap. MLB.com has covered the team for more than a decade, of course, and The Athletic, which began covering local teams across the country in the past two years, started a Bay Area edition in 2017. So there are four beat writers currently covering the team on a regular basis, along with several outlets that provide coverage just of home games.

* * *

Young reporters often ask me for advice when they're getting into the business. I usually keep it simple with something that can apply to any job in any industry: When you get your first job or internship, always get there on time (or early), stay late, and learn every aspect of the job and other people's jobs, too. If you make yourself indispensable, you might wind up sticking around, and if you learn other skills, you'll expand your options.

I like to remind young writers to watch and listen first. See what the veterans are doing, how they go about the job, and always be polite and friendly. The last thing anyone at any company wants is a new hire or intern showing up and being a know-it-all or a nonstop talker. Learn as much as possible and pick your spots to give your two cents. I've seen otherwise capable interns lose jobs because they came in acting overly entitled. Remember the people who've done the work for years might have a decent idea what they're doing. If you think you know better, well, let your work speak for you.

Dressing appropriately is important, which might seem strange, considering the cliché of slob sportswriters can be pretty close to the mark. It's fine to dress casually for some sports, particularly baseball, with a long season played in hot weather. (Standards for the three other major pro team sports are much higher, especially on game days.)

Even with casual attire, though, a reporter should appear to be professional in order to be taken seriously. This can be especially tricky for women, and I'm blunt. I tell women entering the business: Do not dress like you're going clubbing or heading out on a date. It does not send the right message. You want players to think of you as a reporter and nothing more, otherwise you cannot do your job correctly. The best way for any reporter to dress is to not draw attention to yourself—you want to be part of the background. Only one reporter completely ignored that advice when I gave it to her, and she was out of baseball several years later.

I was part of a committee that Major League Baseball put together to come up with a dress code before the 2012 season. The guidelines were common sense, but there was a lot of misinformation in the wake of the announcement during the 2011 Winter Meetings. Some reported, erroneously, that the league wanted to avoid any issue with scantily clad sideline reporters after an incident with the New York Jets and a female TV reporter. The truth is much more mundane, and involved a male reporter who had worn flip flops throughout the previous year's World Series. Baseball's bigwigs were unhappy that some media members weren't attired properly for the sport's jewel event. Thus, the dress code.

I can say, having been on the committee, that every possible care was taken to be gender neutral: skirt length and shorts length were both addressed, among other things. Some items, such as no undershirt-style

T-shirts, shredded jeans and team-logo attire were geared more specifically toward photographers and camera people who often show up in the sightline of TV viewers.

Wearing logo clothing of *any* team is a major sticking point with most reporters. Journalists are supposed to be objective. And yet every postseason, in particular, there are reporters from local TV stations wearing team gear. It's maddeningly unprofessional.

So there were reasons for the dress code, even if it was misunderstood. One national publication wrote an entire story based on the false premise that sandals were prohibited, despite talking to me beforehand and being told in no uncertain terms that sandals and other women's footwear are fine (though spike heels aren't the most sensible choice on a baseball field, and groundskeepers hate them). Only backless shoes—flip-flops, shower shoes, and the like—are not allowed, and that's only during the regular season and postseason. Spring training, when work includes long days in the sun, flip flops are okay per the league, although at least one team has banned them during the spring.

I drew some flak myself for being sexist in the wake of the guidelines' announcement. I told the Associated Press that the idea was to "not dress like a hobo or a ho." I said it just to be funny, but yes, I guess the issue of scanty attire can be seen to be gender specific. However, for a long time, the most notoriously underdressed writer in Arizona every spring was a Northern California sports columnist—male—who wore short-shorts everywhere. And, as a woman, I worry that publications that toss around accusations of sexism where it does not exist will wind up cheapening the notion and won't retain a voice of authority when there is real discrimination at hand.

Meanwhile, the joke around the A's after the dress-code guidelines were published was that Billy Beane would not pass muster—he's in flip flops year round.

CHAPTER 9

BOB MELVIN: CALM, COOL, AND COLLABORATIVE

Bob Melvin was hired as the A's manager on an interim basis midway through 2011. The following year, Melvin, who is from Menlo Park and played at Cal, led Oakland to an improbable AL West title on the final day of the season and was named the AL Manager of the Year, becoming the sixth man to win the award in both leagues. Two more playoff appearances followed in 2013 and '14, and in 2018, Melvin took a young team to a surprise postseason spot after a 97-win season, the A's highest victory total since 2002. After the season, Melvin earned his third Manager of the Year Award from the BBWAA.

When did you first realize you might want to become a manager?

I was playing for Johnny Oates in Baltimore in 1991 and it was either the eighth or ninth inning, and they had a left-hander on the mound. We had a left-hander leading off the next inning, so I asked Johnny, "Why don't they just send the left-hander out to make us make a move?"

Bob Melvin and Ken Korach taping the manager's show, 2018. (Michael Zagaris)

Johnny said, "I've been meaning to tell you this. Walter Alston told me the same thing one day: I believe you're going to manage one day, with the interaction we have, the way you watch the game. I feel like you have what it takes to be a manager one day."

I thought he was crazy for a minute. It's not like all of a sudden I did an about-face and had an epiphany and said, "That's what I want to do," but that was the first time it ever crossed my mind.

I started thinking about the way I watched the game. My last year in Baltimore, Cal Ripken Jr. signed a bat for me and wrote on it "To BoMel, you're the smartest man in baseball (not me)—future managing material for sure." That was the second time I thought, "Maybe there's something to this."

Not to downplay Johnny Oates, because he was a great manager, but when Cal Ripken says something like that to you, it gives you some confidence. It's like an inspirational little boost. I thought, "Maybe there's a different track here."

How did you get your first job after your playing days were over?

Three people were really responsible: Bud Selig, Sal Bando, and Phil Garner. I wrote a letter to Bud when I was out about potentially trying to get back, maybe do something in the coaching ranks. Sue Selig, Bud's wife, played bridge with my great aunt, so I knew the family. Bud was the commissioner by then, because Wendy, his daughter, was in charge of the Brewers, and I knew Wendy, too. The next thing I knew, I heard from Sal, who was Milwaukee's general manager. I joined Phil's staff in 1999.

What are your recollections of your first big-league managing job with Seattle, when you took over after Lou Piniella requested to go to Tampa Bay?

My biggest trepidation was I wasn't much older than most of the guys who were there. It was a veteran team that was on its last legs. I think one of the reasons I was brought in was to give these guys a little bit of a break. I don't want to say anything negative about Lou, but I think they thought, "These guys have had enough of that, they might need somebody a little bit more low key, who played in close proximity to them and might do some things a little differently to take some of the pressure off."

My biggest fear was: Will these guys respect me at the age of 41? With some of the older guys, it took some time because a lot of them were really close with Lou, and I was the complete opposite of Lou, but I think the younger guys appreciated it.

How did you learn to walk that delicate line to be both liked and respected? That's a tough balance to achieve.

You can't just throw the balls out there and let them play. When guys make mistakes, you have to hold them accountable for it, and that's probably something you learn along the way anyway. It hit me in the face when I was let go in Seattle that you're going to have to do some things a little differently if you're going to get another chance. I knew why I was there, and it was hard for me to go and hold Edgar Martinez accountable for something.

Even toward the end, I came down on some guys there, and I had some blowups. I felt like early on there that if I did have some epic blowups, it would be trying to look like Lou. I knew you can't fake that stuff. It has to come from the heart.

You're not the best you're ever going to be in your first year. That's what experience is all about. Every year, you feel like you can get better and do some things differently to make your team better.

How was your next job, with Arizona, starting in 2005, different for you?

I think that right away I felt like I was the leader there and the guys knew it, as opposed to kind of easing my way in Seattle. Now I had experience. I took solace in the fact that I was let go in Seattle, but there were positives from that because now I had done it.

What was your departure from Arizona like after five seasons?

Arizona hurt more than Seattle did. I didn't feel that way at the beginning, but later on, I really realized—it was almost like I didn't want to acknowledge the fact that it hurt when they let me go. The hardest year I ever had was the year that I was out. (Melvin did not manage during the 2010 season.) I gained a lot of perspective from that year. I was way better for it. I was invigorated. I was inspired. All the things that maybe when you do this job for a period of time beat you down a little bit, all went away.

I was completely inspired when I got back doing this. I realized how lucky you are to be able to do this job.

What happened there?

I thought we had a really good team. We got off to a slow start in 2009. I almost felt like I was a little invulnerable and I found out the hard way that I wasn't. I butted heads with the GM, and I didn't think there would be repercussions, and there were. I had a year and a half, almost two years left on my contract and they let me go. I was Manager of the Year just a year and a half before that with the youngest team in the league, got outscored and had a low payroll, the whole bit. I learned that no day in this job is promised to you.

What was your reaction when Oakland called?

When Billy called me, I knew within five minutes I was going to have that job. A psychic told my wife that I was going to have another job and it was going to be on the West Coast, so I looked at all the West Coast jobs, and I told her, "You're crazy. There is absolutely no way." She also told Kelley that our next house would have a view of water.

When Billy called, I knew this was going to happen, not because of anything in particular that he said, but during the course of the conversation, it all kind of came together. We had two conversations. He said he wanted to know what my thoughts were about being interim. The next day we reconvened, then I was talking to David Forst about a contract right after that.

What was your first day on the job like?

I'm in the dugout, and I literally didn't know anybody. I had to wait until they walked by, and if they had a jacket on, I still had no idea. We had four games in Chicago, and then we came home. We had an advance meeting that first day at home, and I kept telling Adam Rosales, "The pitchers' meeting is over *there*." I thought he was Brad Ziegler.

I started to get upset. I remember that first day in the dugout thinking, "This isn't going to go very well. I don't know anybody here. I don't feel comfortable."

Two or three days later, I started feeling comfortable. I remember that first day, the left-hander [Bobby Cramer] came in and I had to send him down. I don't recall ever having to do that by myself before, there'd always been someone from the front office there. He was pleading his case and he was emotional.

The last play on the last day in Chicago, we had a guy thrown out at first, and I thought he was safe. I was out there for a long time screaming and yelling at the umpire to the point where some of my coaches felt like they had to come get me. It felt right then. When we got home, it felt a lot better.

What are your memories of your first full year with Oakland in 2012?

That was a pretty amazing season. I felt like a couple months in, there was something there with the group that we had, then they started getting us more guys too.

The Kurt Suzuki trade hurt me a little bit, but Derek Norris came up and did a great job for us. That trade made me realize that my job description was different there. A lot of the other stuff, I had more input, but I knew this is the way it was going to be. I'm not saying that's good or bad, I'm just saying that's the way it is here. I learned that pretty quickly.

The second half of that season was as magical as any few months of baseball I've ever been a part of. I was worried the night before the final day because we had clinched the wild card the night before and watching these guys celebrate, I thought, "We have no chance tomorrow." I almost felt like trying to break it up a little bit. Then they came out and it was 5–0 Texas really quickly. But we just came storming back. As soon as Josh Hamilton had that infamous play in center field, there was no chance we were going to be denied that day.

Bob Melvin is sprayed with champagne as the A's celebrate winning the 2012 AL West.
(AP Photo/Ben Margot)

You played for many well-known managers: Sparky Anderson, Frank Robinson, Roger Craig, Buck Showalter among them. What did you learn from them that you use now?

Just as much negative as the positive—including what I *didn't* think was the right way to handle people. I'm not going to talk about the guys I took the negative stuff from, but I think that was just as important as maybe some of the other more positive things I picked up about managing people and games.

How have you changed over the years?

I used to have to do everything. I remember my coaches in Seattle would say, "We can help" all the time. I ran spring training, I did it all. Now I feel like I delegate as well as anybody. For a while, that was the hardest part, delegating because you knew you were accountable for everything.

How has the relationship with players changed over the years?

When I first came up, Sparky Anderson, to me, was unapproachable. I wouldn't even try to talk to him. If we had a conversation, it was instigated by him. I would never even think about going up and talking to Sparky Anderson.

Now, I think that the players have to be very comfortable with me. Therefore, it is my job to make them comfortable. There's been an influx of younger players like there's never been before. An influx of younger players who are way more important to the team than they were back then.

Younger players, you didn't hear from them when I was coming up. It took a few years to be a leader in the clubhouse. Now there are certain guys who have been here for less than a year that are very instrumental in our clubhouse.

It's not just about the players now, you have to be able to relate to the people above you and even ownership. When I first got to Seattle, Pat Gillick insulated me from all of that: "You deal with the players. I'll deal with you, and I'll deflect everything else." There are a lot more layers you have to deal with now. I feel like I'm capable of doing that, but maybe I wasn't earlier in my career.

What's the most important thing you emphasize to players?

The effort level. You need to have an effort level that would suggest to the other team that you're always playing hard, and we have that here now with this group. That's always been important to me, the effort level. If you're tired, I'll give you a day off, but I need that 90 feet. The other team needs to know that we're coming all the time.

How has the rise of advanced metrics impacted your job? Front offices have much more input in day-to-day decisions than in past decades.

I don't know if metrics have changed my approach all that much. Data gives you more of an objective snapshot of how things are done, but there are so many nuances that sometimes outweigh the objective snapshot that you get on a day-to-day basis, say if you know a guy is tired or just not swinging well.

How much can you use gut instinct in today's game?

For me, gut doesn't mean I'm just reaching. Gut means I might not be able to write it down mathematically, but it's all of my experiences in baseball that tell me—a red light goes off, something needs to be done here and it might not jibe with some of the information you're looking at.

You and Billy Beane have developed an excellent working relationship over the years. What's been the key?

You have to let him know that you're analytics-based in what you look at, because that's what we're famous for and that's a big reason we've been successful. Understanding that's important for Billy, but he also understands that I played and I know some of these nuances. As long as you communicate and have a reason for what you want to do, he definitely listens. As long as you have a reason that you can explain to him—you learn that along the way. At this point, I don't know if our relationship has ever been better.

The pressure associated with big-league managing jobs is immense, and not everyone handles it as well as others. How have you managed it?

There's a lot and you need to insulate from that. I don't look at social media about myself. When I was in Seattle, I made myself look at the message-board stuff to get a thicker skin. After that, I knew that that did no good. There are certain things that you have to stay away from. I very rarely watch MLB Network. I very rarely watch a lot of baseball during the day and/or after games because I don't want to be affected by people that don't know. There are too many outlets now where people are just trying to say something to make a name for themselves, whether it's fact or not. It's not that important now to be right. It's just to be controversial. You have to know what affects you and what doesn't.

What is your typical day like?

I get to the park by noon, do my lineup, talk to the coaches, talk to the front office, then I go work out. That's my thoughtful period. I do a little workout, come back, confirm my lineup. Then it's probably another hour and a half in my office depending on if it's a day with advance meetings or not. I'll talk to a few players who I might feel I need to check in with that day, communicate whatever it is I need to communicate. After that, I'll do the manager's radio show with Ken, then meet with the media, watch batting practice and throw to a group. It's a full day before the game even starts.

How has your relationship with the media evolved?

When I first got to Seattle, Pat Gillick was the GM and he made sure that my media time was condensed. He didn't want me spending too much time on it.

I had formed relationships during my playing career that were helpful then and now. The two beat writers in Baltimore were Ken Rosenthal and Tim Kurkjian, and I actually supplied them with trade rumors sometimes; we would all sit around and talk about what might make sense.

Dealing with the media is part of the job, and you have to do it well, in my opinion. Everybody has a job to do. If you don't understand what somebody else's job is, then you're missing the whole totality of what baseball is all about. Our message needs to get out. People need to write and talk about your team.

Earlier in my career, the manager's radio show was two minutes. I was just trying to get out of the way. I didn't even step back and say, "People are actually listening to this and this might be an important time." It took years for me to figure that one out. Since I've been here, I take it seriously every day.

How do you maintain an even keel?

It's hardest part of the job, because there may be time you have a great day, and the next day, you come in and it's completely the opposite. You have to put on the same face because over 162 games, players need to know that you're the same every time, that there is a routine and you're not moody. If you're in a good mood when you're winning and a bad mood when you're losing, your whole clubhouse feels that.

At times you have to manufacture who you are on a particular day in order to stay consistent. That's probably the hardest part of the job. It can take a little bit more time to get to that place that you need to be in. That starts when you go home, when you get up in the morning. All my workouts and pregame preparation, I try to stay consistent, so my days are the same. That's why I'm so routine-oriented. The players need to know you're disciplined with what you do, too.

I tell the coaching staff that our personality permeates in here. Each and every day, no matter what happened the day before and no matter who we're upset with, we need to make sure that these guys come in and know we're on it. I tell my coaches in spring training, "Dig in there and be with them. If you expect them to respond to criticism, you better give them positives, too, or they won't. If you only talk to them when it's something negative, they won't listen the same way."

I think that preparation leads to going out there with a positive outlook and a dedication to knowing that you're going to win every day. You know you're not going to win 162 in a row, but there isn't a day you go out there that you don't think you're going to win. The players need to feel that, too.

CHAPTER 10
COOPERSTOWN: KINGS AND ANGELLS

Ken Korach

Tom Brokaw recorded a promotional spot for the National Baseball Hall of Fame in which he says:

> "Tucked away at the north part of the U.S. there is a small town where tomorrow never comes. Here the warm glow of bygone days are collected and stored for all time. Our story lies within these walls, triumphs of spirit, artifacts of greatness, legendary tools of a beloved trade, but whenever the present turns its eyes towards the past, the most coveted treasures are heroes."

There's no doubt about any of that. Time has stopped at the Hall of Fame in Cooperstown, and it's as if a mystical spell is cast over every baseball fan who enters the city limits.

We've all experienced times in which the reality of an event doesn't match the excitement of the anticipation. If possible, however, the weekend of the 2017 induction ceremonies exceeded expectations. Being part of the Bill King celebration was a magical, emotional time that left all of us who were there with memories that will last forever.

* * *

It was my second time in Cooperstown. The first was with the White Sox in 1992 to call a game that never should have been broadcast: They used to play an annual exhibition game on a Monday in August called the Hall of Fame Game, and that year's featured the Mets and the White Sox. We were broadcasting the game because the Sox had had a spring-training game rained out and the team and our flagship station, WMAQ, decided this would be a make-up game to satisfy contractual obligations to their sponsors.

The Sox played a day game in Chicago on Sunday, August 2, then we hopped on a charter flight to Utica, New York. It was my first time on a charter and I was blown away. This was well before 9/11, of course, but still, the ease of boarding—the team bus drove right up to the plane—and the first-class seats and ample food and drink reminded me that travel is the biggest difference between the big leagues and the minors. We bussed to Cooperstown the next morning, got a tour of the Hall, and then walked next door for the game.

Even though there was a nice crowd on hand, the Hall of Fame Game was truly an exhibition and it came at an awkward time on the schedule. The goal was to get out of there as quickly as possible. It was almost as if the hitters were fined if the count went past 1-1. If a regular was in the lineup, he got just one at-bat, and the pitchers were mostly minor-league call-ups for the day. I remember approaching Gene Lamont to tell him that we had to do a pregame manager's show. His response was succinct: "Why?"

Still, it was a thrill being in Cooperstown, and broadcasting at quaint, cozy Doubleday Field, which hosted its first game in 1920, took me back to a much simpler time. Ed Farmer and I literally broadcast the game from the stands. Ed and I sat side-by-side in the bleachers while our engineer set up the equipment one row behind us. Except for the presence of an engineer, it reminded me of when I broadcast high school games in Petaluma a dozen years earlier.

* * *

Fast forward to 2017, and the A's played a four-game series in Toronto at the end of July. Denise flew up for the series, which was a nice bit of scheduling by the baseball gods because she had worked closely with the Blue Jays while they were affiliated with the Las Vegas 51s of the PCL. We rented a car and drove down to Cooperstown after the final game of the series.

Cooperstown during induction weekend is a little like Masters week at Augusta. Many of the locals flee the town and rent their houses. It's crazy. Our room at the Holiday Inn Express was going for almost $500 a night. (Thankfully, the A's picked up the tab.)

The headquarters for the weekend was the elegant Otesaga Resort, which was built in 1909 and is another reminder of the absence of time in Cooperstown. The Otesaga's history is woven into that of the Hall itself. I remember hearing tales when I was a kid of how the legends would hang out on the balcony that overlooks the patio restaurant and Otsego Lake, spinning endless yarns and reveling in the Arcadian setting that makes everyone feel like a kid again. I saw Bob Gibson shortly after we arrived, but I didn't see Gibson at 81, I saw him firing wicked fastballs in the 1968 World Series. For the greats of the game, as Orlando Cepeda told me, "Every year, this is like coming home."

Denise and I were there, along with our group of Bill King fans, media, and family, to celebrate Bill's career. I think it's perfectly okay and probably less confusing to say that Bill was going into the Hall, but, technically, he was receiving the Ford C. Frick Award for broadcasting excellence.

It was posthumous, of course, which was the only bittersweet aspect of the weekend.

* * *

Leading up to the event, the *San Jose Mercury News* asked me to write some of my thoughts as their advance story for the weekend:

Editors note: This is the author's 22nd year with the A's and his 12th as the team's lead radio announcer. His book, Holy Toledo! Lessons from Bill King: Renaissance Man of the Mic, *helped establish King's case for Cooperstown.*

By Ken Korach

Because I spent 10 years as his radio partner, people often ask me what the late Bill King would think about being honored by the National Baseball Hall of Fame.

That in itself tells you a lot about Bill: Every time I mentioned the Ford C. Frick Award, the highest possible honor a baseball broadcaster can receive, he would modestly change the subject.

Bill was a rigid guy who lived life solely on his own terms, and as the July 29 ceremony in Cooperstown approaches, I can certainly understand the sentiment from those who thought Bill would have said something like, "Screw it. Take your Hall of Fame and shove it." He was that iconoclastic, of course. And, let's face it, he didn't exactly bow down at the foot of most institutions.

In the least, we know that Bill never campaigned for the award. As Johnny Stephens, Bill's stepson emphatically told me, "Bill broadcast because he loved it and not because he wanted the adulation. He didn't need the Hall of Fame. He was fulfilled because he strove to meet his own standards and not anyone else's."

But to those who listened to him or were mesmerized by him or loved him—or broadcast next to him—the Hall of Fame honor represents a worthy and overdue coronation. King, who died in 2005, spent 25 years captivating A's fans with his brilliance, wit, and enthusiasm.

It was Bill's adherence to the tenets of his profession that drove him, alongside with his insatiable thirst for talking. His commitment to his craft was one major reason why I felt so strongly about Bill and the Frick. If chosen, there would no doubt be a greater examination of Bill's career and learning about him would be instructive for aspiring broadcasters.

I can tell you what the honor means to his family. Bill's daughter, Kathleen Lowenthal, spent a nervous early morning at her home in Marin County on December 7, 2016.

She had grown jaded from her experience of waiting by a phone that didn't ring over all the years Bill had been a finalist for the Frick Award. Still, she fought a battle with her feelings. On one hand, she knew what the disappointment felt like and braced herself for it once again. On the other, it was hard to stave off the anticipation that maybe—just maybe—this might be Bill's year. She knew the call, if it was to come, would happen between 7:00 AM and 7:45 AM Pacific Time.

Kathleen kept looking at her watch and the time seemed to pass in slow motion. Around 7:40, her hopes were running out.

But at 7:43 the phone rang. It was Jeff Idelson, the president of the Hall of Fame. It was Bill's time. She had no idea how she would react, but immediately the tears started to flow.

My phone didn't stop ringing for the next three days. The experience was incredibly heartwarming and took me back to the day Bill died in 2005. The Bay Area was in a state of shock and the grieving reached emotional levels one would expect for a family member. There are thousands of Bill King fans who look back on that day with such a profound sadness that the memory is still painful.

I got a bunch of messages and media requests back then, too, of course.

But now, instead of sadness, there was full-on jubilation.

As for all those questions about how Bill would react: Anyone who has read my book or listened to me speak knows I believe he would be deeply moved by the Hall of Fame honor.

Bill had an encyclopedic knowledge of the history of the game, and it's hard to think he would shun an award that means so much to baseball itself.

This became crystalized in 2004 when Bill made the trip to Cooperstown for one of the great weekends of his life. That was the year Dennis Eckersley and Lon Simmons were honored.

Eck, of course, entered the Hall as one of the great pitchers of all-time and Lon received the Frick. Bill had great fondness for both men. And when he returned from the trip, he was still glowing from the experience.

That time in Cooperstown was so meaningful to him, not only because he shared it with Eck and Lon, but because of the feeling of being in a place of such sublimity. Bill wasn't devout in any way, but for a man whose love of baseball was so deep that he felt it down to his bones, the augustness of Cooperstown almost felt like a pilgrimage to him.

As Hank Greenwald told me: "It was obvious to me from the outset how deeply baseball was in his blood. For that reason alone, I know Bill would be thrilled at being recognized by the Hall of Fame, not for the award itself, but for being embraced by the sport he loved so much."

Beyond the award, one of best things about Bill's honor is that more people will get to know about his career. Learning about him would be instructive for aspiring broadcasters.

Before the final vote, Jon Shestakofsky, the point person at the Hall for the Frick Award, arranged a conference call so that any member of the voting committee could talk about the finalists. Giants broadcaster Jon Miller was on that call and relished the chance to share his thoughts about his boyhood idol.

Jon told the story of listening to an A's game and being struck by the accuracy and detail in Bill's description of a great play by Miguel Tejada. Jon felt like he was at the ballpark watching the play as he listened to Bill and he couldn't wait to see a replay of the call that night on ESPN. When he saw it, he thought to himself, "That's exactly the way I pictured the play unfolding while listening to Bill describe it."

The word that I used most in any conversation about Bill and the Frick Award was "impact." There are plenty of good announcers, but how many of them impacted their fan base the way Bill did?

When it came to a game's denouement, you wanted Bill in your ear. Bill was a brilliant man, and as I said at his memorial, his wide range of interests added texture to his broadcasts. But the main reason Bill resonated was the passion and commitment he brought to every broadcast.

Bill immersed himself in life and his work and his broadcasts took listeners through the chapters of a season with a storytelling style that would rival even the most acclaimed authors. You can't hide over the course of 162 games. Anyone going through the motions will inevitably get exposed. There was no chance of that happening with someone as authentic as Bill.

The outpouring of love and respect for Bill after the Frick announcement validated the committee's vote.

As Dale Tafoya wrote in a message:

"I've been an A's fan since 1981, and the late Bill King finally winning the Frick Award will go down as one of my favorite moments in team history.

"For me, it's like witnessing one of my favorite A's players enter Cooperstown. It's truly special. I was so joyous and happy when it was announced. I met Bill a few times, but listening to him call A's games was a huge part of my life. I was addicted to A's baseball."

In January, Andy Dolich, who always referred to Bill as "the Triple Threat" because of his virtuosity in baseball, basketball, and football, organized a party in honor of Bill at Perry's Restaurant in San Francisco.

The party turned into a Who's Who of Bay Area sporting royalty, as luminaries like Roy Eisenhardt, Wally Haas, Tom Meschery, George Lee, Hank Greenwald, Ted Robinson, Gary Hughes, and Miller came to honor Bill.

A very proud daughter was at the party as well. Kathleen wrote a thank you note to Dolich after she received her invitation. It read, in part:

"He never in a million years expected that he would someday be in the Baseball Hall of Fame. I wish that he could walk out of that Iowa corn field in *Field of Dreams* and see for himself the tremendous respect and fondness his fans and colleagues still hold for him."

Holy Toledo, indeed!

* * *

We had access to the Otesaga for the weekend, which meant we could hang out with Bill's daughter, Kathleen, and her husband, Barry, who were among the dignitaries and invited guests staying at the hotel. We had lunch with them on the patio a day before she delivered the acceptance speech on behalf of Bill.

She was the perfect choice. Bill had officially married Kathleen's mom, Nancy, late in life, but the two were together for decades. Technically, Kathleen was Bill's stepdaughter, but anyone who spent time around them knew to remove the "step" preface. They were close and drew even closer after Nancy died in 2002 and when Bill suffered a terrible hip injury during spring training of 2005.

He couldn't travel for the road games, but, despite being in great pain, persevered through the home games and was sharp as ever. As the A's former broadcasting director Ken Pries used to say, "Broadcasting was Bill's oxygen."

Kathleen drove Bill to the games and back from Bill's home in Sausalito. They'd preview the games on the way over and re-hash them on the way back. It was Kathleen's baseball education. Sometimes they changed the mood and popped in an opera or another of Bill's favorite musical selections.

"Once in a while he'd get in the car and he'd say, 'Let's listen to this,'" Kathleen said. "He'd put the opera *La Traviata* in the CD player, or arias by Anna Netrebko, and we would drive in complete silence, enthralled by the music. We never ran out of things or people to talk about—or music to listen to."

Not that she needed it, but Kathleen got validation of the mark Bill had made on the game during the Hall of Fame weekend, especially during those times on the patio.

Don Sutton, one of Bill's all-time favorite players, was sitting with his family two tables from Kathleen and Barry on Friday and after they finished eating, he came over and explained to Kathleen that he was equally fond of Bill.

Sutton, who was inducted into the Hall of Fame in 1998, initially had balked at joining the A's when they had traded for him in 1985 because he wanted to pitch closer to his home in Southern California, so Sandy Alderson fined him for reporting late to camp.

Sutton was open about saying that the main reason he continued to play at the age of 40 was his pursuit of 300 wins. He began his year with the A's at 280, and he was intrigued by Alderson's hope that he would mentor the A's young pitchers.

He quickly endeared himself to Bill because he had the qualities Bill respected: Sutton loved the game and was a tough-as-nails competitor. Before he was dealt to the Angels in mid-September of '85, Sutton, featuring more guile than pure stuff, won 13 games for a team that finished with only 77.

They were kindred souls when it came to old-school thinking about subjects like pitch counts. And I have to say, the fact that Sutton was a connoisseur of fine wine didn't hurt his relationship with Bill either. He was a civilized man, as Bill liked to say.

"Civilized people," Bill used to tell me, "prefer dining at 8:00 PM or later." We used to argue that point and most of our dinners were preceded by a negotiation over when we would meet.

The scene with Sutton and Kathleen was repeated several times over the weekend with Hall of Famers who had ties to the A's and the East Bay, like Tony La Russa, Dennis Eckersley, Rickey Henderson, and Joe Morgan.

Bill King and Ken at the Coliseum, 2003. (Michael Zagaris)

Joe, who grew up in Oakland and attended Castlemont High School, had the responsibility of introducing Kathleen and presenting the Frick Award plaque at the ceremony. It was a huge honor for Joe and something he had requested to do. "I started listening to Bill in the early '60s," Joe told me that evening. "I had to do that. It was very special for me to be up there with Kathleen."

Twenty-five years after that Hall of Fame game between the White Sox and Mets, Denise and I were seated near second base at Doubleday Field, facing a stage that had been erected in short center field.

Bill's great friend and longtime basketball broadcast partner Hank Greenwald was seated with his wife, Carla, to our right. Marty Lurie was there along with former A's broadcast manager Robert Buan, as were A's president Dave Kaval and chief of staff Miguel Duarte. Mike Marquardt, who engineered many of Bill's Warriors' broadcasts (and "Watergated" the infamous "Mother's Day" basketball tape in 1968), made the trip from Reno. A's luminaries past and present like Wally Haas, Sandy

Alderson, Walt Jocketty, Dr. Elliott Schwartz, and Ken Pries were also on hand. My co-author, Susan, was there as well—not just to cover the event for the *Chronicle*, but because of her fondness for Bill.

One by one, the Hall of Famers were introduced and took their places in rows behind the podium. One of the first was Sandy Koufax, looking like he could still pitch at 80. Seeing Koufax completed a baseball full-circle for me, in a way. My first memories of the big leagues are from when the Dodgers moved to LA and played at the Coliseum in 1958. My grandmother knew nothing about the game, but she considered it a holiday whenever her "Sandala" pitched. Now, almost 60 years later, my longtime broadcast partner and close friend was about to be honored by the Hall of Fame.

Kathleen nailed the speech. Here is what Susan wrote in the *Chronicle*:

> "I think this is a 'Holy Toledo' moment," Lowenthal said, using King's catchphrase with dozens of Hall of Fame players and managers applauding behind her on the stage. "It is for me. Holy Toledo."
>
> Lowenthal said that while King was famously unconventional, "when it came to baseball, he had tremendous respect for its traditions. And he would have been tremendously moved" by Saturday's honor.

Of all the unforgettable moments from the weekend, the first one that comes to mind was what happened when Kathleen's speech ended. In a split second, all the Hall of Famers rose to a standing ovation. I think that's when it hit me hardest and my eyes watered the most—to see the respect for Bill and his place in the game. I wished so badly he could have been there to be part of that scene.

As soon as he got to his feet, Cal Ripken Jr., who was sitting right behind Kathleen, bent over and told her what a great job she had done. She'll never forget that.

The honor bestowed on Bill was part of a perfect afternoon that also featured the wonderful baseball writer Claire Smith receiving the Spink Award—the writing equivalent of the Frick—and Rachel Robinson, Jackie's widow, being honored with the Buck O'Neil Lifetime Achievement Award for her tireless work in many realms, including the establishment of the Jackie Robinson Foundation.

The parade of Hall of Famers on Main Street was next on the schedule and that was followed by a reception at the Hall of Fame—which was like a trip through the pages of baseball history. Everywhere you turned, there was a Hall of Famer dining or mingling with other invited guests.

Denise and I sat with Cepeda, Marty Lurie, and longtime scout and executive "The Legendary" Gary Hughes. (I capitalized "The Legendary," because to me, it's part of his first name).

I wanted to thank Joe Morgan and I found him at a table with Frank Robinson and Henry Aaron. Those are moments that remind me that as baseball fans, the sense of wonder and awe we felt as kids may sometimes be dormant but is never too far below the surface.

The day ended with a reception that Sandy Alderson orchestrated at one of the meeting rooms at the Otesaga. There were about 25 of us and we went around the room telling Bill King stories. They were all touching, especially when an always earnest Dennis Eckersley reminisced about growing up in the East Bay and how much Bill had been a part of his childhood—then Bill called his games during Eck's greatest years.

There are many adjectives that would be apropos to describe both Bill and Eck. I think "authentic" is the first that comes to mind.

Kathleen was the last speaker and as she began thanking everyone, the doors to the room swung open behind her and in strolled a beaming Rickey Henderson. She realized at that moment that there would be no point continuing and it was fitting. Rickey Henderson, the Man of Steal and the living embodiment of the Hall of Fame, stole the show.

* * *

Susan Slusser

For any baseball fan, Hall of Fame induction weekend in Cooperstown is heaven on earth. I've been lucky enough to attend three inductions—and even got to take part in one.

In 2012, while vice president of the Baseball Writers Association of America, I introduced the great Canadian sportswriter, Bob Elliott of the *Toronto Sun*, when he was presented with the J.G. Taylor Spink Award, the top honor for a baseball writer.

It was an unparalleled pleasure, not least because I admire Bob Elliott. He's a funny, kind, and gentlemanly sort whose hard work and diligence set a standard for baseball writers for four decades or more, and he has mentored many women reporters throughout his career. Plus, as a hockey fan, I was tickled to be able to get some hockey references into my introduction speech—I'm hopeful that's a Cooperstown first.

At one point, I mentioned during the introduction that Bob's "laser-like focus on baseball famously makes him forget things in his day-to-day life—such as the whereabouts of his phone, even when he's holding it… or talking on it."

That got some chuckles from the Hall of Famers on the stage, which helped the nerves disappear.

Being part of the induction program is extraordinary. Participants attend all the private pre-induction events (except of course the Hall of Famers-only dinner) and stay in the Otesaga Hotel, which, for the weekend, accepts only past and present inductees and their families.

Introducing an award-winner is a very minor task—my speech was about two minutes—but riding on the bus to the event, surrounded by the game's greatest, and then sitting on a podium with them is an intimidating I-don't-belong-here-at-all feeling. A blast, but with the subtext that there was some major misunderstanding.

Then there are the nerves. Writers typically are best hiding behind their laptops. Only a few are really at ease on TV. A speech, however short, is mind-bogglingly stressful, then add in the large audience in person and on TV—while standing a few feet away from all the game's greats—well, my stomach and knees were jelly. I was convinced I'd pass out, as I once did giving a book report in front of the class in sixth grade.

Somehow, I made it through. The next morning, in line for breakfast, Al Kaline said, "Great job with the speech!"

I said, "Oh my gosh, I was so nervous."

"Yeah," he said. "We've all been there."

* * *

In 2014, my idol, Roger Angell of the *New Yorker* was presented with the Spink Award. My husband, Dan Brown, and I attended, ostensibly to cover the inductions of former A's manager Tony La Russa and former Oakland DH Frank Thomas, but our main emphasis was Angell, whom I'd nominated for the Spink. Before the BBWAA cocktail party in his honor, we sat and chatted with Roger and his then fiancée, now wife, Peggy, an absolute thrill. I wish I could remember the entire conversation but I love him so much my brain was basically frozen. It's a little unfair that when you'd like to be at your most quick-witted and charming, you can't remember any words—especially when you're talking to someone who knows *all* the words.

I do have a nice keepsake from the event: The *New Yorker* gang there for the weekend gave me an "Angell's Angels" t-shirt, which I won't wear because I don't want to sully it.

The night before the players are inducted, there is a gala at the Hall of Fame, a private party actually inside the museum. It's remarkable. Legends around every corner, top executives hobnobbing with the most high-profile media members. I always have to remind myself to not walk around mouth agape at this event. "Be cool!"

The town itself, wonderful any time of year, is just spectacular during induction weekend. Former players sit at tables up and down Main Street, signing cards. Pete Rose is a fixture, along with many of the best players of the 1970s—guys who just missed out on the big contracts that came with free agency. Often, players, executives, and baseball media members are selling recently released books. There are memorabilia shops galore, good restaurants, and better bars, all jammed full of baseball photos and relics.

If you don't mind packed streets, make a point to go to Cooperstown one induction weekend when a favorite player or broadcaster is inducted. If you prefer to avoid crowds, go any other time. It's magical.

* * *

Dan wrote a travelogue about our first trip to Cooperstown in 2012. Here are some highlights:

FRIDAY

I wake up at 10:00 AM, peek outside my hotel room, and see stars. Ferguson Jenkins and Jim Bunning are on the veranda in rocking chairs.

As I duck out for a run, I spot Gaylord Perry in the lobby telling stories. If Gaylord moved from this spot—or stopped telling stories—over the next three days, it wasn't for long.

Later, at a Carousel Party hosted by Jane Forbes Clark, Susan chats with MLB spokesman Pat Courtney, but I spend the entire time watching conversation between Mike Schmidt, George Brett, and Paul Molitor. My inner child starts banging on the walls, begging to get out.

This scene here is incredible. Throw a fastball in any direction and you'll brush back a legend. Whitey Ford. Brooks Robinson. Andre Dawson. Lou Brock. "This party is like walking around with your baseball cards," writer Jack O'Connell says.

Susan says hello to pal Rickey Henderson, who gives her a peck on the cheek. (Stealing a kiss?)

Whitey Ford sits down next to Yogi Berra. Susan sneaks a photo.

I tell Steve Carlton that Mike Krukow (his '83 Phillies teammate) is always singing his praises. "Don't believe anything Krukow says," Carlton replies. I'm pretty sure he's joking. I tell him that Krukow and I were recently discussing sliders and sinkers. 'Sinkers or stinkers?" Carlton says. We talk some more, but those are honestly the last words I understand. "Nice meeting you," I say as I make my awkward retreat.

A portly senior citizen walks by with his hands full. He looks like a human dessert tray. Susan: "Did you see that guy? He was carrying four ice cream cones." Me: "Did you see that guy? He was Gaylord Perry."

Fearful that Perry didn't leave us any, we get in the ice cream line. Brooks Robinson, Jim Bunning, and Al Kaline are there, too. When it's Robinson's turn, I resist the temptation to shout, "Oh, and Brooksie makes an ice cream catch!" But it's not easy.

SATURDAY

I keep taking the elevator in hopes of sharing a ride with a legend. I keep getting the same laundry guy, who looks as disappointed in me as I do in him. Sluss, in contrast, keeps returning to the hotel room and recounting conversations like this one:

Susan: "I just wanted to say hello, I'm Susan Slusser."

Elevator passenger: "Nice to meet you. I'm Bob Gibson."

Susan: "I know!"

I give up and start taking the stairs.

Sluss goes to a rehearsal for that evening's ceremony. I go for a run. Half-a-mile in, I blow past another stolen base champ. I ignore the fact that he's walking and declare myself faster than Rickey Henderson. I resist temptation to stop in front of Rickey, pull something out of the ground, hold it over my head, and shout, "Today, I am the greatest of all-time!" But it's not easy.

Time for the real thing, the Awards Presentation at Doubleday Field. Sluss steps on to the stage and sits down on a folding chair in front of Wade Boggs and Ryne Sandberg. Sluss loves the '80s.

Sluss crushes her speech. I've heard this speech many, many times over the past few weeks—around the house, in the car, in the hotel room—but here it sounds like something new. The jokes land as lightly as feathers. The rhythm and pacing comes from some unseen orchestra conductor. The crowd eats it up. (Television replays would later confirm that Robin Yount is laughing.)

Ceremony ends. I turn around to see that everyone has left the stage except for two people deep in conversation: Susan Slusser and Carlton Fisk.

I sneak up for photos. I am so sly and undetectable that Susan shouts: "Hey, there's my husband." Fisk waves emphatically. Is this guy always waving emphatically?

Party at the Hall of Fame Museum. This is where reality breaks from its moorings and drifts out to sea. The ballplayers are stepping through the cornfield.

This is a private reception, so Susan and I tour the museum alone. But after a few minutes, we have interlopers: Steve Carlton (329 wins) and Rollie Fingers (341 saves). They marvel at the same stuff we do. When they spot the famous pine-tar bat, they recall with glee just how mad George Brett was.

Within minutes, Dennis Eckersley arrives and stands right in front of an A's exhibit. As Jennifer Eckersley takes a few photos, so do we.

Soon, I'm in a conversation with Eckersley and Tony La Russa, both of whom are fond of my boss, Bud Geracie. La Russa says, "You know what we used to call him? 'Bum.'" I point out that it's really not a nickname. "You're right," La Russa allows, "it was really more of a description."

Back downstairs, the guy from the poster that used to hang on my bedroom wall praises Susan: Lou Brock touches her on the arm and says, "Really good job with the speech."

Michael Weiner, the executive director of the player's association, seeks Susan out, too. He introduces himself and says that his teenage daughter is the world's harshest critic when it comes to women in media. "But in you, she has someone she can look up to," Weiner tells Susan. That is pretty damn cool, even if I didn't have a Michael Weiner poster on my wall.

On the bus ride back, veteran writers tell us that it's worth checking out the hotel bar. Paul Molitor has been known to sing Springsteen, karaoke style. Stan Musial has been known to break out his harmonica. "You never know what might happen," one writer says. What happens is that we stand in a dark corner talking to paunchy, middle-aged baseball writers, just like we do at home. We're gone within 15 minutes. But later that night, I hear "Dancing in the Dark" and wonder....

SUNDAY

I return from a run but Susan is gone. When she steps back into the hotel room, she says: "I just spent an hour-and-a-half on the veranda talking to Carlton Fisk." Such absurd statements are now the norm. The same goes for what she says next: "Remind me to take a few business cards in case I run into Fisk and Joe Morgan again." Of course, we *did* run into them again, and she gave them *San Francisco Chronicle* business cards.

(Side note: Do baseball players collect business cards?)

In the hotel lobby, the once-in-a-lifetime bus arrives again. Charlie Sheen is posing with Dave Winfield and Andre Dawson, but I fumble with my camera and miss the shot. No matter. Sheen proceeds to pose with Ozzie Smith, George

Brett, Rickey Henderson, Whitey Ford, Yogi Berra, and several of their amused wives.

Sheen is on our shuttle bus to the induction ceremony. Susan takes many photos of the back of his head.

The induction ceremony is lovely: Ron Santo's widow delivers a note-perfect tribute that gets a sustained standing ovation and generates buzz for the rest of the weekend. Barry Larkin's speech is strong, too, in part because he tells lots of Eric Davis stories.

After the ceremony, we race to get lunch at hotel restaurant but Susan has to drop off stuff in the room. I find myself at a table with nothing to do… except listen to Willie Mays and Gaylord Perry, who are two tables over swapping stories about the early 1960s Giants.

Perry tells a favorite I'd only read about: In dismissing Perry's hitting skills, Alvin Dark said in 1964 that "they'll put a man on the moon before he hits a home run." Perry wound up hitting the first home run of his career on July 20, 1969—just minutes after Apollo 11 touched down.

Mays suddenly gets hacked off—40 years after the fact—that the Giants traded Perry to the Indians for Sam McDowell in 1971. Perry points out that he won 43 games over the next two years. In fact, I hear him point that out at least three times.

MONDAY

We spend much of breakfast talking to the widow of Eddie Mathews. Judy Mathews still comes to the inductions every year. Not long ago, she asked George Brett how many home runs he hit. "317," Brett said. "Is that all?" Judy replied. (Her husband hit 512.)

Eddie Mathews died in 2001. Now, when Judy comes to the events at Cooperstown, her dance partner is George Brett.

We get on the shuttle to the Albany airport, albeit reluctantly. One last thrill: we're joined by Hall of Fame umpire Doug Harvey and his wife, Joy. Players gave Doug the nickname of "God," but apparently the players never met his wife, the true omnipotent one. She is smart, tough, opinionated, and a little scary. She and Susan get along famously.

* * *

In 2017, Bill King received the Frick Award for broadcasting—an event much better told by Ken Korach—and Claire Smith won the Spink Award, becoming the first woman baseball writer with a plaque at the Hall of Fame.

I went to cover King's induction for the *Chronicle*, and tears came to my eyes hearing some of his greatest calls played there in Cooperstown. The party in King's honor later at the Otesaga was just perfect—fond reminiscences shared, stories about King's many talents and quirks, jokes and laughter. A celebration of the greatest sports broadcaster of all time, what a day and night.

For me, the best part of that day and evening was watching Ken Korach soak it all in. Ken likes to downplay his involvement, but there is no doubt in anyone else's mind: Ken is responsible for Bill King getting the Frick Award. He sent out testimonials and tapes to voters, he made pleas, he did publicity—he wrote a book, for goodness sake! The Frick Award was the culmination of years of hard work, a testament to love and friendship. Beautiful.

For me, Claire Smith was always an inspiration. She was in the wave of first women to cover baseball full time—she first worked for the *Hartford Courant*, then the *New York Times*—and as an African American, Claire had even more to deal with. She endured all sorts of slights, insults, and outright obstacles, and did so with a patience and grace that I, possessing neither quality, can only marvel at. Claire earned the respect of everyone in the sport with the quality of her reporting and her impeccable professionalism. Her speech was phenomenal—touching, funny, and inspiring. Watching from the press area and wearing hats Claire had brought along to honor the late and much-loved MLB executive Katy Feeney, Alyson Footer of MLB.com and I were both wiping away tears.

Bill King and Claire Smith honored, on the same day. Remarkable. They mean so much to so many people, their influence enduring. Hall of Famers, both.

* * *

Another fun Hall of Fame–related event is the dinner that the BBWAA's New York chapter throws at a midtown hotel in January for that year's award winners—MVP, Cy Young, etc.—and the upcoming inductees. It's open to the public; tickets are available on the BBWAA website, and it's a great evening of speeches and jokes.

I've twice introduced people at that event: Bob Melvin, when he was the AL Manager of the Year in 2012, and Angell, in 2014. The best part of that evening was hanging out beforehand with Roger and *New Yorker* editor David Remnick, who is just a tick below Angell on the personal pantheon of deities. At one point, Roger asked Dan to go find "Rem" for him. I've never seen anyone happier to be sent on an errand or beaming so much once the mission was completed.

The best New York writers' dinner was one I attended mostly for fun but also as a reporter, to cover the A's Big Three—Barry Zito, Mark Mulder, and Tim Hudson—getting the Willie, Mickey, and the Duke Award, which is presented annually to figures forever linked in baseball history. A blizzard nearly wiped out the event—the streets were shut down, and public gatherings were all cancelled for safety concerns—so the dinner wound up consisting of honorees, their families, baseball executives, and media members and it was moved into a small, auxiliary room.

My best friend, Christine Winge, and I slogged four blocks through the blizzard, trudging right down the middle of closed-off Sixth Avenue, the snow several feet thick and coming down hard, to get to the Hilton; we brought a change of clothes—and more important, shoes—with us.

"Do you remember that movie *Alive*, where they have to hike out of the Andes?" Zito said after hoofing it all the way from lower Manhattan with his wife. "Amber and I were doing the version of hiking out of the Andes. We hiked a long way."

With almost no one in attendance, everyone had a marvelous time catching up and celebrating baseball's best, which that year included a former A's player, Josh Donaldson, that year's AL MVP, as well as Carlos Correa, the AL Rookie of the Year. Correa and his family had never seen snow before, and he posted video of himself and his dad, also named Carlos, racing around, throwing snowballs and plunging into snowbanks. "Snow can't stop baseball!" Correa said.

During the ceremony, Zito stole the show by unveiling his "All Dreamy Team," which included Cy Young winner Jake Arrieta of the Cubs ("You edged out Cole Hamels," Zito said) and Nationals outfielder Bryce Harper, the NL MVP. "Congrats," Zito said to Harper of his All-Dreamy honors, leaning over to shake his hand.

Donaldson, when presented with the AL MVP award, nodded at Zito. "I told Barry that he's one of the reasons I'm here," Donaldson said. "In the middle of 2012, I looked up at the scoreboard [in a game against the Giants] and saw he was hitting 40 points higher than I was, so I figured I had to change a few things."

CHAPTER 11

MICKEY MORABITO: STEINBRENNER, MARTIN, AND THE A'S REAL MVP

Mickey Morabito began his career in baseball in 1970, as a ball boy, and he joined the A's in 1980, the same year as the team's new manager, Billy Martin. One of the best-known figures in American League press boxes, Morabito is friendly with everyone in the game, from execs to players, from umpires to reporters, and he's a repository of knowledge about restaurants and bars across the country. He chatted with Ken and Susan on a trip to Chicago in June 2018.

How did you become a ball boy and then become a full-time employee?

I was a big Yankee fan growing up in New York, so I wrote a letter to the director of stadium operations at Yankee Stadium about being a batboy or a clubhouse guy. I was called in and interviewed, but they only hired two positions that year.

The following year, I got called in again. They must have thought I did okay, and they hired me. Most of the time I was a ball boy right by the Yankees dugout, running balls out to the umpires and stuff like that.

I also called the lineup changes upstairs to the press box. The umpire would tell me and I would call Bob Fishel, who was the Yankee PR director at the time, to let him know. When I got out of school, they put me part-time in the PR department.

I did that for a couple of years, then there was a succession of people leaving. Bob Fishel left to go to the American League office, and Marty Appel got the head PR job, so they made me the assistant PR director.

Two years later, Marty left, and I didn't know if I would get the head job. I was 25 years old. I give George Steinbrenner credit because he went with me. Gabe Paul, the team president, told him no, we have to look around, and Steinbrenner said, "Let's go with Mickey. I think he can do the job."

In 1976, we hosted the All-Star Game and all of a sudden, after being crappy, the Yankees are hosting a playoff series—and then win the World Series the next two years. I got thrown right into the fire.

When Billy Martin came in, he and I hit it off. He trusted me and I helped him out with the media in New York. When Billy got fired and went to Oakland in 1980, he asked me to go to Oakland with him.

I asked Steinbrenner for a raise. He didn't give it to me. I resigned and came to Oakland. Here I am in Oakland now.

What was Steinbrenner like as a boss?

I really can't say anything bad about working for George. He fired me two or three times, but he always rehired me the next day. He would scream and yell, but it was his club. He was bombastic and he would go off on some things, but he took a chance with me at a pretty young age, giving me a job that gave me a lot of exposure.

The Yankees were always a great organization, but there was a period of time in the early '70s that they were pretty bad. Under George, the Yankees all of a sudden were a great team again. I never forgot that.

When I left, I really think George knew what he was doing—he didn't really want to make it rough for me. The day I went in to tell him I had another opportunity, he put his arm around me and said, "I really think you should think about this. Let's talk tomorrow."

Deep down, I think he thought I wanted to leave. He didn't want to stand in my way and keep me there.

That night, I went out with Phil Pepe and Moss Klein and Murray Chass, all the Yankee writers, and I said, "He made no effort to keep me. I've got to go." And I went in the next day and I told him I was leaving.

Every time I went back to New York, I would go into the ticket office and the ticket guys would roll their eyes, "I don't know what you got, but Steinbrenner sent down extra club boxes for you and Billy. He wants you to have these good tickets because he knows you have family here."

George thought about things like that. That was pretty cool. Whenever I was there, I would always walk down to his little box to say hi to him. He couldn't have been nicer.

What was it like being the PR man when Martin and Reggie Jackson got in that famous dugout fight?

It pretty much was a circus. I'll never forget that day in Fenway. George was somewhere in Indiana, he had a farm there or something. It was the Game of the Week on TV, so he was watching this whole thing. Back then, we didn't have cellphones, so he was calling the switchboard at Fenway Park. Helen was the switchboard operator; they always said they built Fenway Park around her, and she was tough to get calls through. She wouldn't send him to the clubhouse or the press box and George was screaming, "Put me through. I have to talk to Mickey in the press box!"

He finally got a hold of me and said he needed Al Rosen, the GM, to reach him right away.

After the game, we went back to the hotel, and I went to Billy's room to try to solve this whole thing.

Situations like that, I just got used to them. I used to call it the vicious triangle. I would come in one day and I wouldn't know if it was Billy and George hating Reggie, or maybe the next day it was Reggie and George hating Billy. You never knew which side to be on. I'm sitting there, from a PR standpoint, like, "Who's mad at who today?" There were times Billy and Reggie would be lovey-dovey and moaning about Steinbrenner. There would be days where it would be Billy and Steinbrenner talking like, "What a jerk Reggie is."

When I left, it was kind of relaxing. In 1980, our first year in Oakland, Charlie Finley was basically an absentee owner. We could never get a hold of him. Billy was kind of like the manager and the general manager. He was running the show. One day, Billy wanted to bring a player up and he couldn't reach Charlie and he was getting angry.

I said to Billy, "Think of what you're saying right now. We just left a situation in New York where the owner was omnipresent every day and now you've got an owner you can't find. Why don't you just enjoy it?"

How did Martin go about asking you to come with him to Oakland?

I was with the Yankees at spring training in Fort Lauderdale and Dick Howser was the manager. I loved Dick, and I was kind of actually looking forward to working with him because he had been Billy's third-base coach.

Billy calls and he says, "Mickey, there's no staff out here. Charlie says I can hire whoever I want. I'd really like you to come out here with me."

Then Charlie calls me and the first thing he tells me is, "I can't pay you what they're paying you in New York." I told him what I was making in New York and he laughed. He said, "Oh, I can pay you that, but you're going to do both jobs. You're going to do public relations and be the traveling secretary."

I said, "That's fine, Mr. Finley." It wasn't like I had an interview. Billy just hired me and told Charlie, "This is what I'm doing."

That 1980 season was one of my most fun years in baseball. The A's had been one of the worst teams in baseball in 1979, they lost 108 games under Jim Marshall. Then, with Billy, they were almost in the playoffs in 1980. In '81, we got into the playoffs.

When did you move over to the traveling secretary role full time?

I did both jobs for the first year, and at the end of the year they sold to the Haas family, and I told them, "If you're going to split the jobs up, I'd rather just do the travel."

I liked the logistics of it, and to be honest, after coming from New York and the whole media circus, I just didn't feel like dealing with the press on a day-to-day basis anymore. It wasn't like we had a big media entourage, but I just felt more inclined to stick with travel.

I did some of the travel arrangements in college. I went to Hunter College and I was manager of the basketball and baseball teams, so I set up the baseball team for our southern trip every year. One year, I called [Yankees great] Bobby Richardson and he gave me a game at the University of South Carolina, where he was coaching. We played Virginia Tech, Virginia Commonwealth. Most Eastern teams would look for colleges in Florida and the Carolinas to go to early because you couldn't play in New York with the weather. I did the same thing with the basketball team. I was booking Holiday Inns and La Quintas back then, but I really enjoyed doing that.

What was it like when you first got to Oakland?

I didn't come until the end of February, so Carl Finley [Charlie's cousin and right-hand man] had set up all the flights and the hotels. When I went through it all, there were times we were like a Triple-A team—we were getting up and flying on the day of the game to places on commercial flights. We were changing planes.

We chartered a few flights, but back then a lot of teams still flew commercial, and the players still had to fly first class. Say we're going to New York, Boston, Toronto. Back then, SFO had nonstop flights to New York and Boston that left about noon. They were wide-bodies and some had 30 to 40 first-class seats, so I was able to buy the whole first-class cabin. It was almost as good as a charter. Back then, first class was actually first class. Now you fly first class and they'll only give you a soda.

We flew a lot of commercial flights, a lot of day-of-game stuff. I remember one time in Dallas, after a Sunday night game, we had to take a 7:00 AM flight to Cleveland. We were on the bus and Billy was in one of his hungover moods. Everybody was bleary-eyed. We're on this bus going to the airport at 6:00 AM and Billy gets up screaming about Charlie Finely being a cheap son of a bitch for not getting us a charter.

Billy said, "We're never doing this again. We'll all chip in, right? We'll get our own charter."

After that, except for the trans-con flights where I could get an all first-class flight, we started chartering a lot.

Even into the early '80s, we always had a mix of commercial and charter flights. We would walk through terminals like regular people. I would get all the boarding passes in advance and hand them out, so we could board first.

The airlines tried to take care of us the best they could. When we landed, we didn't have to go to the carousel and wait for our luggage, our trucks were able to go to the plane and pick it up.

With some of the more high-profile A's teams, what was traveling like?

In the late '80s, we were rock stars. We used to stay at the Adams Mark in Kansas City across from the ballpark. They had a little school bus that they would shuttle us around in. It had baseball players painted on the side. It was really kind of cute, but we would go back over after a game and there would be all these A's fans in the lobby. It was brutal.

There were a few times where I had to change hotels because of the security situation with the big stars. There were some hotels where we would go in and there were service elevators for the players to use. After we picked our keys up, they would take to the back elevators that they used to bring room service up. It worked okay.

There was a time in New York where Jose Canseco was caught on the front page of the *Post* leaving Madonna's apartment on the West Side early one morning. We're staying at the Grand Hyatt and Jose walks on the bus in frayed jeans and a suede jacket. The guys are looking at the paper and looking at Jose: He's wearing the exact same thing that he had on that was on the front page of the *New York Post* that day.

How did your current airplane arrangement come about?

We used to fly America West exclusively for a while, then we went to Swift Air, which had three or four teams and a couple of planes that they used. One time, about six or seven years ago, there was a conflict so they got the Mavericks plane for me on a sub-service.

I got on, and I said, "This is nice." I started talking to one of the pilots and he said, "Call so-and-so in Mark Cuban's office. See if they are willing to charter it."

I called and they said, "Right now, we have no intention to use the plane other than for the basketball team." So I kept pushing and pushing, and I said, "This would be a great opportunity to marry a baseball team with a basketball team. The plane gets usage all year. It's not sitting dead in the summer."

Their money people said, "That's not a bad idea," and they must've gone to Cuban. He said, "If you think it's a good thing to do."

They ended up getting a second aircraft and the Rangers and Dallas Stars share them. We've had a couple of multi-year contracts with them and, hopefully, I can renegotiate it and we can use it moving forward.

How many commercial flights do you typically have to book throughout the season?

Just this week, three guys flew in in one day. Two were coming off of rehab assignments and one was a call-up. Any time a starter goes out in the third inning, I'm thinking, "Did we blow out a pitcher? Are they going to bring somebody else here?" I need to immediately consider the logistics, think ahead because I know our front office is doing the same thing. If a reliever goes into a game and pitches three innings, they might be sent out after the game. Chris Bassitt just called me from the Oklahoma City airport, and his flight to Chicago was cancelled and he was going to miss his connection. We ended up voiding that ticket and putting him on a Delta flight, Oklahoma City to Minneapolis, Minneapolis to Detroit. Those are things that happen when you're dealing with commercial flights.

How has your job changed with advancements in communications, particularly cell phones?

In baseball, you never know how long the game is. In the old days, a game was over and I would call the next hotel from the press-box phone and that was it. They didn't hear from me again. If we were delayed in traffic or there was something mechanical with the plane on the other end, or with the bus or the truck, the hotel would be sitting there twiddling their thumbs. I had no way to get in touch with them. [Technology] has definitely been a help. Right now, on a getaway day, you're sitting there saying to yourself, "Bus here, airport here, then we're going to land. Do I have the bus, truck, airport and hotel?" You're trying to keep them all in line. At the end of the game, I can call the airport here and tell them we're on our way and to meet us at the gate. When I'm on the plane before we take off, I'll call the bus driver, the truck driver, the hotel, and give them an update on our arrival time.

It just makes things go smoother. There's less chance of something getting screwed up by keeping everybody informed as you go along.

How many people are on each trip?

Right now, we basically travel with around 52 people on each flight: players, broadcasters, support staff. In the '70s and '80s, you had the traveling secretary, the equipment manager, the PR guy, and one trainer. Now you've got two trainers, two conditioning coaches, massage therapist, two PR guys, an interpreter. The traveling party has grown as the needs of the players have grown.

How is the seating decided?

We do it by seniority for the seats in the front section. At one of our last spring-training meetings, I go through the seniority list and I tell the guys, "Here are the seats in the front, this is what we're going to start with, but if there's a card game going on that means you need somebody up front who doesn't have seniority, you guys police yourselves." For example, Mark Canha is up at the card game, but he doesn't have the seniority to be there. The card game is Stephen Piscotty, Jed Lowrie, Marcus Semien. Maybe no one else wants to play cards, so it's fine that Canha is up there. The other day the players all realized that Edwin Jackson (a newly arrived 15-year veteran) needed to sit up front, so someone went to the back and let him take their seat.

How does the catering work for the flights?

Our lead flight attendant and our nutritionist are involved, and we work with different caterers in each city and they'll send me a menu at the start of the month for the next month's flights. The nutritionist might say, "We had sliders on our last flight and let's move away from the breaded chicken fingers. Instead of potatoes, can you do rice as a side for this?" The flight attendant knows what the guys are eating, and if something doesn't go over well, she'll say, "The guys didn't eat that at all. We need to do more of this other thing." A lot of times, if we are flying after a day game and they eat dinner in the clubhouse after the game or if we're getting to a city in time for dinner, we'll really knock down what we're going to have on the plane. Otherwise, so much food is going to go to waste.

Do people in the general public understand your job or do you wind up having to explain it?

I think people understand that I'm the guy that books the flights and the hotels. I don't know if they understand everything that's involved. Obviously, there are so many other things involved: arranging for players' tickets every game, handling payroll and per diems, dealing with spring-training preparations, being the point person for the spring-training schedule and the regular-season schedule. There are lots of other things involved in the position.

What are your pet peeves?

Last-minute requests, that's the big thing. As we're getting on the plane, the player who comes up and says, "I need a car when we land back in Oakland." Or, as we're getting on the plane, who says, "My wife is going to be at our hotel with her family and I need two extra rooms." How about telling me about this two days ago?

Our guys are mostly pretty good, but they're forgetful, too. Those are the things where I wish I had more notice.

What is the best part of your job?

I still really enjoy the travel and the cities. I can go out and sight-see and go to good restaurants. In baseball, you do have some time to because you're usually in a city for at least three days.

I'm going to all these great cities, and I'm staying in nice hotels. Somebody is paying for my room. It's kind of cool to be able to go to places that if I did this on vacation, it would be on my dime.

CHAPTER 12

MONEYBALL: "IT'S INCREDIBLY HARD"

Ken Korach

The IMDB listing for my role in the movie *Moneyball* has the following information: Ken Korach is an actor, known for *Moneyball*.

IMDB is the bible of the movie business, the primary source for information on movies and actors, but that's probably the most misleading sentence in the history of Hollywood.

It should probably say: Ken Korach is a would-be actor, whose role in *Moneyball* currently resides on the cutting-room floor.

Not that I can blame the producers of the movie for cutting me out. The camera and I have never been great friends and, let's face it: They had a movie to make. Bennett Miller, who's been nominated twice for an Academy Award for Best Director, didn't earn his reputation by awarding gratuitous roles to awkward novices like me.

Maybe that cutting-room floor revealed a bit about why I'm on radio instead of TV and I suppose this is a good a place as any to answer a question about television.

I had a goal when I started to get consistent broadcasting work: I saw myself as a radio announcer who occasionally did television. I've been lucky that it's worked out that way, because you can't always map out a career.

A good example would be my two most recent jobs. I did more than 400 UNLV basketball games and I would guess that around 50 of those were on TV, including several simulcasts in the first few years. And I was Greg Papa's fill-in during my first decade with the A's. Greg was a multisport talent and I would take his spot on the A's telecasts when he was away with basketball or football.

I've always been more comfortable on radio. Even with all the games I did, I never took to doing television. And, there is nothing more fulfilling for me than describing the action on radio. As Bill King said: "On television you are an instrument of the director and you caption the pictures." That's not a knock on television or the folks who produce the games. I've worked with some brilliant production talent over the years and I have great respect for TV play-by-play announcers who do it well. It's just that the mediums are different.

The A's have been so great to me and there are many examples why. One is their acquiescing to my desire to stay on radio, even after some serious imploring from the front office and ownership to make the switch to television in my earlier years. That was a big concern; I didn't want to let the team down. But, they understood that radio is where my heart has always been, and I'm grateful for that.

* * *

One of the best things about *Moneyball* is that it provided another showcase for the amazing Bill King. People from the Bay Area knew he was great, but a hit movie starring Brad Pitt helped reveal him to a whole new audience.

Bill always said that his strength was in the descriptions and trying to quantify his best call over his 25 years with the A's is impossible. I don't think, however, there is any doubt that his call of Scott Hatteberg's home run that crowned the A's 20-game winning streak in 2002 is the one folks remember most. It was the perfect call to immortalize on film.

Hatteberg's home run was the climax of the *Moneyball* movie. The producers went out of their way to bring authenticity to those scenes. They culled through hundreds of hours of radio and television play-by-play, and that's the reason the A's broadcasters are heard in the movie. They didn't have to do that. They could have saved tons of time by having someone voice over those plays in the studio. It was that desire for authenticity which impressed me so much while spending an hour with Bennett Miller.

David Rinetti, the A's VP of stadium operations, was the catalyst in working with casting to give Greg Papa, Glen Kuiper—the current TV voice of the A's—and me a shot.

We showed up one morning at the Coliseum and had our little taste of Hollywood. There were trailers in the parking lot with tiny dressing rooms and, nearby, we were directed to the trailer for hair and makeup. That meant some predictable sitting around and waiting, so we got to spend some time with Brent Jennings, the wonderful character actor who played Ron Washington.

It's Jennings who delivers one of *Moneyball*'s most oft-repeated lines. Brad Pitt, as Billy Beane, is trying to sign Hatteberg and convince him that he could easily make the transition from catching to first base. Part of Beane's pitch is to have Wash confirm this. Jennings (as Wash) responds: "It's incredibly hard." If you close your eyes and listen to Jennings, you'd swear it was Wash.

They converted an unused broadcast booth in the press box for shooting some scenes, and that's where I was assigned to report. Miller came in with a cadre of support personnel. The camera seemed like it was three times the size of TV cameras I was used to.

The sound technicians and other crew members crowded onto a short flight of stairs that overlooked the desk where Miller and I sat. It felt like the giant camera was right over my shoulder.

Miller got right to the point. He said, "It's Opening Day, 2002, the A's have lost Jason Giambi, Johnny Damon, and Jason Isringhausen. Open the broadcast and set the scene."

There was very little direction beyond that. Miller said, "You're the expert and I'm not. Tell me what's happening, how things are different this year, what fans should expect, and do it as if you're in your booth starting the first broadcast of the year."

I left the booth feeling like it went okay, not great. Miller made things as relaxed as possible, but I remember thinking that it was a good thing I can make a living on the radio. The acting thing isn't exactly in my comfort zone. It was a great experience, though, even if that tape probably wound up in a dumpster long ago.

* * *

When the movie was released in the fall of 2011, it received generally positive reviews and earned six Academy Award nominations.

My biggest beef has been with the portrayal of Art Howe. The late Philip Seymour Hoffman was a gifted actor and I'm sure his performance was what Miller and the producers were looking for. But there is no way, in appearance or personality, that he resembled Art Howe.

Art was deeply hurt by the characterization and for good reason. Art is tall and athletic and as fine a person as I've ever met. Hoffman was schlubby and his character's mulishness bore scant resemblance to Art. But in an effort to develop their characters and with generous Hollywood license, the script accentuated the differences between Art and Billy and the dissonance that grew between them.

Art Howe and Ken at Fenway Park in 1996. (Michael Zagaris)

It's also easy to point out how the movie glosses over stars such as the Big Three (Tim Hudson, Mark Mulder, and Barry Zito) and the finest left side of the infield in Oakland history—Miguel Tejada (the league MVP in 2002) and Eric Chavez. (That's a point that's open for debate, as I'm sure there would be support for Campy Campaneris and Sal Bando. Walt Weiss and Carney Lansford had good years together, as did Jed Lowrie and Josh Donaldson.)

But this was a movie about the economics of baseball and, from that standpoint, the film did justice to Michael Lewis' book. And the book has had a profound influence on the game and 16 years after the 2002 season, there isn't a team in baseball that isn't deep into analytics. Billy Beane and the A's get credit for that.

It wasn't just the emphasis on finding value where others didn't and using objective analysis and out-of-the-box thinking to quantify it. Look around baseball: Front offices are comprised differently than before. Someone like Farhan Zaidi, the Giants' new GM and Billy Beane protégé, has a PhD in economics from UC Berkeley. That would have been unthinkable in the old days.

The world premiere of *Moneyball* was a big event for Oakland. Hollywood came to town. The screening was held downtown, at the Paramount Theatre, on September 19, 2011. Denise, Emilee, and I arrived an hour early and had to navigate our way through several hundred fans who lined the streets to try to spot stars Brad Pitt, Hoffman, Chris Pratt, and Jonah Hill.

TV production trucks were everywhere, with news and entertainment shows capturing the red-carpet spectacle.

The scene inside the theatre was wild. A's fans mixed in with the invited guests, and as the scenes of the winning streak built to a crescendo, you would have thought we were inside the Coliseum. Papa and Kuiper did a very nice job with their parts, by the way, and Greg's narration added a classy bit of storytelling.

The place went crazy when Bill's call of Hatteberg's homer rang out.

When Chris Pratt, as Hatteberg, took the grand tour of the bases, it took Hatteberg back to that moment when all he heard were "the bells and whistles inside my head."

You hear me for about 90 seconds, primarily as Miguel Tejada's heroics propelled the A's to walk-off wins in games 18 and 19. Emilee was sitting to my left, and we had a touching father-daughter moment when she turned and said, "Dad, you had a pretty big part to play there."

As a broadcaster, it's serendipitous: Think of all the announcers whose calls rarely get heard because their teams aren't successful. The A's gave me nine postseasons in a 19-year stretch, a 20-game winning streak, a perfect game, and a no-hitter.

That's a pretty good résumé for Billy Beane, and the focus on the book and movie highlighted the debate over Billy's place in the game.

Is he a Hall of Famer? He gets dinged because the A's haven't won a World Series and only advanced past the ALDS once in all those tries. I suppose there is some fairness in the criticism, but Beane's influence, as

Emilee Korach and Ken in Tokyo for the season-opening series in 2008.
(courtesy Ken Korach)

delineated in the book and movie, was seminal. And those great teams wound up in situations that would have been hard for any team to overcome. Who knows what might have happened if Derek Jeter doesn't make one of the most famous plays of all time in Game 3 with "the Flip" in 2001?

And, in case you're wondering about whether the movie padded my pocketbook, I made $1,000 for acting the scene with Miller. (There was no pay for the radio calls of the streak's highlights. As my old boss with the A's, Ken Pries, once told me, "Once you say it, we own it!")

Even though my part was cut out, I'm still an official member of the cast, which means the residual checks keep trickling in. I've made about $1,000 in residuals, although the amount keeps shrinking. The last one was for $15.23.

Susan Slusser

In 20-plus years of covering the A's, the topic I've written about most often is "Moneyball"—the book, the movie, the misperceptions of the term. Team trends get the Moneyball analysis, then there are anniversaries of the book, the movie, and the 20-game winning streak.

All of those run together at times. One big blob of Moneyball.

That's why the book, in particular, is so genius... despite some flaws. Michael Lewis, with his 2003 bestseller, captured all sorts of things: the dawn of advanced analytics in baseball (and eventually pro sports, politics, and all sorts of other ventures); Billy Beane's intense personality; an outrageously fun year for the A's; a unique 2002 draft class; and the A's franchise-long penchant for doing things differently.

Sure, there are the obvious issues: Lewis focuses on Scott Hatteberg and Chad Bradford as difference makers for the A's but downplays the Big Three and Miguel Tejada—in a season in which Tejada was the AL MVP and Barry Zito the Cy Young winner. (One Tejada reference calls him "Miguel 'swings at everything' Tejada.")

"To just focus on the peripheral pieces is like talking about the kind of wax you're putting on your Mercedes," Angels manager Mike Scioscia told me when I asked him about *Moneyball*.

The book's description of longtime, well-respected scouts is far too dismissive, and the disdain for scouting in general is misplaced—scouting-reliant teams that have since enjoyed great success, such as the Giants and Royals, will tell you so. And in both the book and, especially, the movie, former A's manager Art Howe is portrayed unfairly, as Ken mentions in his section. Howe wasn't a stuck-in-the-past simpleton; he was one of the most perceptive and warmest people in the game.

Where Lewis' book really shines is in his depiction of Beane. His insight that Beane became devoted to metrics rather than scouts because Beane himself never panned out to be the player scouts had predicted was, for someone who has covered Beane his entire time as GM, absolutely fascinating. Is that truly the driving force behind Beane's embrace of analytics? I don't know; I think Beane's extreme competitiveness makes him want to use any extra edge to win and Oakland's limited financial resources force the team to be especially creative. But I love at least considering the idea that, ultimately, Billy Beane is using numbers to avoid drafting or trading for himself.

The primary misinterpretation of the idea of Moneyball is that it's about on-base percentage. It's not. The A's just happened to have determined that OBP was an undervalued asset in the early 2000s. (And yes, of course earlier baseball executives had used on-base percentage as a key evaluation tool.) What Moneyball really represents, at heart, is an exploitation of market inequities, any market inequities. What can Oakland afford that richer clubs are overlooking?

Because the A's became less vocal about their plans after the Moneyball revolution, it's been fun over the years trying to figure out what the team thinks that untapped market is. One year, it was defense. Some years, it's drafting college players, others high school players, and always the moves are based on an advanced proprietary system, algorithms that weigh whatever the team wants to emphasize in a given draft or season. Recently, the A's have focused on drafting and trading for the best overall athletes.

Moneyball the book, as it turned out, did not help the A's, as even Lewis acknowledged; he told me in 2011, "The book probably cost the A's an opportunity or two." Wealthier teams took Oakland's methods and spent far more than the A's ever could, wiping out many available market inequities. Boston was already on the analytics track, though, and Lewis said the book probably just accelerated something that would have happened eventually.

The book's importance can't be understated. It's taught in business schools. It's brought world-wide attention to the A's—I regularly run into fans who became aware of the team through the book, including AthleticsNation.com founder Tyler Bleszinski—and it brought Beane fame even before Brad Pitt played him in the movie. The book transformed international sports at the executive level, with Ivy Leaguers with advanced degrees getting top jobs over former athletes and coaches.

Like every Michael Lewis book, *Moneyball* is just a fun read, an in-depth look at the way an entire industry works based on one particularly interesting example—and the fact that the A's reeled off 20 wins in a row that season provided a strong rooting interest.

I always remember something else Scioscia told me about *Moneyball*: Had Lewis focused on the Angels in 2002, that team also had plenty of interesting secondary contributors found in non-traditional ways— Brandon Donnelly came from an independent league, for instance. "If there was ever a band of misfits, it was our 2002 team," Scioscia said. "And at the end of the book, we'd have won the World Series."

* * *

The movie was a different animal. When there were initial reports that director Steven Soderbergh planned to film the book, the general reaction around the Coliseum was, "What the hell?" How do you make a movie about what is, at heart, a business book? Soderbergh then revealed

Billy Beane and Brad Pitt at Columbia Pictures' Premiere of *Moneyball* to Benefit the Fight Against Cancer with Children's Hospital & Research Center in Oakland and Stand Up to Cancer at the Paramount Theatre of the Arts on September 19, 2011.

(Photo by Eric Charbonneau/Invision/AP Images)

he wanted key people—Howe, some coaches and players and scouts—to play themselves, and the enterprise sounded even wackier. The studio balked, Pitt's production company took over, and those of us around the team remained baffled.

What emerged—an eminently watchable movie, thoroughly enjoyable (except the portrayal of Howe), and nominated for multiple Academy Awards—was extraordinary. I remain amazed that screenwriter Aaron Sorkin and director Bennett Miller turned *Moneyball* into such a good film.

Pitt's performance as Beane is spot-on. They don't look much alike, but Pitt captures Beane's expressions and gestures, his command of a room, his occasional temper flares, and his drive. Also: his tendency to spill food on whatever he's wearing. There were times during the screening I attended when I gasped because Pitt got even just a quick glance exactly right. It's a shame that Beane wasn't a major celebrity when the movie came out, because Pitt's performance would have been hailed as a tour-de-force.

Parts of the movie were filmed at the Coliseum, which was delightful for everyone who spends time there and is accustomed to hearing the building described as decrepit and run down. (I'm the same age as the Coliseum, so I always feel a little sad when people talk about the crumbling infrastructure and bad plumbing. You and me both, sister.) The production designers, the location managers, all the artistic parts of the crew raved about the Coliseum—the quirks, the colors, the dark hallways opening out onto fresh green grass and bright sky. It was nice to hear some appreciation for the old girl.

Some of the regulars got to help out, too. The production used the A's bat boys, who got a huge kick of being on the field for filming. Equipment manager Steve Vucinich, the legend, gets a quick cameo. The look of the Coliseum in 2002 was replicated exactly, down to the signage and the scores on the out-of-town scoreboard.

Well, almost exactly. One day, the beat writers arrived to find that the crew was still filming a scene in the press box. We waited briefly as they wrapped up, and when we got in, we discovered a bunch of extras playing members of the press: a dozen or so 40- to 50-year-old white guys wearing blazers. One even had a fedora on.

The diverse group of A's beat writers and other local media members wearing jeans and khakis and polo shirts chuckled. All that time spent making sure the outfield advertising was right, and no one thought to check out what a press contingent looked like? Plus, *Moneyball* takes place just eight years before the movie was filmed, who would possibly think the press box was still a bunch of middle-aged white guys?

No press-box scene exists in the finished film. It must have been pretty obvious they whiffed on that one. (And for the four people who still don't know: The A's do not and never have charged players for sodas in the clubhouse, as was depicted in a David Justice scene. There was quite a bit of dramatic license taken.)

* * *

The studio held a press junket at the Coliseum the day of the movie's premiere, which for the local sports media was an entrée into a whole different world, a culture shock similar to what I imagine it would be like for a lifelong movie critic suddenly flung into a baseball clubhouse. Proper entertainment journalists were there—even some of the Hollywood Foreign Press Association members you hear about during the Golden Globes.

Thankfully, the studio arranged cast and crew Q and A's that were limited to sports media, or I'm sure the entertainment journalists would have rolled their eyes at our clueless questions about the production. It was a blast: Pitt and Beane did a session together that was informative and funny—"In this story, we have a terrible professional baseball player," Pitt said, looking at Beane, then adding, "I'm so kidding."

Hatteberg-portrayer Chris Pratt—before he was *the* Chris Pratt, and still just "that goofy guy from *Parks and Recreation*"—took part in a delightful Q and A along with Hatteberg. "Is this where my home run landed?" Pratt asked, while seated high above right-center field.

"Maybe about 180 feet short," Hatteberg said.

The premiere, at the Paramount Theatre in Oakland, was fantastic. For the first—and I imagine only—time in my career, I covered the red-carpet portion of an event. As it turns out, it's weird. You set up next to a barricade, jostling for position, and then you holler at actors and other luminaries to come over to talk to you. It's utterly haphazard. Philip Seymour Hoffman blasted right past us, but many of the lesser-known actors, particularly those portraying players, talked to every single outlet.

Best of all was Pitt. He stopped to chat with me and Dan, seemed to remember us from the Q and A, and he and I talked about his portrayal of Billy Beane and the friendship he and Beane had developed during filming. The entire time, he had his hand on my arm. *Brad Pitt!* I spent most of the rest of the night texting photos of my arm to my friends.

This is why they don't allow sportswriters to cover movie events. Well, that and we don't know anything about cinema.

(Here again, I imagine an entertainment journalist might be excited to talk to Shaq or Tom Brady or the like, while sportswriters are utterly nonchalant about pretty much any athlete you could name. But... *Brad Pitt!*)

Dan was less enthusiastic about Brad Pitt having his hand on my arm. (Editor's note from Dan: "Step off, bro.")

Pitt raved about the Oakland fans, the reception the production received, and said he'd become attached to the team.

"I feel a bit romantic about the A's," Pitt said.

(Editor's note from Dan: "What did I just say?")

CHAPTER 13

CLAY WOOD: GROUNDSKEEPER'S FIELD OF DREAMS

Clay Wood became the A's head groundskeeper in 1995 and is entering his 30th *season overall with the organization. Wood has a particular challenge at the Coliseum because the A's share the field with the Raiders. It's the only remaining dual-purpose surface in the major leagues. He spoke to Ken and Susan in the grounds crew's shed next to the dugout in July 2018.*

Is there a specific path to becoming a groundskeeper? How did you wind up with the A's?

I think it varies a lot. For me, it was all about timing. I was in Arizona at Scottsdale Community College playing baseball. During spring training, the other catchers and I would catch bullpens for Wes Stock, the minor-league pitching director. I started to meet a bunch of A's people through that; the facilities were right on the campus.

The summer after my freshman year, I got a job as a part-time groundskeeper. Then I transferred to Arizona State, and I didn't play baseball, so I just started working full-time at spring training. Next thing I know, after I graduated, I became head groundskeeper in Arizona, and a year and a half after that, my old boss Mark Razum left Oakland to open Coors Field and I ended up getting the head job here as a 24 -year-old kid.

There was a lot of hard work, but there was some luck in being in the right place at the right time. There are guys who go to school for turf now. It's a very specialized major for golf-course and sports-turf specialties. There are a lot of different ways to go about it, but getting a Major League job, there has to be some luck involved—there are only 30 of them.

With no previous background or specialized degree, how did you learn the business?

Everything was hands-on; I had to learn it all from scratch. I had been a catcher, so I had learned to maintain home plate and the batter's box, and I had mowed yards as a kid, but that was the extent of it.

I learned everything I know from Mark Razum. I self-amended that throughout the years.

The agronomy aspect, I did some research and read some books. I never actually took agronomy classes. Mark taught me all the basics and everything I needed to get started in the industry. He was a great mentor all the way through. While I was working in Arizona, I was exposed to a lot of the different multi-use things before I got up here—I used to take trips up to Oakland when the Coliseum had concerts. It was still a major surprise when the Raiders came back in 1995.

You kind of had to be a groundskeeper with your name. How often do you hear that?

It is kind of ironic. People do mention it from time to time. "How perfect is your name for your job?" But I don't really think about it too much.

What is the most difficult part of the job? Or the toughest part of the year?

Getting ready for baseball at the beginning of the year after the monster-trucks events, the stadium is just a mess. That's very challenging. This year [2018], especially, we had the driest February on record and torrential rains all of March. It was very difficult to try to get a new field in with those conditions.

Besides that, the three months of sharing the stadium—September, October, November, depending on where the A's are, if they make the playoffs, which we've done plenty of years since I've been here—that's an absolute nightmare for everybody involved. Not just for the grounds crew but also for everybody who works in the stadium. Everything has to change. It's super stressful, physically, mentally, and it's hard on the players, too. They go from pristine conditions to difficult conditions, especially in center field. You can play 50-plus baseball games on a field and it's perfect, then we have one conversion and the field takes a beating. That's hard to deal with.

How much did the Raiders' return change things?

When I got the job up here, the Raiders were still in LA. The following February, they announced that they were coming back. It was kind of a scramble to try to figure things out. The first year, we didn't have the Mt. Davis structure out there, so the football field ran from home plate toward center field. The only thing we had to take out was the main pitcher's mound. The bullpens didn't have to move. It wasn't until 1996, when they built the east-side structure, that the Raiders played all their games north to south and we had to take out the bullpens and the bullpen mounds.

Everything comes into play now. The infield was less in play in 1995, now it's the heart of the football field. It made everything more challenging once they came back and expanded and built the structure.

What is the field conversion like, going between baseball and football?

It's around the clock. Sometimes it's around the clock for *everybody* who is working. I try to give my guys a break as far as the field goes. What we'll usually do is we'll work until we get to a point where we can't do anything else. There comes a time when we're absolutely stuck. You have cranes on the field. You have plywood. There's no access onto the field to get the pitcher's mound in. At that point, we'll shut it down and go home for six or eight hours and come back early in the morning and start back up then when we have access to get through the center-field tunnel.

Have you found some workarounds to make the conversion a little easier?

Having our mounds built on steel plates makes a huge difference. It would be impossible to build the pitcher's mound and two bullpen mounds the next day and have them be major-league quality; it just wouldn't happen.

We have a lot of space in right-center field. We take them out on a trailer and park them out there. We have a trailer that was specially made for it. The plates that the mounds were built on were specially made. That's a huge lifesaver.

There's been a lot of creativity on the crane company's part to make the changeover go faster. Some of the machines that they've used and the modifications they've made to the bleachers to make them easier to get in and out, that's helped a lot.

Other than that, you're in survival mode once football starts. You're trying to make the field as playable and the best that it can be for baseball and football and trying to keep everybody happy—but in the process keeping nobody happy.

How often do you re-sod center field after football games?

We've done that at least once a year for the last 20 years, usually two or three times, and if the A's get to the playoffs, four. When we were making those playoff runs from 2000 to '03 and '12 to '14, we were re-sodding the entire area where the bleachers sit—that's almost 30,000 square feet. We're doing that when the A's are on the road. One time, we didn't even know if the A's were going to come home. They went to Minnesota during the playoffs in 2006 and they had to win to stay alive. We re-sodded center field just in case. They ended up coming home.

With a multi-use facility, what sort of grass to you have to use?

The base is Bermuda and it's over-seeded with perennial rye grass. The main advantage for us is it's a very hardy grass for football, it really stands up and gives the green appearance year-round. It's just a really solid turf for both sports. I think the field looks great but it doesn't have a lot of the dark characteristics some of the bluegrass fields have. I used to have bluegrass, but we were having trouble with bluegrass during football. As the season got later and we started getting into the rainy season, it just didn't hold up. During the 1997 football season, I re-sodded the middle of the field with Bermuda and I've never gone back.

Where do you get the dirt?

This dirt came from Corona, California. You're looking for a certain consistency. There are probably four or five different infield supplier sources for the major-league fields. You're looking for a certain amount of sand, silt, and clay, not necessarily the source.

We're on it every day. We're fixing it after the game and we're fixing it in the morning before the next game. When they're taking batting practice, they're using these mats over the dirt, which makes a huge difference.

I work on my son's Little League fields all the time and they have huge holes. It's hard to work on those fields, because it's frustrating. Part of our job is to make sure we don't have those huge holes. There are some days we still get huge holes if it's really hot and windy and guys are digging in.

The playing surface is 21 feet below sea level. How does that impact your job?

It affects us a lot. The field stays wet when it wouldn't otherwise. We don't necessarily have water coming up from underneath, but things stay wetter in general and when it does rain, it takes a little longer for the water to go through. The whole stadium drains to the same place the field does.

We also have the Mt. Davis structure and the new scoreboards, which create pretty big problems with shadows, especially as we get later in the year. During football, parts of the field never get any sun whatsoever.

There are all kinds of challenges. The nice thing is we're at a really good climate to grow grass and we have that advantage. There's good air circulation.

There are some effects with the tide. Once you get to really know the field, when you're walking on it, you can tell if it's low tide or high tide. A full moon will get crazy moisture up and through. It's pretty amazing.

Are there some years you tailor the field toward the personnel? Make it play faster or slower?

The A's have never been a team that's bunted a lot but we've had requests over the years to do certain things for certain pitchers, ground-ball pitchers might want it softer in front of home plate. Unless you grow the grass a certain way, it's hard to tailor it day to day. We can maybe not mow it a certain day and let it grow out a little bit. It's not going to make that much of a difference.

Grounds crew personnel sweep water off the tarp at Oakland Coliseum before a game against the Houston Astros, which would end up being postponed due to rain.
(Kelley L Cox-USA TODAY Sports)

You can tailor the field to your home team and that is one of the beauties of baseball. One of the great jokes is that people used to accuse Raiders owner Al Davis of having the grounds crew water the field down back in the old days. Why would we want to do that? We had the fastest team on the face of the earth. It was just the conditions of the stadium. The drainage system wasn't as good back then as it is now, so we replaced it.

Football you can tailor the field, but it's not the same as baseball. You can water down the first-base area if you're playing a team that has a great base stealer. You can make it mud at first base and nothing says you can't. There are little things groundskeepers do or have been asked to do over the years. It used to happen a lot.

With as little rain as there is at the Coliseum, how often do you have to replace the tarp?

A tarp can last 10 years if you take care of it. The problem we have here is not from overuse, obviously, but it's from underuse and from moving it around during conversions. We have to slide it around on the dirt when we go from baseball to football. We can't really take it off the field. In the winter, it will sit there and mice will get in it and chew holes in it. We usually get three to four years out of a tarp, but there are Midwest teams who replace them every year.

They're not cheap. They're $7,000–$10,000 depending on the material and how big they are.

Do you have to have tarp drills, since it is used so little?

We actually have to tarp a lot for football, usually on game week, but the tarp isn't great for the field. The turf can't breathe underneath it. The NFL is pretty strict about the 72 hours before a game, they want to try to control conditions as much as possible.

I'm an A's employee, but we do maintain the field for the Raiders; it would be really hard to have someone else come in and say, "We're going to take care of the Raider game." It's something we've adapted to. We're groundskeeper professionals and we do the best we can for every event that comes in here, whether it's high school baseball, the A's, or Raiders.

You seem to have very little turnover on your crew, how much does that help when it comes to consistent field maintenance?

I've been very fortunate to have great people working with me and that they've been able to stay around a long time. I've had some turnover lately, but we've got basically seven full-time guys and an assistant, Zack Ricketts.

With a small staff, the management side of it is fairly easy. It's more on-field management, trying to keep everything right on the field. The off-field, business side of it is not too stressful.

How has technology changed your job?

It's still pretty old school when it comes to maintaining a field. There have been new products, soil conditioners, irrigation systems, moisture monitors, and a lot of other stuff that's come into play, but when it comes to maintaining a field on a daily basis, not a lot of it has really changed over the last hundred years.

Are there many misperceptions about the job?

A lot of times I tell people what I do and they go, "Oh, you chalk the lines and water the field before the game." That's kind of what people see when they come to the stadium. They see that last 15 or 20 minutes before the game, but the amount of hours that go into it—people don't realize we're here at 9:00 AM for a 7:00 PM game and we don't go home until 11:00 or 11:30 PM at night. People just don't know how much goes into keeping a field but when they get onto the field they say, 'Oh, *wow*."

Do you have any pet peeves? Does anything drive you nuts that people do on the field?

Spitting sunflower seeds, things like that are time consuming for us to clean up. It doesn't seem like much when you sit in the outfield and spit a bag of seeds, but it takes a while—there's no easy way to pick them up.

Our baseball culture here, you come into a dugout after a game and it's a disaster. I was in South Korea in 2015 and went to a playoff game. Afterward, we walked by the dugouts, and I had to ask somebody if the dugouts had already been cleaned, because they were spotless. There was no garbage. They spit their sunflower seeds in a cup. It was mind-boggling to walk by and see a dugout that clean.

I've mellowed out a lot. Everybody has a purpose here so if you have to be out on the field, that's fine, but it's little disrespectful, with as much time and effort we put in, when people mess things up. It can be frustrating.

Have you had any real disasters?

I've had a few nightmares. I've had a couple come to life. It's hard to watch other groundskeepers struggle, too. You see highlights of a football games where the field is all torn up or the crew can't get the tarp on the field. Your stomach turns into knots. You know what they're going through.

Do you get any complaints from players?

Frankie Montas was pitching for us, and if you talk to our pitchers, they'll say Frankie digs a big hole at the rubber where he pushes off, and he's a big boy and he spins out a little. Zack Greinke was the opposing starter and he happened to be pitching on the edge of Frankie's hole. These guys, they're locked in on that mound. They pitch from the same spot every time. They want their landing hole the same.

Grienke is not going to move where he is on the rubber, so he asked us to come out and put some clay in the hole, to fill in where his toe was. When my assistant went out to fix it, Greinke said, "Sorry guys, I just wasn't pitching very well, so I needed an excuse."

That's happened over the years. Some guys twist and make a bigger hole and you need to make repairs in game. That's why we're here.

What's the best compliment you've received?

It's kind of funny, because when Torey Lovullo was the bench coach for the Red Sox, he mentioned to me one time, "Dustin Pedroia loves your field."

So I was walking across the field when they were in town and it was during their early batting practice; Torey said, "Hey, Pedey, there's Clay. He's the head groundskeeper."

Pedroia walked right up to me and said, "This is the best surface I've ever played on." Someone told me later it's not like him just to throw around compliments.

What's the best part of your job?

Every day, getting to come to a major-league stadium. Every baseball player as a kid dreams of playing in the majors, right? Well, there's only a few of these jobs. Getting to come to the stadium and put in all this time and effort—people don't realize what goes into maintaining the surface, the amount of hours we spend here and everything we do.

But once the game starts, it's the most gratifying thing. All the work is done, the first pitch is thrown. As the groundskeeper, you're the only one who can really have an effect of the game. Everybody who works here in the stadium makes the whole thing happen, but when it comes to the game—it's played on the field. That's pretty cool.

CHAPTER 14
THE BEST GAMES
WE EVER SAW

Ken Korach

I get asked all the time about the A's and their history of trading players or losing them in free agency and how difficult it must be for me. I understand the question and the sentiment behind it, and I admit, it's been tough to see so many great players go. As Dave Kaval has said, the A's can't put their fans through another cycle of building and tearing down. One of a broadcaster's jobs is to help foster a relationship between fans and players. You hope fans develop an attachment and a familiarity with the roster.

But even the most cynical of A's supporters would concede there have been tons of thrills along the way. Don't feel sorry for me. Not only have the A's treated me great—I've been incredibly fortunate to do my job for 23 years without any interference from the front office—but I've broadcast some of the most memorable games of the last two decades.

The A's had eight postseason appearances over a span of 15 years beginning in 2000. I've called a perfect game, a no-hitter, and a 20-game winning streak. If it all ended tomorrow, it's been an incredible run.

How do you quantify the greatest games? I've tried to do that in this chapter, and every time I think I have my list pared down, someone reminds me of a game that was tucked away in my memory. There have been that many to consider, one reason taking a fan poll was so interesting and instructive. Susan and I asked the A's to assist in a Twitter questionnaire, asking fans to list their top games from the last two decades (to coincide with the time Susan and I have covered the A's) and we were thrilled by the variety of responses. The results are listed in this chapter, but one game stands heads and shoulders above the rest: the last game of the 2012 regular season, "Hamilton Drops the Ball," when the A's beat the Rangers and stood in first place for the only day of the season that mattered.

No-hitters are fresh in my mind, because Sean Manaea threw one in 2018 for the A's and because Dallas Braden's perfecto left such an indelible emotional mark.

This chapter begins with those two masterpieces.

* * *

Capturing Perfection

Dallas Braden wanted to throw just four more pitches. He was back home in Stockton in 2006, on a rehab assignment from shoulder surgery, and he was on a 75-pitch limit. He'd reached 71 without allowing a baserunner, and in the dugout, Braden pleaded with pitching coach Scott Emerson to let him go back out and start the next inning. Emerson would have none of it. He approved of Braden's doggedness, but he wanted him to see the larger picture. "You won't remember this game," Emerson told Braden, "when you throw your perfect game in the big leagues."

Emerson's prescience was more than idle talk. He spent countless hours with Braden while Dallas was climbing the minor-league ladder and was witness to the left-hander's potential. He also knew just getting to the majors from where Braden was that day in Stockton would be considered accomplishment enough.

Braden had pitched well the previous year at Double-A Midland in the Texas League, but his left arm was bothering him, and postseason surgery confirmed an unusual problem. He was diagnosed with a defect of the humerus bone and, as Susan reported in the *Chronicle* in 2007:

> The bone at the top of the arm looked as if someone had hollowed it out using an ice-cream scoop, according to Braden. Or "like someone chipped at the humerus bone with a pitching wood," he said. He literally has a chip on his shoulder.

There is no way to know how that happened, but to fix the problem, "They basically took a cheese grater and shaved the bone until it bled, to stimulate bone growth," Braden said.

The operation was successful enough that the next year Dallas was back in Midland, where his teammate was an old college rival named Cliff Pennington. By 2009, they were both in Oakland, and Pennington and Braden always will be linked because of how flawlessly Pennington fielded the grounder that ended the perfect game the following year.

That's one reason I've always felt a perfect game is at the top of the list of baseball's single-game accomplishments. Sure, the pitcher gets all the glory, and there's no disputing the rarity of the feat. Baseball had been played for 110 years in the modern era when Braden threw his gem, and it was just the 19th, including Don Larsen's perfecto in the 1956 World Series. But a perfect game is a true *team* accomplishment. The fielders need to do their jobs. Can you imagine the ignominy Pennington would have faced if he had booted Gabe Kapler's grounder? That's a case of serious pressure.

"You're just as nervous on defense as you are for the pitcher," Pennington told me outside the Angels' dugout in Anaheim, where he played in 2016. "That last ball Kapler hit had a little bit of cue-ball spin, and when I got it, I just threw it as hard as I could down low to [Daric] Barton. Obviously, it was a good throw and the celebration started.

"I was definitely nervous. I figure sometimes we have to trick ourselves as players. 'Hit the ball to me, hit the ball to me.' And then he hit to me, and I was like, 'Oh, man, I better make this.' To be a part of that play, that day, is something I've never forgotten."

No other feat brings baseball's superstitions to the fore like a no-hitter. Pennington went to the end of the A's bench after every half-inning. He didn't dare to change seats or talk to Braden. That's forbidden. Vin Scully, as he described the ninth inning of Sandy Koufax's perfect game in 1965, remarked that, to Koufax, the pitcher's mound at Dodger

Stadium "must be the loneliest place on earth." That's what it's like in the dugout for a pitcher with a no-hitter in progress.

"I always sat toward the end, where the helmets are, as the game was going, trying to stay out of Braden's way," Pennington said. "No one was talking to him, he was kind of on his own. No one was mentioning it, no one was getting near him, we were just letting the game play out and every inning, he'd go out there and get three guys out and come back in and we were like, 'Oh man, all right,' just getting more excited for him as it got closer and closer."

Similar traditions were observed down the left-field line in the A's bullpen. Lefty Craig Breslow was down there:

"I've had a chance to be in the bullpen for a couple of pretty historic outings," Breslow told me. "Clay Buchholtz's no-hitter in Boston is one that comes to mind. In a number of those scenarios, you feel something magical is unraveling. But that one was a little different, because I don't think anyone thought of Dallas as someone who was bringing no-hit stuff out to the mound. He wasn't a guy who would go out and dominate in terms of swings and misses. He was a guy who relied on command and guile. It wasn't until pretty late in the game we all realized he had a perfect game going.

"Once we did, we kind of recognized how incredible it was to be a part of. Then you incorporate his grandmother being in the stands and it being Mother's Day, it really was a storybook finish to that game and one I'll remember—even though I had very little to do with it—for the rest of my life."

Braden pitched in only three big-league games after 2010, when his shoulder finally gave out for the last time. But he stayed in the game as a broadcaster, first for ESPN and now with the A's telecasts on NBC Sports California.

The A's season-long celebration of the team's 50th anniversary in Oakland in 2018 included naming the 50 greatest players in Oakland A's history, as voted upon by the fans. Despite his brief career, Braden is on the team. He's honest about it, though, tweeting:

Dallas Braden ✓
@DALLASBRADEN209

Follow ⌄

Let's be real. This ain't got nothin' to do with the back of my baseball card. Which is why I appreciate this honor even more. Oakland will ALWAYS be home & I have the amazing fans to thank for that! Here's to 50 more! #RootedInOakland 🌳 #BAYseball #HomeGrown

9:14 AM - 31 Mar 2018

46 Retweets 639 Likes

There's no denying the impact of his perfect game. Because it was such a moving and transcendent story, Braden often hears from people who were there or whose own experiences made the accomplishment relatable.

The best messages, he told me, are from kids and families who are reminded of Braden's relationship with his grandmother and the power of love. "I've heard from Little Leaguers who tell me they were inspired and thinking about me when they did something good on the diamond," Braden said. "A couple of times there were no-hitters and it was like, 'We did what Dallas did and he showed us what was possible!'"

Dallas and I have spoken many times since May 9, 2010, and he confirmed that, before then, Mother's Day never had been a great day for him, as it wasn't for me, with our shared history of losing our mothers at an early age.

But there is also a funny and serendipitous story that links us on that magical day:

It's crazy to think that when Dallas was one out away from perfection he lost track of the count in the Kapler at-bat. It was stuck in his mind that an earlier close pitch was a strike and thinking the count was 2-2, he threw a fastball to Kapler. Braden thought Kapler would be looking for an off-speed pitch since Dallas was known for pitching "backward"—which means, in the baseball vernacular, throwing something other than a fastball in a fastball count.

In reality, the count was 3–1.

I had a split-second sinking feeling when I heard Dallas talking about me after the game. Had I messed up the count? Dallas, in the immediate aftermath, said he heard my call, which became a sidebar story to the events of the day.

Tyer Kepner, the fine baseball writer for the *New York Times*, wanted to get into Dallas' thinking before making the critical 3–1 pitch to Kapler.

"Braden, though, was blissfully ignorant," Kepner wrote. "Unbelievably, this is what he said about the final pitch:

> "It was 2-1, and I threw a fastball on the outside part of the plate that I thought looked good. The umpire disagreed. He thought it was a ball. I thought it looked so good that I think I told myself it was a strike, and I thought the count was 2-2, to be totally honest. So I threw a fastball, and it worked out. I didn't know until I heard the replay of Ken Korach: 'And the count, 3-1, Braden comes set.' And then I'm going: 'It was 3-1? Oh my God, I would have thrown the guy a changeup.'"

Now, when Dallas sees me, he'll often say: "Korach, it was the biggest call of your life and you screwed up the count!"

* * *

Manaea's Masterpiece

There was no such confusion when Sean Manaea was one out away from a no-hitter against the Red Sox on April 21, 2018, at the Coliseum. But there was plenty of intrigue and much to debate, as there so often is with famous sporting events.

For instance, my dad's first memory of hearing sports on the radio came on September 22, 1927, when he sat with his family in Los Angeles in front of a large crystal set, glued to Graham McNamee's NBC Radio call of the "Long Count" heavyweight title fight between Jack Dempsey and Gene Tunney from Soldier Field in Chicago. Dempsey, famously, had been slow to move to the neutral corner after knocking down Tunney, delaying the count. Tunney fought back later and won the match in a unanimous decision.

Now, 90 years later and 20 miles northwest of his childhood home, my dad was listening to Vince and me on his satellite radio as Sean Manaea was navigating his way through a red-hot Red Sox lineup.

In the A's dugout, Bob Melvin, as usual, had his scorecard in his hand. He's always meticulous in making notes and keeping track of substitutions. By the seventh inning, he started to make sure his writing was as neat as possible, just in case Manaea completed the no-no. If so, Melvin's card would become a treasured souvenir.

Down in the bullpen, with Manaea's pitch count mounting in the ninth inning, Melvin got closer Blake Treinen up after a two-out walk to Andrew Benintendi. That meant if the next hitter, Hanley Ramirez, reached base, J.D. Martinez, one of the best power hitters in the game, would come up as the potential tying run.

Treinen never threw a pitch in the pen, however. He didn't want to disrupt the karma or the game's flow, especially if he bounced a warm-up pitch and the ball rolled away and caused a stoppage in play.

"If I was coming in, my warm-up was going to be my eight warm-up tosses on the mound and that was going to be it," Treinen told me, relieved it didn't come to that.

Manaea's no-hitter pursuit had already had one moment worthy of debate. It wasn't exactly the Long Count, but there was plenty of spice.

With two outs in the top of the fifth, Red Sox catcher Sandy Leon hit a pop fly into no-man's land in left center. Shortstop Marcus Semien raced out, steadied himself with his back to the infield, had the ball for a split second and dropped it. Official scorer Art Santo Domingo ruled the

Sean Manaea celebrates with Jonathan Lucroy and Matt Chapman after throwing his no-hitter against the Red Sox on Saturday, April 21, 2018. (AP Photo/John Hefti)

play an error, prompting a collective exhale from the 25,000 fans (save a few thousand Red Sox faithful) at the Coliseum. On the air, I said that Santo Domingo likely had adhered to the old theory that the first hit needs to be a clean one.

The call was much debated, although Santo Domingo said the next day that he had fielded very few questions about it. Official scoring is a tough job and it's often subjective. I suppose, if there hadn't been a no-hitter in progress, Leon might have been credited with a hit, but it would have been a shame to lose a no-hitter on such a close call. No less an authority than A's television voice Glen Kuiper, a former minor league infielder, said when I asked him: "Error, for sure." There were others who felt differently, but there are often three or four calls an official scorer makes during a game that aren't clear-cut. Bottom line: There's no way it was a bad decision.

It looked as if the no-no was over in the bottom of the sixth when Red Sox left-fielder Andrew Benintendi dribbled a ball down the first-base line. Manaea had no chance at it, so it was up to first baseman Matt Olson to make the play. He did his best, fielding the ball and lunging at Benintendi 10 feet short of the bag. Benintendi went into foul territory to evade the tag, then dived on the bag with his left hand. Safe, first-base umpire Adrian Johnson ruled.

Melvin, on top of everything, came racing out of the dugout to challenge the call, contending Benintendi was out of the baseline. Up in the press box, longtime National League umpire Eddie Montague, now an umpire supervisor for Major League Baseball, said he wished he could have called down to the field because he was certain that Benintendi was out of the baseline.

The home-plate umpire was veteran Hunter Wendelstedt, but Johnson had made the call. Montague explained the next day that either could have made the call—it was up to the one who had it. Although Wendelstedt would have to acquiesce to change the call, Melvin saw when he approached Johnson that he might be willing to confer with the other umpires—and all a manager wants, in that situation, is a chance.

Johnson had been more focused on whether Olson had made the tag and when Benintendi had gotten to the bag than he was the baseline issue, and in this case, the chalk lines weren't in play. The runner establishes his own baseline, and a big thing that helped the A's case is that Olson, at 6-foot-5, has a huge wingspan. Given that, Melvin contended, Benintendi had moved out of the lane he'd established by more than the three feet allowed. After a long conference, thanks to the teamwork of Johnson and Wendelstedt, the call was overturned.

Red Sox manager Alex Cora, managing his 20th game in the big leagues, spent the inning break arguing, repeatedly saying, "No way, no way."

In something of an irony, the umpires weren't allowed to consider going to video replay—even though one reason replay is in place is because of a missed call during an ongoing perfect game. With Detroit's Armando Galarraga one out from a perfecto in 2010, first-base umpire Jim Joyce ruled that Jason Donald of the Indians beat Galarraga to the bag when the pitcher was covering first. Replay would have saved Joyce, one of the best and most respected umpires of his time, from forever being associated with the call that cost Galarraga what would have been the 21st perfect game in major-league history.

Because of a quirk in the rules—you can't replay something that happens in front of the base umpires—there was no challenge available on the Benintendi play.

* * *

What a great sport baseball is to broadcast. The time between pitches, especially if you have a lengthy inning, affords room for stories that mine the game's rich history. And, for me, that often means it's almost as if Vin Scully is inside my head.

Watching Wendlestedt talking with Johnson took me back a half century to May 31, 1968, when, as a 16-year-old, I was listening to Vinny as Don Drysdale was trying to complete his fifth consecutive shutout.

The Giants had the bases loaded with nobody out in the ninth and Drysdale had a 2-2 count on Dick Dietz, when Drysdale came inside and hit Dietz on the elbow. But, hang on, wait a second: Harry Wendelstedt—Hunter's father—invoked a seldom-used rule, determining that Dietz hadn't tried to get out of the way. Wendelstedt summoned Dietz back to the plate, he flied out and the runners held. Drysdale got the next two outs and the scoreless streak reached 45 innings. The Giants fumed, of course, but Drysdale continued for two more games until the streak ended at 58⅔ innings.

Now, as the A's were batting in the eighth, I reflected on the air about Harry Wendelstedt's famous call, and how, almost 50 years to the day, his son was involved in another controversial decision that came as history was unfolding at the ballpark.

My approach in the top of the ninth for both the Braden and Manaea games was the same: I did everything I could to clear my head and concentrate on calling the action. I borrowed from Vinny's call of Koufax's perfect game in 1965 by mentioning the date at the start of the inning of both games but refrained from giving the time of day as the inning was unfolding—that's Vinny's and his alone. When I set the A's defense, I was also borrowing from Scully. I've always been taken by how brilliant and magnanimous that was. He wanted the players on the field to have an audio recording of their participation if they wanted one.

I've never intentionally tried to copy Scully, except to have some fun with lousy impressions or by paying homage as I did by giving the date and setting the defense. But when Manaea walked Benintendi and then fell behind 2-0 on Ramirez, I said, "You can't blame Manaea if he's pressing, trying to throw perfect pitches."

I had no memory I had said that until I listened back to the Ramirez at-bat a week later, and it sounded oddly familiar to me. I went back and checked the transcript from the ninth inning of Koufax's perfect game. Needing one more out, Koufax fell behind 2-1 to Harvey Kuenn, and Vin said, "You can't blame a man for pushing just a little bit right now."

As I said, there are times he's inside my head and I don't even know it.

* * *

Making History

THE STREAK, GAMES 18 AND 19 (SEPTEMBER 1–2, 2002, AT OAKLAND):

Miguel Tejada's heroics during the 20-game winning streak always will have a special place in Athletics lore and solidified his MVP candidacy. With the A's trailing 5–4 going to the bottom of the ninth, Tejada hit a three-run homer off Twins closer Eddie Guardado on September 1, sending 38,000 fans into delirium.

The A's, perhaps emotionally drained, fell behind early the next day, and trailed Kansas City 5–0 after four innings. Royals starter Runelvys Hernandez lit a fire under Oakland, however, when he came up and in on Jermaine Dye, who was leading off the fifth. Awakened, the A's rallied and won another cliffhanger when Tejada singled to center against a five-man infield, a 7–6 victory.

I wasn't at win No. 20. It was a planned vacation day and the only game I missed in 2002. The broadcast featured Bill King and Ray Fosse (who was on radio because the game was nationally televised) and the great ending, with Scott Hatteberg's dramatic homer, was fitting—it allowed Bill to return from his vacation and deliver an exclamation point to his Hall-of-Fame career.

* * *

Postseasons and Pennant Races

GAME 2 OF THE 2013 ALDS (OCTOBER 5, 2013, AT OAKLAND):

Justin Verlander of the Tigers went seven innings and Sonny Gray went eight for the A's. Combined, they K'd 20 and allowed eight hits and no runs, but it was catcher Stephen Vogt's night. With one out in the top of the fifth, he gunned down Jose Iglesias trying to steal second on strike three to Austin Jackson. Then, after Rick Porcello was summoned from the bullpen with the bases loaded in the ninth, Vogt smashed a single to left-center and the A's won 1–0. The crowd: 48,292. The atmosphere: electric from the first pitch.

THE FOSSE SCREAM (OCTOBER 10, 2012, AT OAKLAND):

The A's had their backs against the wall against Detroit. Trailing 2–1 in the best-of-five ALDS and down 3–1 going to the bottom of the ninth, Oakland mounted a stirring comeback. Seth Smith doubled to left-center, scoring Josh Reddick and Josh Donaldson to tie it up. After Tigers closer Jose Valverde retired George Kottaras and Cliff Pennington, the stage was set for Coco Crisp. And when Avisail Garcia bobbled Coco's single to right, Ray Fosse let out a primal scream that obliterated my call. It was okay: Smith scored the winning run, the fans went nuts, and the series went to Game 5 the next night. (The fifth of six Game 5 ALDS losses for the A's in 14 seasons.)

Ray apologized profusely, but I told him if anyone had the license to do that, it was him. It was unvarnished, raw emotion and the fans loved it. But Ray, don't ever do it again!

FUN BUNCH, THE 2006 ALDS VS. MINNESOTA (OCTOBER 3–6, 2006):

This was a trilogy of excitement that was right near the top of the fans' list. The A's won the first game, Barry Zito vs. Johan Santana, thanks to Frank Thomas' two home runs. Game 2 at the Metrodome featured Mark Kotsay's inside-the-park home run, with Vince Cotroneo making the call. The A's swept the series back home, where Marco Scutaro starred. He doubled twice and drove in four runs as the fans chanted, "Mar-co Scu-tar-o, Mar-co Scu-tar-o!"

BEST FOR LAST (OCTOBER 3, 2012, AT OAKLAND):

After more than 20 years with the A's, it's pretty tough to single out the two or three best games, but this one is the zenith and easily topped the fans' list as well. It was the only day the A's resided in first place all year and the culmination of a miraculous run in which Oakland gained five games on the Rangers in six days. Game 162 featured Vince's "Hamilton drops the ball!" call in the fourth, when, after trailing 5–1, the A's rallied for six runs. In the eighth, Brandon Moss's single—plus an error by Nelson Cruz in right—scored three runs, and I said something I had never said before and haven't since: "That's worthy of a Holy Toledo!"

THE SIX-HOUR GAME (AUGUST 9, 2002, AT NEW YORK):

This was the A's fifth win in a stretch of taking 29 of 33, but at the time, they were in third place, four games behind the Mariners and in a wild-card battle with Boston and the Angels. As the action played out at Yankee Stadium, however, there also was drama back in San Francisco.

The A's were sharing a Fox regional cable channel with the Giants, who were playing the Pirates that night, creating a potential issue if Oakland's game ran late. Even more problematic: Barry Bonds was sitting on 599 home runs and the Giants and the station had a ratings bonanza on their hands. But the A's were in the middle of a postseason chase and playing on the grand stage before 54,000 fans.

What happened changed the face of Bay Area cable television, because our game went six hours and was one of the most suspenseful in A's history. Meanwhile, in San Francisco, a tug of war was taking place. Ken Pries, the A's vice broadcast of broadcasting at the time, remembers Giants chief executive officer Larry Baer lobbying for his game to be shown as much as possible. The A's, of course, reasoned that Fox Sports Net Bay Area had an obligation to stay with their game until its conclusion. Pries held his ground: "I knew from an historical standpoint why they wanted to carry the game, but I thought that I should dig in my heels because I knew at some point the decision would go over my head," he said. That's what happened, with phone calls involving both teams leading all the way to commissioner Bud Selig.

Jeff Krolik, the general manager of Fox Sports Net Bay Area, made the right decision. He stayed with the A's game until its conclusion, but we wound up tossing back and forth like a cross-country TV football. We went back to AT&T Park for updates and short segments of action and carried all of Bonds' at-bats live. I was on TV that night with Ray, and since it was an intense night and we needed to be keen to directions and audibles from producer Tim Sullivan, I never left the booth. My prostate was a lot younger then. Couldn't happen now!

Bonds hit number 600 off Kip Wells in the sixth. It was 12:25 AM in New York, and the A's and Yankees were still battling. In the 16th inning, Mark Ellis' single scored Jermaine Dye, who had doubled off Sterling Hitchcock. Micah Bowie finished out the game and the A's won 3–2 at 1:15 AM. Tim and director Tommy Adza brilliantly maneuvered through a very tricky night.

The fallout: The A's and Giants now have separate channels, the A's on NBC Sports California and the Giants on NBC Sports Bay Area, and fans and announcers won't have to endure another complicated broadcast.

Game 161 Clincher (October 1, 2000, at Oakland):

This game has a short sidebar: Earlier in September, Oakland had a road game postponed at Tampa Bay because of Hurricane Gordon. So the last Sunday of the season was actually game 161, not 162. Entering the day, the A's were locked in a three-way battle with the Indians and Mariners. If they lost, the A's would have to fly to Florida to play a dreaded "if necessary" game Monday. An Oakland win, however, would eliminate Cleveland and put the Mariners in the wild-card spot. The A's, who had drilled the Rangers 23–2 the previous day, arrived at the Coliseum with their bags packed for a cross-country flight they were desperate to avoid. Oakland took a 3–0 lead into the ninth, with Jason Isringhausen trying to close it out.

Bill: "Strike three called, the A's win the West!"

What ensued, as clubhouse manager Steve Vucinich has noted, was the greatest clubhouse celebration in Oakland's glorious history of celebrations. I was there doing interviews and getting drenched at the same time. It was the most raucous, spontaneous outpouring of emotion I have ever experienced, as against long odds, the young A's wrapped up the division title—and didn't have to go back to Florida.

Bill King's Greatest Hits

August 12, 2001, at Oakland:

The A's were trying to complete a weekend sweep of the Yankees and a win would be their 11th in a row. The crowd: 47,725. The game went to the bottom of the ninth tied 2–2, with reliable Yankees southpaw Mike Stanton on the mound. Then, Jason Giambi, looking for a slider because he had the feeling Stanton was trying to strike him out, hoisted a long drive that landed in the right-field seats.

Bill: "Jason Giambi is THE MAN, in capital letters. He has beaten the Yankees with one swing of the bat. Sweep! 11 victories in a row!"

July 15, 1999, at Oakland:

This was one of Bill's greatest set-ups to a call (rivaled, unfortunately, by his observation that Dennis Eckersley hadn't thrown a backdoor slider yet to Kirk Gibson in Game 1 of the 1988 World Series). The A's and Giants were in the bottom of the ninth with the potential winning run, slow-footed John Jaha, at first base. Olmedo Saenz was up. Robb Nen was on the mound.

Bill: "Raines at second the tying run, the winning run at first base and that's Jaha. But it's tough for him to negotiate that distance in very much quick time. The only way Saenz can avoid that problem is to take it deep. Nen has no idea that's going to happen. It may have happened. There's a swing and a deep drive way back into left-center field! And it's gone! Olmedo Saenz has beaten the Giants with a three-run homer! The

A's are pouring out of the dugout! The Athletics have won the ballgame by a score of 11–9. Hooooly Toledo! What a finish!"

October 1, 2003, at Oakland:

This call came during the ALDS that featured the A's and the Red Sox, a series that, of course, went five games. Game 1 was tied 4–4 and starters Pedro Martinez and Tim Hudson were long gone, when, with two outs in the bottom of the 12th inning of an absolute gem of a game, Ramon Hernandez came to the plate with the potential winning run at third. Third baseman Bill Mueller was playing back, and Hernandez stunned everyone with a perfect bunt down the line. Bill, always ready to capture the moment, delivered a line that christened the game: "The element of surprise reigns supreme!"

Honorable mention: On Cinco de Mayo of 2000, the game that sent Bill over the top and led him to skip as many trips as possible to Texas ended 17–16 Rangers. It was a brutally windy night, and the A's led by eight runs in the seventh, but Texas scored 10 runs in the final three innings, and Mike Lamb finally won it for the Rangers with a pinch-hit single, "on a night you wouldn't conjure in your wildest alcoholic dreams," Bill said.

(My note: Obviously, Game 20 during the 2002 winning streak would be at the top of any list, along with Bill's call of Hatteberg's home run. Sticking with the premise—best games I've seen—that bit of radio magic will hold its special place in our hearts, if not officially on this list.)

* * *

Heartbreaker (October 13, 2001, at Oakland):

You'll know this as the "Jeter Flip" game. I've mentioned it plenty of times—there is no doubting its historic place in the game. What I remember most, besides the Flip, is how beautiful the night was. It was one of those perfect October early evenings in the Bay Area and the crowd of 55,861 was locked in from the start. Also unforgettable: the brilliant pitching of Barry Zito and Mike Mussina. Yes, it was a brutal loss for the A's, but, still, it was a beauty of a game.

WILD WILD CARD GAME (SEPTEMBER 30, 2014, AT KANSAS CITY):
The A's limped to the finish line in 2014, finally punching their ticket to the postseason on the last day, when Sonny Gray beat the Rangers in Arlington. The wild-card game had more twists and turns than a Hoyt Wilhelm knuckleball. With second-half acquisition Jon Lester on the mound, Oakland led 7–3 in the eighth inning. A roller-coaster ride ensued, the Royals scoring three in the eighth and one in the ninth to tie it up before the A's reclaimed the lead in the 12th. The game ended—along with the A's season—in the bottom of the inning on Salvador Perez's dribbler down the third-base line. Christian Colon, who stole the Royals' seventh base of the game that inning, scored the winning run. It was a bitter loss, especially because at one point Oakland's season held so much promise (an incredible run differential, seven All-Stars) but kudos also go to the crowd; Kauffman Stadium was as loud and intense as any place I have ever been, and nobody left, even when the Royals trailed by four late.

* * *

The Fans Vote

Several games stood out in the fan polling (many thanks to the A's and their Twitter handle, @athletics).

One game was head and shoulders above the rest, and it's no surprise, since it tops my list: Game 162 in 2012, the A's only day in first place. @JenniferTrumpp: "I bawled happy tears during that moment. 'Let's Go, Oakland!' cheers continued from after the game ended all the way to the BART platform."

Most of the rest of the items on my list also showed up in the fan voting, and it's fun to see what other games stick in fans' memories:

2) The 2006 ALDS vs. Minnesota. @mlleaimee and @derekC5 "When the whole stadium was chanting Marco Scutaro during that playoff game!"

3) April 29, 2013 at Oakland, the 19-inning game between the A's and Angels. Brandon Moss won it with a walk-off in the 19th after 6 hours and 32 minutes and 597 pitches thrown by 16 pitchers. You know it's a long game when Dick Callahan, on the PA system, announces (well before the game ended), "If you need to go home, the last BART train is about to leave." Moss' homer gave the A's a 10–8 win at 1:41 AM.

4) Bill's "element of surprise" call, Ramon Hernandez's bunt vs. Boston. @TeegSoAs: "My co-worker ran from one end of the third deck to the other and back, and the crowd noise had not abated one decibel, we were still screaming just as loud. I just got chills remembering that night, still have my 'I survived the Walk-off Bunt' shirt somewhere." @derekc5: "I advocated the bunt from the bleachers." @RussellsRitings: "The greatest game I have ever seen in person, hands down." @shawcochrane: "I was there and it got so loud in the Coli that I thought the whole thing would crack apart."

5) Coco Crisp's hit, Game 4 of the ALDS. @diaryofmac10: "The most joyous I've ever seen the Coliseum."

6) Stephen Vogt's walk-off, Game 2 of the ALDS.

7) Games 18, 19, and 20 of the streak. On No. 18, @themikeandersen: "I had chest pains for hours from screaming. My wife thought I gave myself a heart attack." @matthewjsegal: "Strangers literally embracing at the Coliseum."

8) Dallas Braden's perfect game. @dprnesq: "Dallas Braden pitches a perfect game on Mother's Day when I was there with my son—and we were both keeping score. We were over the (moon emogi)."

Also receiving mentions, in no particular order:

- Nate Freiman's walk-off vs. Mariano Rivera, 2013. Freiman's 18th-inning broken-bat single completed Oakland's three-game sweep, the A's 11th win in a row at home, putting them a season-best 14 games over .500, their best start since 1990.

- Josh Reddick cameos as Spider-Man, July 25, 2012. Oakland wins 16–0 at Toronto, the A's seventh straight win. In the second inning, Reddick scaled the wall by digging in cleats and clung on with one hand while catching a drive by Travis Snider. "Why yes, I'm part spider," he said afterward.

- Brandon Inge's walk-off grand slam off Toronto's Francisco Cordero on May 8, 2012, with the A's trailing by five in the ninth. Oakland went on to win 7–3. Inge was acquired on the A's previous road trip and was playing in his first home game. As one fan kindly mentioned, it was my first game of the season after knee replacement surgery.

- Reddick's three-homer game at Toronto, in consecutive at-bats, fueled Oakland's 14–6 win on August 9, 2013.

- On July 22, 2012, the A's completed a four-game sweep of the Yankees in the 12th inning on Coco Crisp's base hit to left center. It was the A's 11th walk- off of season. A's had trailed 4–0 earlier in the game.

- Barry Zito vs. Roger Clemens, Game 4 of the 2001 ALDS at Yankee Stadium. Trailing 2–1 in the series, A's won 11–1 to force a fifth game in Oakland. Zito went 5⅔ innings and allowed one run.

- On April 15, 2006, the A's went back-to-back-to-back in the sixth inning: Eric Chavez, Frank Thomas, and Milton Bradley homered on consecutive pitches from Texas' Vicente Padilla. Oakland won 5–4.

- Down 12–2 against the Twins on July 20, 2009, the A's came back to win 14–13. Matt Holliday's grand slam was the highlight of a seven-run seventh. Minnesota made a last-ditch push but the game ended on a disputed play with Michael Cuddyer thrown out at the plate.

- Josh Donaldson, who'd had a dustup with Orioles third baseman Manny Machado earlier in the season, hit a three-run walk-off homer against Baltimore on July 18, 2014, and Oakland won 5–4.

- On September 29, 2012, vs. Seattle, Brandon Moss hit a three-run homer in the 10th, the A's 14th walk-off win of the season. Vince Cotroneo: "Oakland is the walk-off capital of baseball!"

- With the A's trailing 3–1 in the ninth, Josh Reddick provided a walk-off hit with the outfield and infield playing in, giving Oakland a 4–3 win over the Astros on April 19, 2014.

- On May 12, 2000, the A's beat the Mariners 9–7 on Matt Stairs' walk-off homer off Mariners closer Kaz Sasaki.

- Derek Norris' first career homer came off Giants reliever Santiago Casilla on June 24, 2012, and helped the A's beat the Giants 4–2. A.J. Griffin made his big-league debut in the same game.

- Mark Ellis hit a walk-off grand slam in the 12th inning and Oakland beat the Angels 7–3 on June 8, 2008. It was the A's first walk-off slam in 13 years.

- On April 15, 2007, with two outs and the A's down by two, Marco Scutaro hit a three-run homer off Yankees closer Mariano Rivera, a drive off the foul pole in left to give Oakland a 5–4 at the sold-out Coliseum.

- Barry Zito made his debut on July 22, 2000, and he finished up his appearance by striking out Mo Vaughn, Tim Salmon, and Garrett Anderson in a row in the fifth. He allowed two hits, six walks, and one run, and struck out six.

- On September 11, 2012, with the A's in the playoff hunt, reliever Jerry Blevins turned in quite an escape act, taking over with two on and no outs, striking out Kendrys Morales and getting Howie Kendrick to hit into a double play. "That's the biggest moment, most exciting, I felt pure jubilation," Blevins told Susan: "That was one of the biggest screams I've given on a baseball field." That improved Oakland's record to 81–60.

- On June 10, 2014, Yoenis Cespedes made one of the greatest throws of all time after initially misplaying Mike Trout's drive to left. Cespedes launched a throw from deep in the corner to nail Howie Kendrick at the plate to keep game tied in the eighth inning.

- On June 24, 1997, Mark McGwire hit a 538-foot home run off Randy Johnson at the Kingdome, the greatest collision of a fastball and a bat I've ever seen. Johnson struck out 19, but the A's won 4–1.

- Milton Bradley smacked a two-out, three-run walk-off homer off B.J. Ryan of the Blue Jays on July 30, 2006, to give Oakland a 6–5 win and a half-game lead in the AL West.

- As Angels closer Francisco Rodriguez dropped the throw back to the mound from catcher Jose Molina, Jason Kendall raced in with the winning run on August 11, 2005, and the A's had a 5–4 victory: Bill: "Bonehead number one!"

Susan Slusser

I don't have a secret list of top games no one else has thought of—they bump up against everyone else's. But Ken's list and the fans' voting made me curious to go back and see what I had written about some of those top games in the *Chronicle*. Here are some of my recollections and snippets from the most entertaining games of the past 20 years.

Dallas Braden's Perfect Game:

For a reporter, this had it all: drama, color, and loads of fun. The embrace shared by Braden and his grandmother, Peggy Lindsey, who raised him after his mom died, was as tender a moment as you'll see on a baseball diamond—on Mother's Day, no less.

Grant Balfour and catcher Derek Norris celebrate after their 12–5 win over the Texas Rangers to clinch the 2012 AL West title. (AP Photo/Ben Margot)

And we soon learned that Peggy Lindsey is every bit as feisty as her grandson. The previous month, Braden had been embroiled in a feud with Yankees superstar Alex Rodriguez after taking exception to Rodriguez's shortcut across the Coliseum mound on his way back to first after a foul ball. Braden screamed: "Get off of my mound," and followed up with more choice words for A-Rod after the game. Rodriguez responded by saying, "I've never quite heard that, especially from a guy who has a handful of wins in his career."

That was still on Lindsey's mind after Braden's sensational accomplishment, though she initially downplayed the Rodriguez kerfuffle:

"I'm thinking, 'Let's forget it, let's forget it,'" Lindsey said.

But then she paused and said, "Stick it, A-Rod."

The perfect ending to a perfect day.

THE FINAL GAME OF THE 2012 SEASON:

You know all the details. Here's how the *Chronicle*'s game story started:

Oakland's outlandish 2012 season now includes the American League West title.

The A's, overlooked and unloved during the spring, are now baseball's darlings after tearing through the past week to snatch the division crown from the Rangers, the fearsome two-time defending league champs.

The A's completed their sweep of Texas on Wednesday with a 12–5 victory that was a perfect snapshot of their methods: They got down early and all looked bleak—then Oakland bounced back with gusto, took the lead, and handed things to an ironclad bullpen.

"It's kind of like the story of our whole season," reliever Sean Doolittle said of Wednesday's comeback win. "At the end of June, we were 13 games back, we had injuries, young guys stepping up, and we were never out of it.

"It wasn't if we were going to do it. It was how or when we were going to do it."

The previous day, Oakland had clinched a playoff spot. That might be my favorite game story I've written. Billy Beane liked it, too—he quoted from it in a group interview the next day after the A's won the division.

An improbable, implausible, absurd season for the Oakland A's churned out one sensational story after another, and at last comes the most fantastic tale yet:

The 2012 A's are going to the postseason.

Yes, the club that traded three of its top pitchers, all All-Stars, last winter. The team that lost its starting third baseman on the first full day of spring training and three starting pitchers in the past month and a half.

Oakland's third baseman is a catcher, the first baseman is an outfielder, the former shortstop is at second base, and the top left-hander in the bullpen was a first baseman until last fall, for crying out loud. There are five rookies in the A's rotation. Five of them.

This group of castoffs and youngsters beat the two-time defending AL champion Rangers 4–3 Monday night at the Coliseum to claim, at the least, the second wild-card spot. The team celebrated with a sight familiar in its home park: wildly jumping around in a tight bunch.

"We've shocked the world," said Monday's winning pitcher, Jarrod Parker, one of the rookie five. "And we're not done."

THE JETER FLIP:

I haven't kept many scoresheets over the years. I tucked away the one I filled out during Braden's perfect game, I'll hang onto the one from Sean Manaea's no-hitter. And I still have the one from the Jeter Flip game, because as the play was unfolding, I wrote down in the margin, "What's he doing over there?"

No one could remember a shortstop going well into foul ground on the first-base side as Derek Jeter did to get the overthrow by Shane Spencer. He then famously shoveled the ball home to get Jeremy Giambi, going in standing up, in Game 3 of the 2001 ALDS.

After the game, Giambi argued that sliding would have slowed him down. But catcher Ramon Hernandez was signaling for him to slide from the on-deck circle.

From my story in the *Chronicle*:

"I was getting ready to make contact and didn't pick up Ramon," Giambi said. "That's where I made my mistake."

As it was, Jorge Posada got the tag on Giambi's right calf, just before Giambi crossed the plate. But the real key was Jeter's alertness in backing up the play when right fielder Shane Spencer overthrew both cutoff men, second baseman Alfonso Soriano and first baseman Tino Martinez. As the ball rolled past first in the grass near the baseline, Jeter appeared out of nowhere, picked up the ball, and, in the same motion, made a backhand flip to Posada, a play

Scott Hatteberg watches the ninth-inning home run that defeated the Royals 12–11 on Wednesday, September 4, 2002, setting the American League record with 20 consecutive wins. (AP Photo/Paul Sakuma)

that Oakland general manager Billy Beane likened to a quarterback's pitch to a running back.

"My biggest question is what the heck is Jeter doing running over there?" A's center fielder Johnny Damon said. "That's pure instinct. That's why he's such a great shortstop. He just made a great play—a play that saved their season."

Third-base coach Ron Washington had a definite opinion on Giambi's decision not to slide.

"What Jeremy had to do was finish the play off," Washington said. "If he did that, you [reporters] wouldn't be talking to me. Anytime you're going home in a 1–0 ballgame and it's going to be close, you hit the dirt."

GAME 20 OF THE STREAK:

It seemed as if every game leading up to the A's then-AL record 20th consecutive win was equally tense—Oakland kept having to storm back late to keep the roll going. The A's upped the ante in what turned out to be the final game of the streak.

Twenty wins in a row is improbable enough. The method, inconceivable.

With a record crowd at the Coliseum, the A's zoomed to an 11-run lead over the Royals after three innings, but by the ninth, they had somehow given it all back. Kansas City's Mike Sweeney poked a three-run homer down the left-field line off Jeff Tam in the eighth, and the Royals tied it in the ninth against closer Billy Koch, who had set an Oakland record with 11 saves in August.

Then, with one out in the bottom of the ninth, pinch-hitter Scott Hatteberg, no part of the earlier shenanigans, punched a 1–0 pitch from Jason Grimsley out to right for an insane 12–11 victory—and an American League record for consecutive wins.

"Best moment I've had in baseball," Hatteberg said. "Unbelievable. We just keep rolling. It's a phenomenal experience, tough to put in words.

"There's always doubt. We'd just given up 11 straight runs, it wasn't looking good. But we were still confident.... I couldn't wait to get around the bases and hug the guys."

Kotsay's Inside-the-Park Homer:

Over the past two decades, the A's have few first-round memories on the positive side of the ledger—the Jeter Flip, the base-running gaffes against Boston, Justin Verlander, those moments tend to stand out more.

Then there's Mark Kotsay's dash at the Metrodome during the 2006 ALDS, a great individual feat, and remembered all the more fondly by fans because it came in the team's only successful division series.

MINNEAPOLIS: By the time he hit third base, Mark Kotsay was getting winded. He kept going, though, pushing as hard as he could.

The A's center fielder crossed the plate, huffing and puffing, then gleefully celebrated his inside-the-park home run with fellow playoff newcomer Jason Kendall, who also scored when Kotsay's drive to center got past Torii Hunter. That rip-and-run off Dennys Reyes in the seventh inning turned out to be the decisive moment for Oakland in a 5–2 victory over the Twins and a 2–0 lead in the American League Division Series.

* * *

Before Mark Ellis' injury, the mood was upbeat, particularly after Kotsay's frenzied dash around the bases. With the game tied 2–2, he smacked a 3–1 pitch from Reyes to center and Hunter, a Gold Glove outfielder, dived for the ball and missed it. It rolled to the wall, easily scoring Kendall, but Kotsay had to bust it for all he was worth. Kendall motioned for Kotsay to get down as he approached the plate, then the two friends "acted like two-year-olds," Kendall said of their enthusiastic reaction.

"For the ball to get by Torii… I was like, 'Let's go, let's see what you can do,'" said Kotsay, who gave himself an added degree of difficulty by hesitating out of the box. "I was gassed. That was all I had. I asked for some oxygen, but there wasn't any. If this were a football game, there would have been some oxygen on the sidelines and I could have sucked some down."

"I just made sure I got him a glass of water," teammate Nick Swisher said.

THE WILD-CARD GAME:

Back to a bitter outcome for the A's and their fans—but what a great game to cover for a reporter. Back and forth, tension, lead changes, an electric atmosphere. Everything but an Oakland win on September 30, 2014.

KANSAS CITY, Mo. — If you missed Oakland's regular season, you got to see the condensed version at Kauffman Stadium on Tuesday.

For the 2014 A's, nothing was ever easy. Ever.

And a 9–8 loss in 12 innings in the American League wild-card game pounded that home, especially with the team losing two players, catcher Geovany Soto and center fielder Coco Crisp, to injuries before the end of the game.

"We got off to a fast start, were able to take a big lead, and, unfortunately, down the stretch, we weren't able to nail it down," closer Sean Doolittle said. "That's kind of the way the season went as a whole."

MANAEA'S NO-NO:

When Sean Manaea threw a no-hitter on April 21, 2018, he was blissfully unaware he had one going for much of it.

Sean Manaea didn't just throw a no-hitter Saturday, the seventh in Oakland history and the A's first since Dallas Braden's perfect game in 2010.

Manaea did so against a Red Sox team that came into the Coliseum winners of 17 of their previous 18 games and averaging more than six runs a game. Better still, the A's left-hander had no idea for a good chunk of the game that he even had a no-no going.

Perhaps that's why Manaea, whose lack of focus and killer instinct occasionally affected him in previous years, looked as calm as he could be in the later stages of the A's 3–0 victory while dominating baseball's hottest team.

When shortstop Marcus Semien "dropped that ball in the fifth, I thought it was a hit," Manaea said. "Until the eighth I thought it just like was a one-hitter. I looked up in the eighth and saw there were still zeroes and thought, 'Weird!'"

Hey, whatever works.

BRANDON MOSS ENDS 19-INNING GAME:

For anyone working at a baseball game, extra innings can be a drag. For writers, extra innings are especially problematic—each half inning means another potential re-write, on what is, by then, an extremely tight deadline.

On April 29, 2013—and April 30, too, as it turned out—it was all worth it, because Moss, the A's first baseman, was so delightful after beating the Angels 10–8 with a two-out, two-run homer.

"It's one of those things where you just want to quit, but you don't want to lose, so you keep fighting through it and hope they throw a ball into your bat," Moss said. *"I don't even know how I hit it, I was so late on everything after the 10th inning."*

Moss did get the customary whipped-cream pie in the face, but Josh Reddick handed him the pie tin and Moss smacked it against his own face. Nutty stuff happens after 1:00 AM.

"Reddick was too tired to pie me, so yeah, I did pie myself," Moss said.

The other fun fact from that 6-hour, 32-minute game: Brett Anderson was scratched from starting that game because of an ankle injury. He wound up in the game anyway and worked 5⅓ innings, going longer than starter Dan Straily.

"That's probably the best outing I've had all year," Anderson said, *"and it was in relief. It's baseball. Weird things happen."*

YOENIS CÉSPEDES' THROW:

The most amazing thing I've ever seen on a baseball field happened on June 10, 2014, at Anaheim. Like the rest of the writers, I was busy filling in a run for the Angels in my scorebook after A's left fielder Yoenis Céspedes kicked a drive by Mike Trout into the corner, sending Howie Kendrick toward the plate.

I looked up, and saw a blur heading toward the plate, and for a second I thought it was a bird plummeting down, or that a fan had thrown something out of the stands.

It was Céspedes' extraordinary missile of a throw. It plopped right into catcher Derek Norris' glove as if it had fallen from the sky.

With the game tied 1–1 in the eighth, Luke Gregerson walked Howie Kendrick with one out. Then Mike Trout hit a rocket toward the corner in left that Céspedes couldn't come up with cleanly. It appeared as if the A's had made yet another costly error in this series.

Instead, Céspedes uncorked an ungodly great throw to the plate to get Kendrick. It didn't seem possible, but the high-arcing throw came down right into Derek Norris' mitt, and Kendrick was out, a call confirmed on replay. It was astounding, staggering. A thesaurus' worth of such words, and maybe a few expletives.

* * *

Céspedes, asked if he's ever made a better throw, said in English, "Here? No. In Cuba? Yes."

His teammates remain flabbergasted. Gregerson saw Céspedes lose the ball into the corner and ran behind the plate to back up the play.

"As I was standing there behind home plate, this giant beach ball is coming in, and I was like, 'Oh, my goodness! That's the most incredible thing I've ever seen,'" Gregerson said. "I really thought it was a run, and the ball comes flying in. I was like, 'How did that get here?'"

Norris said he realized immediately that the ball had the height to reach him.

"I knew it was right to my chest—or hitting a fan behind me 30 rows up," he said. "It went from being a debacle at the beginning to a tremendous play, so it was even more impressive. Everyone in the stadium was cheering because they thought they'd scored a run, and all of a sudden it was so quiet. Everyone was like, 'What just happened?'"

STEPHEN PISCOTTY'S FENWAY PARK HOMER:

On May 15, 2018, Stephen Piscotty returned to the A's after the memorial services for his mother, Gretchen, who had died of amyotrophic lateral sclerosis, or Lou Gehrig's disease, nine days earlier.

In his first at-bat, Piscotty homered over the Green Monster, and as he crossed home plate, he looked toward the heavens and tapped his chest.

"It was pure joy," Piscotty said. *"It's been an emotional week. I've been a little cried out so I didn't tear up or anything. It felt real good knowing family was watching and my mom was watching. Yeah, just pure joy."*

* * *

Against the Astros on May 8, Piscotty had singled in his first at-bat following Gretchen's death. "The hand over my heart, that's something my mom would do when she wasn't able to speak," Piscotty said the next day. "This was just, 'I love you and thank you.'"

So he did the same Tuesday. "Coming around third, I just immediately started thinking of my mom, and I put my hand over my chest like she would do," Piscotty said. "That's kind of going to be my thing, I think, going forward."

I was not alone in tearing up in the press box—including, 30 minutes later, when I saw the best sports photo I've ever seen. Adam Glanzman of Getty captured the exact moment Piscotty gazed upward, and his face is lit from above. The image looks beatific, holy, like a religious artifact. I got goosebumps, and made sure that it was the photo that accompanied the story in the *Chronicle*.

* * *

As a beat writer, I contribute many articles besides game stories. Some of the best opportunities to turn in something different come on the team's days off, or during spring training, which is when reporters provide feature stories and offbeat items.

Here are a few of the ones that have stuck with me over the years.

Gretchen Piscotty:

The Piscotty family was so gracious to allow me and *Chronicle* photographer Carlos Avila Gonzalez to come to their Pleasanton home to meet with them in January 2018.

What struck me most, besides the Piscotty family's closeness, was the good humor Gretchen displayed. She was dealt a dreadful hand and was facing tough odds against a terrible disease, but even though speaking was difficult for her by that point, she was still cracking jokes and gently needling her three boys.

When Gretchen Piscotty was pregnant with her first child, Stephen, she liked to wind up a music-box piano and play "Amazing Grace" for him.

"She thought I could hear it," the new Oakland A's outfielder said. "Amazingly, that's one of my favorite songs. I've always loved it."

In May, Gretchen Piscotty was diagnosed with amyotrophic lateral sclerosis, a neuromuscular disorder also known as Lou Gehrig's disease. The illness is progressing far more quickly than doctors expected, and Gretchen has lost much of her mobility. Speaking is becoming difficult.

So now it's Stephen's turn. He plays "Amazing Grace" for his mother on his guitar and it soothes both of them.

"Whenever I play for her at night, I'll end with that song and it gives me chills, the good kind, when I play it, as well as a calming peace," he said. "It's just crazy the full-circle thoughts and emotions I get when I hear or play that song."

* * *

She and Stephen always have been especially close. "It's funny, it's like what you see on TV, like, 'You're a hawk with the first kid.' On occasion, she calls me 'The experiment,'" Stephen said. "We've always had that special bond, because she was always watching me so closely. That strengthened our relationship. It's hard to describe, but just by raising me, she gave me everything.

"She's so balanced and so fun and pokes fun at us, and she reminds us there is more to life than baseball."

And on those quiet nights when nothing more needs to be said, Stephen can bring out his guitar—it's always close to hand, he said—and play the song that connected them even before he was born.

Tis grace that brought me safe thus far.

And grace will lead me home.

CÉSPEDES' FAMILY ORDEAL:

Toward the end of the 2012 season, Yoenis Céspedes, the A's star rookie outfielder, turned quiet, almost distracted, even as his team was heading toward the playoffs. The next year, he told me why: During that time, his family was trying to escape from Cuba to the United States, and at one point after they'd left the Dominican Republic, he'd lost all contact with them.

From the story that Demian Bulwa and I wrote in the *Chronicle* on July 15, 2013:

Marooned on a tiny Caribbean island, family members of Oakland A's star Yoenis Céspedes feared their journey would end right there under a baking sun.

Their effort to follow Céspedes from Cuba to the United States had gone horribly wrong, leaving them abandoned for two days on a strip of sand more than 600 miles southeast of Florida.

The 10 travelers, including a baby, had no water. They had neither food nor shade. They resorted to catching and cooking an iguana and a seagull, with foul results.

As time wore on and dehydration set in, there were hugs and goodbyes. Estela Milanés, Céspedes' mother, walked away from her huddled loved ones and lay down alone in despair.

Then salvation arrived in the form of a yacht. And the travelers lived on, continuing an odyssey of nearly two years that ultimately reunited them with Céspedes.

Their travels included four countries, six boat rides, two trips to jail, an immigration raid, accusations of human trafficking, and a dispute with a Dominican baseball agent.

The project, which is available without a subscription on the *Chronicle*'s website, includes the details of Céspedes' own dramatic departure from Cuba after one previous failed attempt. The photos, by Carlos Avila Gonzalez, are phenomenal.

BRANDON MOSS MEMORIES:

Sometimes, it's fun just to get random stories from players, and at one point after covering Brandon Moss for two years, I realized I'd heard some doozies about the first baseman/DH. So I just ran a collection of them during spring training, on March 26, 2014. They still make me giggle. Daric Barton talked about Moss abandoning him alone and scared in a hunting blind, Nate Freiman discussed Moss ordering a steak dinner for two and polishing it off, Jed Lowrie detailed Moss' junk food addiction. And from Moss:

The most embarrassing thing that happened to me, my dad (stepdad Todd Milligan) did to me. When I was about 12 or 13, we were at this place called Whitewater, and I was flirting with these girls behind us on the lazy river when my dad yanks my shorts off me and throws them on the bank and I have to swim around the whole thing butt naked in front of the girls I was flirting with.

"Of course the girls were dying laughing and I was like, 'This is awful.' That's a big lazy river, too, I had to go all the way around the park and then jump out and get my shorts."

Moss also detailed his young son belting out country songs about Fireball whiskey in preschool, and, he said, "The teacher was like, 'Okay, Jayden, that's enough singing for now!'"

HOUSE OF A'S:

For a story that ran on October 4, 2002, I was asked to write some copy to accompany photos by the *Chronicle*'s Pulitzer winner, Deanne Fitzmaurice, who'd visited the house shared by Mark Mulder, Eric Chavez, Mark Ellis, Frank Menechino, and Mike Venafro. It was a last-second request, and I remember being grumpy about it. It turned out to be comedy gold.

"The best piece of furniture in the place is the recliner, and it came free with one of the TVs," Venafro said. "The only attention to detail is how the games are organized and how the remotes are stacked."

* * *

Mulder and Chavez took a trip to Target and stocked up on rafts and flotation devices, along with Nerf balls and other things to toss around—but Mulder said that Chavez, a Gold Glove winner, has thrown most of them over the fence.

"Yeah, for some reason, I lose all the toys," *Chavez said.*

The only drawbacks—many spiders and little parking. The guys live together, but seldom carpool. Venafro said that after games there are sometimes races to get home for the three spots in the garage.

"We're not a model of California fuel efficiency," *Venafro said.* "And our power bills are so high, it's unspeakable."

Along the same lines, I did a fun Q and A with Mulder, Tim Hudson, and Barry Zito that ran in the *Chronicle* on March 28, 2002. I had one of those every-reporter's-nightmare moments, though—it was a 30-minute interview, and my recorder was not on. I had to reconstruct it all from my notes, which thankfully were extensive.

Like the other stories, you can find this entire piece online, but this exchange was particularly amusing:

SS: Who is the best dresser?

TH: Definitely Zito... depending on what your sense of style is.

MM: When you wear a blue suit with an orange tie and tan suede shoes and think it looks good...

BZ: I got the pimpest thing ever this winter—a brown corduroy suit with that real thick wale, plus a puke-gold tie.

SS: Which of you is the smartest?

BZ: Me. Definitely me.

TH: You? You went to 12 colleges.

BZ: And I still have four years left.

DUST-UP:

One story that elicited enormous reaction at the time came in late August in 2016, when I learned that designated hitter Billy Butler was injured in a clubhouse altercation with infielder Danny Valencia. Over the next day, I was able to uncover quite a bit of detail about the fight, which left Butler with a concussion.

From the *Chronicle*'s August 23, 2016, edition:

According to the players, the incident occurred before batting practice Friday when an equipment representative quizzed Valencia about a pair of off-brand spikes in Valencia's locker. Valencia previously had been told not to wear those shoes in games.

Valencia told the representative that he only uses the non-issue spikes during pregame workouts. According to multiple sources, Butler, who has an equipment endorsement with a different company, jumped in to tell the equipment rep that Valencia was lying and regularly uses the non-standard spikes. Butler allegedly told the representative that the company should drop Valencia's endorsement deal.

Endorsement deals are typically worth between $10,000 and $20,000, sometimes more.

After the rep departed, the players said, Valencia confronted Butler and told him, "Don't you ever loud-talk me in front of a rep. That was wrong," and walked aggressively toward Butler. Butler turned around, took a couple steps toward Valencia, and according to both witnesses, said, "I can say whatever I want and your bitch ass isn't going to do anything about it."

One player said that the men leaned in, bumped heads and then started pushing each other, then Valencia started swinging and hit Butler in the temple. After the players broke things up, Butler told the players he was okay.

Butler, who then took part in batting practice, was not scheduled to play that night against right-hander James Shields, but he missed the next two games against left-handed starters with what manager Bob Melvin described as nausea and vomiting.

* * *

Clubhouse incidents are not uncommon, although players seldom are injured as a result. And Butler and Valencia have a long-standing loud, joking, back-and-forth relationship that dates back to their time as teammates in Kansas City.

"Those two go at it every day, so in that way, it was pretty normal," one player said. "If Bill had dropped it, Danny never would have done anything. But he kind of kept egging him on. I think it's fair to say he was verbally provoked, very much so. I'm worried about what might happen to Danny now, but at the same time, you don't want to see anyone get hurt."

MOUND VISIT EXTRAVAGANZA:

Ever wonder what happens when pitching coaches and managers visit the mound? That "candlesticks make a nice gift" scene in *Bull Durham* isn't too far off. For this August 7, 2017, story, I asked some of the A's coaches and pitchers to dish. Pitching coach Scott Emerson broke down the difficulty of when and how to go out for a visit, manager Bob Melvin recalled a visit gone awry when he played for the Giants, while A's starter Sonny Gray recalled a funny miscommunication with Melvin. But it was pitcher Chris Smith with the best bits:

Smith said the standard line most pitching coaches provide is, "I'm just giving you a breather."

"You know what, I don't need a breather—I need Billy Wagner's fastball or Trevor Hoffman's changeup right now," Smith said with a cackle. "Or it's, 'Hey, what's going on out here?' 'Well, I'm obviously in some trouble. You're out here for a reason. You're not checking to see where I'm going to dinner.'

"I like having a pitching coach give you something to do.... But if they say, 'Hey, what do you want to do here?' I'm like, 'I don't know! I want to be in the dugout! I don't want to be here. I want to go home! Bases loaded and no outs, you know?'"

CHAPTER 15
KEITH LIEPPMAN: THE MAN BEHIND THE FUTURE STARS

Keith Lieppman, the A's director of player development, started with the club in 1971, when he was Oakland's second-round draft pick, a corner infielder out of the University of Kansas. Lieppman also has managed at every level of Oakland's system, as well as the storied Licey Tigres in the Dominican Winter Leagues.

In 2010, Lieppman was awarded Minor League Baseball's Sheldon "Chief" Bender Award for his distinguished service. He spoke to Ken and Susan in his office at the A's minor-league complex in Mesa, Arizona, in March 2018.

Which A's greats did you play with or manage in your minor-league days?

I was with Rickey Henderson in 1979. He got called up about halfway through. He was focused, athletic, fun to watch. Everybody knew this guy was going to be fantastic. His mindset was geared: There were no distractions. He knew what he was doing, it was easy to watch him play and realize that he was the real deal.

Mickey Tettleton, he was outstanding. Stan Javier. Eric Plunk. There were some guys that developed, some came out of trades.

What were your experiences like managing at Triple-A Tacoma just as many of the cornerstones of the great A's late '80s, early '90s teams came through?

It was almost where we're at right now with a bunch of young players. It has cycled all the way back around again where Matt Olson, Chad Pinder, Matt Chapman… the whole thing where there's a group drafted a couple years apart, then coming up through the system together. That's the way it used to be, there wasn't as much moving around.

Fortunately for this group, they stuck together. They went from Beloit to Stockton to Midland, they developed good relationships with each other, they learned how to win.

Now they're in the same place that that club was back then, although there were more veterans that were assembled around that club.

What are your memories of your first day with the A's?

I was late to practice. I was staying at the Lost Dutchman Motel in Mesa, on Country Club. I had just gotten in the night before, and I overslept my first day!

I remember there was no way to get over here. I had to run more than two miles, all the way from Highway 60 and Country Club Drive, I was five minutes late and was tremendously scolded for my first day as an Oakland A.

Luckily, I was in pretty good shape. It was a little bit discombobulating. You wake up in a panic.

Of all the things to happen. Ever since then, my life has been geared toward trying to get guys to be here on time. It's funny it would turn out like that.

I was picked up in the secondary phase of the Rule 5. Back then, they had a winter draft and a summer draft. I was the second-round pick in the winter draft. I was drafted out of high school by the Dodgers as a draft-and-follow because I was going to go to college to play football, then Atlanta picked me in 1970, and I didn't sign there. I got drafted three times, so I guess somebody liked me.

I played football at Kansas. I started off as a defensive back, then went to strong safety and I punted my last two years. I was fortunate to be on a team that went to the Orange Bowl; it was really a fun team. Pepper Rodgers was the head football coach, John Cooper was a coach on that team, so was Terry Donahue. They were disciplined, very good instructors. They were into it.

Dick Tomey was there, and he was probably my favorite guy. He took a special interest in me because he loved baseball. He would come out and encourage me during the baseball games in the spring because freshmen couldn't play on the varsity team back then. I could go practice baseball, then I would have to take my pads and go to football.

My whole career was an interesting evolution. After my last year in 1979 with Triple-A Ogden, I said I'd had enough. I had been injured a little bit, and I had played nine years. I was substitute teaching in Salt

Lake City and looking for what the next step was. I had a degree in journalism, I was trying to work as an intern for an ad company out of Ogden just making ends meet.

I got a surprise phone call mid-February in 1980 from the farm director, Norm Koselke, saying one of the managers had quit and there was an opening to go to Modesto. Because I was a veteran-type player, people had recommended that I might be a good fit for them. Two days later, I was right back with the organization as the manager of the Modesto A's.

I was fortunate because the year before, Jose Pagan was the Triple-A manager in Ogden. He was kind of a laid-back guy who didn't care much about coaching third, and he let me do it. He let me take the lineup cards out. Sometimes I would help him make the lineups. He saw that I was interested and knew I was at the end of my career as a utility guy.

It wasn't totally foreign, but it was a huge jump. Back then, you didn't have a hitting coach. You had a roving pitching coach, but there weren't a lot of people who were there to help you. You were all on your own. You really got thrown into the fire, especially on a short notice. When we reported for spring training, they would issue the minor-league manager a grocery cart. There would be two fungo bats, pine tar, a bucket of balls and you would push your cart all the way to the field to start your day.

I was there when Billy Martin took over in 1980, and with that came all the changes. He brought all his people in, all the old-school guys. I guess you could say I was demoted. I was put in charge of rookie league Idaho Falls that year. In 1982, I became a roving instructor, and when the rookie league started, I managed there.

Fortunately, one of my first big influences was Bob Didier. He was the manager of Double-A West Haven back then. His dad, Mel, was a really brilliant baseball mind, and he had given a lot of that information to Bob. Bob really taught me a lot of how to play the game and how to manage.

In 1983, things really changed with our player development. Karl Kuehl, Harvey Dorfman, that whole group came in and revolutionized the way we go about doing things. Harvey was a mental skills coach, Karl ran the department and brought this whole new idea of teaching. I was fortunate to be the recipient. You had to show you were willing to pay the price. There was a work ethic involved, and dedication.

I remember we were at Scottsdale Community College back then and we were using an old locker room. They were the regular metal lockers. Karl couldn't stand that. He wanted a baseball atmosphere. Part of our off-season that year, we were asked to go in on our own time and build lockers. We built wood lockers. Everything was geared toward baseball, almost to an excess.

Sandy Alderson got Karl, and Karl was innovative. Then Sandy added an old-school guy, Ron Plaza, from the Cardinals, and St. Louis had the great traditions of the '50s and '60s. He brought in old school and new school. He brought back Wes Stock, a great pitching guy. It was a nice blend of great people who were really interested in promoting new ways of doing things. They weren't afraid to try things.

The next year, I went back to Idaho Falls, and the guy who had replaced me in Modesto, Pete Whisenant, was fired halfway through the year at Albany. All of a sudden, I go from Rookie ball to Double-A. That was a shock. The East Coast fan is far different than the West Coast fan; I had no idea what I was going into. I was full of myself, I thought I knew what I was doing, but I had thin skin. I had never heard the Bronx cheer like that before. It was a rude awakening. You had to learn how to toughen up in that environment. It was good for me.

We had some pretty good young players at that time. After that summer of 1984, the next three years, I was in Tacoma as the Triple-A manager.

What sorts of things did Harvey Dorfman and Karl Kuehl emphasize that you still use today?

There are things like the self-fulfilling prophesy, when coaches' expectations become reality; things such as the art of constructive criticism. These were all Karl's things, he'd read some weird articles and he would bring them in every day. There were a lot of people who looked at him and said, "This man is crazy." A lot of coaches at that point went to other organizations.

They resisted his change. A lot of them didn't want to do the work.

There were days when he would keep Mark McGwire and Jose Canseco out there just to see if they could handle the long work and the pressure and the constant effort. He felt like if you were going to play under pressure, you had to learn how to work and be tired under those influences. We would be standing in the outfield, and he would be throwing batting practice with the sun going down. I think he did it on purpose. It was all about work ethic. Are you willing to pay the price?

I kind of liked it. I'd never had the structure of a program like that. Before that, it just had been, 'Here you go, take your cart out.' This was new information. This was good stuff that I was interested in. In college, I had really enjoyed psychology. That was part of our program now.

When Harvey came along with his new ideas, it was just tremendous. I developed a really good relationship with him and learned a lot about how to deal with people. Creating relationships, that's what he was all about, learning how to listen. That's half the battle, to read keys and understand people. Try to get to a place where you can offer people information in ways they might otherwise resist. The smartest guy in the world can give you information, but if the person you're talking to can't receive it, you're wasting your time.

Those teachings have continued on to today. Our staff is probably more important than the players, because they're the messengers. Everything we do has to be filtered so we're on the same page. We meet every morning just to try to get guys to be likeminded.

There's a lot of confusion, there's a lot of resistance. Guys come out of college programs, and they've been taught a certain way. Change is hard.

Last year, we had everyone read a book called *The Inner Game of Tennis*. It was written in the '70s, and is about how the real growth in a player happens from within. Our job is to teach them how to discover who they are.

There's accountability when it comes to becoming a winning player. That was part of Karl and Harvey's message that I've continued: The best teams are the ones that take care of themselves. A coach or manager can continually bark out instructions, that was the Billy Martin style in the early '80s, but this is more of a matter of understanding the players, letting them monitor each other. They push each other. They discipline each other.

I know there were times when Ryon Healy was the guy who would go off on a tangent and the other guys would bring him back. It wouldn't require the coaches to intervene. They knew what needed to be done. They were skillful enough, and they had fun with it. It wasn't negative. There were times they made him go sit in the corner and turn his back to the group. They made him take a time out. It was done in fun. Sometimes Chad Pinder would be the leader. Sometimes Matt Olson. They all had a way of controlling how the team ran. It was Pindergarten like Kindergarten. Chad was the guy that was in charge of the children. He would get them into place. Sometimes it was sarcastic. Sometimes it was for real.

You have a good manager, Ryan Christenson, who was with those guys all the way through and capable of allowing them autonomy, not caught up on the length of your pants or petty stuff. This was about understanding the dynamic of the team and allowing them to function for the better good.

The pleasure of it all is that you're teaching the staff and teaching the players who are still trying to find their way to do things.

What is your job like when spring training gets going on the minor-league side?

The meetings start a couple of weeks after the big-leaguers report. We'll do some leadership training. Each guy is required to read a book called *Touch Points* about how to create relationships. These two- to three-minute touch points are where you, by design, impart information that you want another person to have—interaction with purpose, because sometimes in this job, you might only have 30 seconds or so in which you can impart something useful. A lot of what we do is moment-to-moment, and it's a whole group of people doing the same thing over an entire organization.

There are always guys who are rogue and renegade and want to do their own thing. We're human, we can get off on tangents. But our roving instructors, whether it was Todd Steverson or Greg Sparks or Dave Hudgens, they always understood the overall big picture. Sometimes, when you're caught up in your team, you can't see all the elements of it. So you have the rovers who can come in and help the staff correct the path a little bit, get them back on target.

I'm more of the idea guy now. I have a knowledge of organization and how put it out on the field. I understand what the coaches and managers have to go through. They're really the key to how this all plays out. Having solid people who are prepared.

We look at all of the statistics from last year. We have a big board that has everybody's name on it with our projections, where we think they should go. Over the course of the spring, David Forst, Billy Beane, and Dan Feinstein will give us information on who is out of options, so our board will fluctuate. Injuries, other things might happen.

Toward the end of the spring, we will have two or three meetings just going over players, where we want players to be to push them. We had some really hard questions this year about what to do with Lazarito Armenteros and Nick Allen. Are these 18-year-olds ready to go to Class-A Beloit? It's a cold environment. Is it better to keep them here and get a little confidence? Send them in May when the weather is better? Is it better to challenge them? There are a lot of questions that start to roll out about what's best for certain players at certain times.

Part of our situation in Oakland is we want to make players attractive because we trade so much. Putting them in a place where they can succeed and continue to hold their value is an important part of that process.

What's the worst part of the job?

I've released so many players in my life. I've lived and died in their moment. It's a life-changing event. I'm the one that gets to tell them that whatever path they were on, they're no longer on that path. It's going to go in a different direction now.

There is shock, dismay. I can't describe the feeling in the room when you totally catch someone off guard. Some guys know it and they're okay with it, but for a lot, this has been a dream since they've been six or seven years old.

The kids that really love it and this is their life, it's tragic sometimes. You get caught up with them. You've been part of their life for three or four years or even longer. We know them. We've motivated them. We've lived their life with them and understood their failures and successes. It's the hardest thing to do.

We've been really good about taking ex-players and bringing them back into our organization. There's a sense of loyalty and a sense of commitment that we are all on the same page. Guys who played in our system and either have been released or traded, we try to reacquire them because they really enjoyed their experience with us. For all of the misery that happens when you release a guy, every spring, I'll have one or two guys who will show up 10 years later and they'll walk through the door and shake my hand and say, "This was the greatest time of my life. I really enjoyed being here." That's the reward. When you're releasing a guy, you know that ultimately, they're going to be successful, that life is going to go on, that they're going to be fine. But in that moment, when it happens, it's crushing.

How well do you remember getting released? Does that help you when you have let someone go?

In the middle of 1977, I was in San Jose, and I got released about halfway through the summer. They called me in, dumped me, and said, "Good luck to you."

Three weeks later, they had an injury and they called me back and said, "Would you mind going back to Double-A?" I had been Triple-A at the time, but I agreed. I ended up playing three more years after that.

I understand the plight. Just being around it as a young player when I first signed in 1971, old guys who were around, like Ramon Webster, had all these catchphrases. "The hog is going to be nipping today." That meant it was cut day.

You'd come to understand the cold-hearted world. You'd walk in and your uniform would be gone or there would be a pink slip on your locker. It was a cruel and inhumane way to do it, but that's just the way it was. *Off you go.*

Guys would walk in and I saw all the misery they encountered as they left the facility. Everybody feared that as a young player. Back then, there were a lot more players at camp and they would release a lot more players. I felt that deeply at that time.

You try to help the players. That goes back to Karl. He had a philosophy that everybody was a prospect, you didn't label people. Somebody saw something in these players. That was part of our teaching. We treated every player the same.

Mike Bordick was not a very good player when he signed, Karl had a nickname for him. He called him "Bubble Bath." At the time, he was a little overweight. He wasn't into it. There were no plans for this late-round draft pick. All of a sudden, he developed and became a star.

You learn that you can't pigeonhole people. That was really stressed with us. As an organization, you don't say, "You're a No. 1 pick and you're a No. 3." You accept people as they are and you encourage whoever it is. With our staff even today, that's part of the premise. We know there are guys who got a lot of money, but who's to say there isn't a Dan Straily late in the draft who can come out and be a viable starter?

What's your work day like during the season?

We have cameras and a program so I can watch every game on real time. I'll catch up on all of our reports. I'll watch targeted selections of games. I'll start my morning with a couple hours of review of what happened the previous night. It might involve player moves or injuries, where to send guys.

I try to set aside a time to call the instructors, the managers, the pitching coaches, the hitting coaches, strength coaches, and trainers. Trying to keep all these people in the loop and trying to have a connection with them and to communicate requires a lot of time. If you want information and you want things to run smoothly, you have to be disciplined.

It gets tiresome because I'll be getting calls about things going on in all sorts of directions. There are problems, maybe a guy didn't run a ball out the night before. We give managers a lot of autonomy to manage their clubs, but sometimes they're looking for background information about what I think should be done.

After that gets done, I'm usually on the road. I spend 100 to 120 days traveling. Around 2:00 PM, I'll go to the ballpark and meet with the staff, watch batting practice, infield work, and watch the game.

It's a full day. It goes fast, and there are so many events that go on that are challenging, sometimes fun, sometimes not so fun. You never know what to expect. Every day has its own mystery about it.

Do you have any pet peeves?

Mine is when guys have their computers up or are looking at devices when we have a guest lecturer come in or someone speaking to the group.

I used to make guys read a book every winter, whether it's John Wooden's or Tony Dungy's. Then I asked each staff member to make a presentation, a 45-minute discussion about what they learned. They hated me for that. No one likes to talk in front of a group. It helped them become better at addressing their own team and maybe looking into things other than baseball. Wooden's pyramid is outstanding. Tony Dungy was a great instructor. The great people in the business that had success, we use their information and pass it out.

The guys who have their computers up and I see them working while there is valuable information being presented, that is the ultimate pet peeve to me. It's like chalk on a chalkboard. Nobody is paying attention to what's going on because there's no test. There's no requirement.

You want to hold people accountable, and you try to give them feedback about how they're doing, but in baseball, you can slide by with bare knowledge and be credible on the field. If you *really* want to be good, you have to get into it. My biggest pet peeve is people that don't pay attention. They disrespect the people that are giving them the opportunity to learn. Aaron Nieckula, who is our spring training coordinator, he said let's make a rule that the phones go off. It's a valuable time.

Same thing with the players: They're always locked into their phones. But in order to be successful as coaches, you have to have relationships, go out and reach these kids because the kids aren't going to reach out to you. When they have a free minute, though, the players are on their phones. Our job is to interact. You have to hear what they have to say in order to respond back to how you think you can best reach them.

What are common misperceptions about your job? Do people understand what you do?

They have no clue. It's a lot different than people think. My job has always been more on the field, I'm not the typical farm director. My title should be more like "field coordinator." More teams have gone to a role in which the farm director is a combination of director of minor-league operations and an information/analytics specialist.

I've been fortunate to be in uniform. People fear me just because I release people, but once I get out there and I'm part of the group, I have a better chance of them getting to know me. When I was a player, there was a mythical figure who sat up in the tower and glared down and had your fate in their hands. I try to get rid of the fear factor. That's part of the way that we do things here.

What's the best part of the job?

I came to enjoy so many aspects of the game that I didn't even understand. It's a constantly evolving business. I see a baseball game almost every day, and something different happens that I've never seen before. I look at different ways to try to make it better. Adapting to all the new information and trying to integrate it and use it is fun.

I'm not so much into the evaluation, that's Billy and David's area. I use the new information more for helping coaches, whether we're talking about spin rates or grips. We try to incorporate that into how we can better help the players. We use launch angle, exit velocities for hitters.

There's no one way to do it. The problem with some of the analytics is you wind up trying to clone people a certain way, but you have to remember there are a lot of different arm angles and a lot of ways of doing things.

I was talking to Josh Donaldson the other day, and he was telling me about some of his transformation. It was fun to hear, because I had tried to make him a little different when he was here. Our plan for him was to try not to be so aggressive as a hitter. We tried to tame him down a little bit. We tried to tame Nick Swisher down, too—but it wasn't right for them. They had their own unique skillset, mindset, attitudes. Sometimes our impressions aren't entirely correct, so you learn from those kind of people.

I tried to make Nick Swisher into Vanilla Swish. He wanted to be the Big Swish. He looked at me like I was crazy. "I'm not Vanilla Swish." Being full of yourself is what he needs to be successful. You learn that whatever it is, analytics or personality, you have to look into that person on a one-on-one basis to understand what they are and what you can do to best help them achieve that.

You can give them ideas, but they have to ultimately buy in and want to be the ones who are going to execute that plan. We're more about setting up good preparation, work ethic, routines, teaching them general information and let them add to their ability.

Donaldson wasn't smooth at all. We laugh about it now, because sometimes it's hard to approach people that aren't having the best of success at the time. There are some confrontations. It requires tough love, a pat on the back, but once you build a relationship with a player, you're able to give them bad messages. Most players are not very self-aware of who they are when they start, and they need to be told the truth sometimes about what we see as their attitudes. Having that relationship where you can give them a hard truth, whether they accept it or not, they respect the fact that you're trying to help them. It's very important.

Josh is a remarkable guy. When he called me, he started the conversation with, "Hey, I've got some news for you about how you can develop players." He wanted to talk about player development, that's amazing.

He was driven. You're not going to change all that, but you've got to guide it. Once he made the switch from catcher to third base, it totally freed him up. Once he left this organization, then he could be who he needed to be. There's no set timetable or absolute perfect place, it's an evolving place and he found it. His confidence is at the highest level.

It's a challenging job, but it's fun. There's a camaraderie with people. There are connections. I listened to Dave Stewart when he spoke to the team, and he explained that he wanted to be something for other people, to have an impact. You want to have influence. You want to add value to people. You want to feel like you're contributing something in this little part of the world. There's something satisfying about watching a program evolve or an idea get expanded.

CHAPTER 16

SUSAN SLUSSER: ALL THE PRESIDENT'S SCRIBES

In 2011, I became the vice president of the Baseball Writers Association of America, and the following year, the president.

I'm the only woman to have served as the president of the Baseball Writers Association of America (which I did from 2012 to '13), a fact that gets brought up a lot and always makes me a little uncomfortable—I'm just a baseball writer, like everyone else in the BBWAA, and I hate to bring gender into the equation. My co-author, Ken, interviewed me during my first year covering the A's and asked me about being a woman in baseball and we still joke about it; I always say he asked, "What's it like to be a woman beat writer?" He didn't actually say that, it was more nuanced and a valid question in 1999, when there were still only a handful of women covering baseball full time. Cheryl Rosenberg of the *Orange County Register* and I were the only ones in the American League. But it's such a strange question to have to answer.

In some ways, being a woman helped at times. When I was coming out of college, many newspapers were trying to diversify their sports departments and were looking for qualified women and minorities. In a business dominated by white males, you tend to stand out on a beat—there were several years when most of the players knew my name but they didn't always know the names of all of the men. And some players seem to be more comfortable talking to women.

The flip side is also true, of course. I had a few issues here and there in the 1990s, none of them too awful and all of them with players who were difficult with everyone, so I always prefer to think that gender wasn't a factor.

One player shoved me out of his way in the clubhouse after his team lost a World Series game; I assume it was out of frustration. One huge NBA star got up, leaned over and screamed in my face after his team lost to the Kings; the team trainer said afterward he was worried that the player was going to punch me. My transgression: asking if said player had a moment to talk before he was fully dressed. The item of clothing he was not yet wearing: cuff links.

The worst incidents were both courtesy of the same baseball player, who once, on a road trip, waved me over to his locker before a game only to shove some porn in my face. "Classy," I replied, before scurrying back to the rest of the writers to implore them not to write about it. This was not terribly long after my good friend Lisa Olson's ordeal with the New England Patriots; a player had harassed her aggressively and, when the incident exploded in a controversy, she moved to Australia because fan response was so heinous.

Several months later, the player who waved porn at me swung a bat at my head when I went over to check with him about an injury he'd been dealing with. I screeched and jumped backward; I'm sure he knew what he was doing enough to not actually hit me, but I felt the breeze of the bat, so it was way too close. I hadn't even said a word to him at that point, I was just walking toward him. "You could just say no comment," I told him. He didn't laugh. He didn't do it as a joke, it was just to intimidate me. But why? I'm sure he didn't know my name or even where I worked; I was just a backup baseball writer and I'm sure he never saw an edition of the *Sacramento Bee*, where I was working at the time. Many others have had bad experiences with that player, but nothing quite like that, to my knowledge.

Over the past decade-plus, more and more women have joined the baseball-writer ranks. The Bay Area always has been ahead of the pack, with Stephanie Salter of the *Examiner*, Joan Ryan of the *Chronicle* and Susan Fornoff of the *Bee* in the first wave of women sportswriters. Annette John-Hall and Kim Boatman covered the A's for the *San Jose Mercury News* in the 1990s, and Anne Peterson did so for the Associated Press.

In recent years, there are often more women in the A's press box than men between me, MLB.com's Jane Lee, AP's Janie McCauley, *Chronicle* columnist Ann Killion, former *Chronicle* columnist Gwen Knapp, and the Athletic's Melissa Lockard, along with several others who pop in from time to time to back up games or write feature stories. The A's magazine did a story a few years ago about how many women cover the team;

Joe Stiglich, who covered for the *Mercury News* and later NBC Sports Bay Area, joked about how outnumbered he was sometimes. "Everyone's always saying, 'Oh, I like your blouse!' to each other," he said. "No one ever asks me about my blouse!"

The locker room question has to be addressed, I suppose. I've been answering it for all of my 30-plus years as a sportswriter, but: Yes, we go into the clubhouse, male and female reporters alike. No, it's not a big deal. Guys wear towels. There is time to change before reporters enter the clubhouse or after we leave (postgame sessions are much shorter than pregame). Almost every professional athlete who has played after 1990 has had women covering them at some point, and it's just a complete non-factor for beat writers—we're in there every day all year from spring training on, part of the background like the other reporters who are there every day.

Every once in a while, a columnist or broadcaster, invariably male, says, "How come men can't go into women's locker rooms?" They can. Almost every major women's sporting event allows all media into the locker rooms—where you'll find that most players are already changed and ready for interviews.

*   *   *

Back to the BBWAA—most fans know the organization because of the postseason awards: The BBWAA instituted the MVP, Cy Young, Manager of the Year, and Rookie of the Year Awards. Two writers from each of the 30 major-league cities vote for each award, and while there are always those who dispute some individual votes and a few years have been controversial, I believe that the organization has done an excellent job over the years in determining the awards. The vote distribution ensures there is no regional bias, and writers take the honor of voting very seriously. I vote for AL MVP most years and I crunch numbers, talk to executives and players and broadcasters throughout September, and put thought into each spot on the 10-man ballot.

We're also the organization that the Hall of Fame chose as its voting body; 10 consecutive years of active BBWAA membership are required to cast a ballot.

This is where things went a little haywire during my tenure as BBWAA president. The 2012 ballot, for the 2013 Hall of Fame class, was the first to include Barry Bonds and Roger Clemens, the two most prominent figures of the steroid era by virtue of evidence presented in their court cases.

No one was elected to the Hall of Fame that year, for the first time since 1996, creating some outrage, and I spent several days talking to

Don Wakamatsu and Susan Slusser at the 2014 World Series at Kansas City.
(Daniel Brown)

media outlets. It was clear what had happened: Many BBWAA members, not wanting to vote for Bonds and Clemens, didn't really know how to approach the ballot. Some chose not to vote at all, most just ticked a few players they believed to be free of any steroid cloud. Over the following five years, the BBWAA voted in 16 players, so there was no lingering effect.

My own approach to the steroid era has changed in that time. I did not vote for Bonds and Clemens during their first four years of eligibility. I believe steroid use is a particularly insidious form of cheating—many people equate it to amphetamine use from the '70s on, but "greenie" use was widespread and right out in the open; I can't tell you the number of times I was jokingly offered the "leaded" coffee in the clubhouse. Many players essentially still take greenies now, with a valid prescription for ADHD medication. Because virtually everyone was taking greenies, the level playing field wasn't affected, in my mind.

Steroids were different. No one discussed them. Everyone denied they used them, they knew it was wrong. It was taboo, secret.

Many people rightly ask why the media didn't write more about performance enhancing substances in the 1990s, but without subpoena power, it was impossible. I asked two different A's players who were rumored to be associated with steroids about the topic; one leaped up and said, "Don't know anything about it! I think I hear someone calling my name! Gotta go hit in the cage!" and the other thoroughly convinced me of his outrage. "These guys are out there cheatin', while I'm working hours in the gym every day trying to put food on the table!" he ranted, and I absolutely believed him. Both were named in the Balco case and wound up testifying about using steroids. It took federal investigations to uncover almost all we know about the era.

I abhor the thought of young players taking steroids to emulate the pros or under pressure to make teams or get scholarships. Steroids are illegal, dangerous, particularly for teens, and their use associated with depression, suicide, and "roid rage." Changing my mind on Bonds and Clemens wasn't easy, nor was it fun and I understand every bit of criticism

I get for it. But as so many members of their era went into the Hall—including several with rumored PEDs ties but no court cases—it started to become very difficult to sort through the candidates. And when many executives and managers who oversaw the steroid era were elected by the Veterans Committee—including commissioner Bud Selig, Atlanta GM John Schuerholz, and managers Tony La Russa, Jim Leyland, and Bobby Cox, in short order after their retirements—I decided that placing the burden of the era on just two players was unsound.

Yes, I believe they absolutely cheated. I think others previously elected did, too. And those in charge should have acted more quickly, the players' own union should have done much more and the media should have pressed the issue more thoroughly. Every entity that is represented in the Hall of Fame in some fashion dropped the ball for too long, and if I'm going to vote for players I strongly suspect of cheating, I'm going to have to vote for Bonds and Clemens.

My hope is that the Hall will provide a permanent exhibit that explains the steroid era and that includes names of the central figures; the Hall never has glossed over the era, but if the main PEDs guys are in, there should be a strong counterpoint right nearby somewhere.

* * *

Most people don't realize that the BBWAA's core function is as an industry advocacy organization, instituted to ensure professional working conditions and adequate access, issues I care about deeply. Writers' access in nearly every sport has declined over the past decade—and that means fans' access has declined by extension. There is less time for interviews, particularly one-on-one; more teams are determining times and places and terms for interviews, and in some sports, declining interviews altogether on many days.

Baseball is still relatively media friendly, and while access has shrunk, it remains better than most sports, and that's due to the BBWAA, which often sits down with union and league officials during labor contracts to make sure that reporters' ability to do their jobs is not affected. Beat writers typically arrive more than four hours before the start of the game, and we need sufficient time to speak to players and the coaching staff in order to provide the best information possible. Correct, thorough reporting—and publicity—is in the best interests of everyone, including the league and teams. And getting to know the local media well can be invaluable for savvy players: It's always a good idea to know which reporters to trust.

But in the 2012 CBA, post-batting-practice clubhouse access was eliminated and pregame access was shortened, and since then, rumors have surfaced occasionally that postgame clubhouse access will be eliminated in favor of press conferences. That would greatly reduce the number of players available to speak after games and make it much easier for them to avoid speaking at all after a critical play or bad outing; fans would be less likely to learn what happened during a big moment in a game or why a specific pitch was thrown, and game stories would be far less accurate. Answers would be much more canned and corporate, because that's what happens in press-conference formats, which are formal and not conducive to natural conversation. Such considerations are precisely why the BBWAA exists.

During my presidency, Angels owner Arte Moreno decided to move the writers' press box from what admittedly was primo real estate—much lower than most press boxes—to a suite next to the right-field foul pole.

We learned about it the weekend before the season, and the A's, coincidentally, were the opponent for the Angels' home opener. The new writers' box is not conducive to proper game coverage: Among other things, it's impossible to see pitches crossing the plate, and if a reporter puts up his or her laptop, the writer to the right can't see the mound, the plate, or first base.

Only one other team has moved the writers' box down the first-base line, but the White Sox's box isn't nearly as far down the line as is the Angels'. It's not great—I hate it—but at least reporters can see what's happening, for the most part.

Most writers there for the Angels' home opener were upset; Scott Miller of Bleacher Report, who is among the nicest and most polite of reporters, swore up a storm on an MLB official's voice mail at one point after a beach ball flew into the box. (A spilled drink on a laptop is every reporter's worst nightmare.)

The Angels PR department, which might be the best in the game, was very helpful in setting up a meeting with team president John Carpino, and John took me around the stadium trying to find a more adequate spot. MLB executive Patrick Courtney flew out to see the arrangements personally, and within a week, the Angels provided a very small box for writers on the broadcast level, with no amenities, not even a TV for replays. It fits about seven or eight people comfortably. But reporters lucky enough to get into the box—it's BBWAA members only—can at least see the plate, even in what is a very bare-bones, cramped spot. With the arrival of Japanese star Shohei Ohtani in 2018, the situation is even worse; many Japanese reporters have been relegated to the press dining room to work, providing them no view of the field at all. They watch the game on an in-house television.

The media-averse Moreno never even bothered to convert the old, terrific press box into a seating area that year. It sat closed, a big thumb in the eye to the press.

* * *

My proudest moment as a BBWAA member wasn't becoming the organization's president, as great an honor as that was. No, my greatest joy came late in 2013, when the *New Yorker*'s Roger Angell was named the Spink Award recipient.

The Spink Award, given by the BBWAA each year for achievement in baseball writing, is presented during the Baseball Hall of Fame's induction weekend in Cooperstown; the recipients of the award are colloquially called "Hall of Famers," because their plaques are displayed in the Hall.

I've been reading Angell's work for more than 40 years, and he's unmatched in almost every fashion when it comes to writing about baseball (or anything else he turns his hand to). Pick up any of his books or look for his work online in the *New Yorker* archives and prepare to be floored by his graceful prose and fascinating character studies. His eye for detail, his lyricism, his mix of the erudite and the conversational—Roger Angell is a national treasure.

Roger Angell of the *New Yorker* speaks after receiving the J.G. Taylor Spink Award during a 2014 ceremony at Doubleday Field in Cooperstown, New York.
(AP Photo/Mike Groll)

As a young reporter, I wondered why Angell had not received the Spink, and when I asked around, I was told that he did not qualify because he never had been a BBWAA member: The *New Yorker* is a weekly publication, not daily, and daily baseball coverage was a prerequisite. (Until the advent of the internet, *Sports Illustrated*'s great baseball writers also were not BBWAA members, for the same reason, which seems crazy. How does a baseball writers' organization not include Roger Angell and Tom Verducci?)

When I mentioned this to the BBWAA's venerable secretary/treasurer, Jack O'Connell, in 2008, however, Jack said, "Spink winners don't have to be BBWAA members. It's just that all of them have been."

I thought, "Well, this will be easy. We've just all thought he was ineligible, time to rectify this injustice, pronto!"

I immediately began lobbying New York writers to nominate Angell for the Spink... and spent four years doing so. Each time, someone from the New York chapter of the BBWAA would tell me, "So-and-so is getting our nomination this year, it's his turn, because last time we nominated this other guy from a different paper." There was already an established pecking order in New York—all newspaper writers. Several people speculated that there was long-standing resentment of Angell because he never had to work with a nightly deadline, he had weeks to write his pieces. ("As if any mere mortal could even approximate what Angell does, given months or even years," I told a few of them.)

Finally, Steve Jacobson from *Newsday* told me he would nominate Angell—and the day before the chapter meeting, Hurricane Sandy hit. Steve's house flooded and he missed the meeting.

Angell had just turned 92 at that point. I was beginning to worry that the greatest of all baseball writers would not get his due in his lifetime. I asked O'Connell if Angell *had* to be nominated by the New York chapter. "Nope," Jack said.

Well, weird as it seemed for the San Francisco–Oakland chapter to nominate the *New Yorker*'s preeminent writer, we set to work. Chris Haft of MLB.com and my husband, Dan Brown, wrote a comprehensive, impeccable bio for the BBWAA's nomination committee to consider and landed Angell one of the three ballot slots.

Voting was held later that year, and on December 10, 2013, at baseball's winter meetings, O'Connell announced that Angell was the Spink winner. I didn't stop grinning all day.

I spoke to my idol by phone that morning—Roger had asked to talk to me, knowing I'd pushed so hard for the nomination. It was difficult not to weep tears of joy while chatting with him. At 93, the best baseball writer of our time—of any time—was finally going to be recognized where he should have been decades before, at the Baseball Hall of Fame.

Dan and I attended the 2014 ceremony, along with the BBWAA cocktail party in Angell's honor, which attracted numerous Hall of Fame players who wanted to pay tribute to Angell, including Bob Gibson and George Brett. We were delighted to spend an hour or so chatting with Angell and his then-fiancée, now wife, Peggy.

"My gratitude always goes back to baseball itself, which turned out to be so familiar and so startling, so spacious and exacting," Angell said the weekend he was inducted. "So easy-looking and so heartbreakingly difficult that it filled up my notebooks and the seasons in a rush. A pastime, indeed."

CHAPTER 17

JONAS RIVERA: THE A'S MOST ANIMATED FAN

Jonas Rivera is the quintessential die-hard A's fan. The Pixar executive, who produced the Academy Award–winning films Up *and* Inside Out, *is from the East Bay. He's the son of Oakland natives, and he's a regular at the Coliseum with his father and with his own children. He even sneaked subtle A's references into* Monsters, Inc. *and the upcoming* Toy Story 4. *In an interview with Ken and Susan at Pixar's headquarters in Emeryville in March 2018, Rivera discussed his lifelong love of the team.*

How did the A's shape your childhood?

I can't think of my childhood without the A's. I was born in '71, just in time for the dynasty. My dad, Mike, was always a fan and has been since the team came to town. As I grew up, I became a really big fan. The time I was really aware of loving baseball and the A's was the Billy Ball era. By then, I'm nine, which is kind of the perfect age. It was Rickey Henderson, Tony Armas, Dwayne Murphy, Mike Heath, and of course Billy Martin. One of my first vivid memories of an A's game was seeing Billy throw a huge fit at second base and seeing him get tossed. We had pretty good seats that day, we were downstairs; Billy came back into the dugout, and I remember seeing things fly out onto the field. I couldn't see the source, we could just see bats and chairs fly out of the dugout. I loved it.

That team was so cool, Rickey and Billy Martin and everyone. When I think about it now, that group seems like a bridge between modern and old-school baseball. So, in a way, I was a kid at the last leg of the old school. Rickey was the first one with the swagger and a kind of new approach. But in my mind, he must have loved being coached by Martin, because Rickey is somehow both old school and new school. I feel really lucky to have grown up around that.

In those days, we didn't have season tickets or anything like that, but my dad always took us to a couple of games a year. Walking into the Coliseum and hearing the games on the radio in those days really defined my childhood.

My son is six now, and he loves going, but he doesn't really get the game yet. He thinks everything is a home run. When you're nine, you lock in and you understand it, I think. For some kids it's earlier, but that's when I really got it.

Did your love of baseball come from your dad?

A lot of it. He loved baseball. He grew up in Oakland before the A's were here and loved baseball, but he liked the Dodgers as a kid. He could get Dodger games on his radio and became a fan. Because of that, I think he developed a very early dislike for the Giants. I completely inherited that from him. I can't stand the Giants, and I pull for the Dodgers in the NL. I'll never understand how anyone in this area can like both the A's and the Giants.

My mom told me the very first baby gift I got from one of my aunts was an outfit with Charlie O. the mule on it. Seared into my childhood is the green and gold, and that mule... then as I started going to games I just fell in love with it. Baseball was a big part of my life, but I never really played it. Honestly, I was never any good at it.... I would play catch and bring my glove to school and all that, but I was never in little league. I sort of regret that. If I could go back in time, I would do that differently, but I think I was too scared or thought I wasn't any good. I loved listening to it, watching it and going there, everything about it, but I never played.

It's sort of like animation, which I obviously love as well without actually being an artist. I always studied animation and knew everything about it—including which animator worked on certain scenes in all the old Disney movies. But I never drew. I came into the animation business as a production person. Anyway, now my son plays baseball and I take him to his little league games in Piedmont, and my wife asks, "Why didn't you play?" I don't have a great answer.

Do you see similarities between the art of baseball and the art of animation?

There is definitely a craft in baseball, a skill. I don't think it's just athleticism. When I see great players, in my mind, it is a little bit like an art form. The real beauty of the game isn't just who is better than who or who can hit the ball farther. It's like a ballet. There's something to it.

There's no doubt some similarities with the art of animation. You don't just write a movie and animate it. Everyone at Pixar has this commitment to what they do. There are a lot of analogies in terms of the teams, the coach and all that.

I think in the actual playing of the game, they're artists. Sports are live theater that never ends. When we make movies at Pixar, we're always asking ourselves: How do we surprise the audience? People always like to tell you that they could see something coming in a movie, and obviously we're trying to prevent that.

When you go to a baseball game or any sporting event, you never know what is going to happen. You may think you do, but you don't know how the game is going to end, and that's what is so great. It's Tuesday night against the Mariners and it's July and they're 10 games below .500, but you still don't know what's going to happen. I get so wrapped up in it as a fan, because it's honestly a different "show" every time.

How does baseball in Oakland relate to the Steve Jobs attitude?

Everything I've ever loved or cared about, I always try to strip it down to its common denominator. There seems to be a renegade/go-the-other-way piece of things that speaks to me.

The A's, to me, are born out of that attitude. This city is born out of that, always in the shadow of San Francisco, and always the underdog. The city of Oakland and the teams here have to fight harder.

Pixar, in my mind, is cut from the same cloth. Especially in the early days. Steve Jobs was all about counterculture and throwing the ball the other way, so to speak. Even his ad campaigns for Apple in those days were "Think Different." That's who he was, and he didn't care what the norms were in the computer business. There's an attitude at Pixar—in fact Andrew Stanton, Pete Docter, and John Lasseter talked about the early days of developing *Toy Story* when they said, "We want to make an animated movie. But let's look at the ingredients of all the Disney animated movies and do the opposite. We're not gonna have songs. We're not gonna have princesses."

Of course, there is way more to it than that, but I thought that was such a cool core guiding principle: Let's do the opposite and still make the best animated movie. There's no doubt in my mind that that's part of the Oakland fabric and DNA and the A's were born out of that. For all of the bad that you could talk about with Charlie Finley—and I'm not defending it—but that's got to be part of it, because he did not care about how he was perceived.

Oakland teams all share that a little bit, which is why it breaks my heart when they leave. I believe they may be miscalculating how important an ingredient Oakland is. I don't think those teams will ever be the same.

I don't think Pixar survives in Hollywood for the same reasons. Pixar was the computer graphics division of LucasFilm back in the '80s when they were playing around with the early days of computer graphics. George Lucas made a conscious decision to move from Hollywood up here, because I think there's something about Northern California, specifically the East Bay, that's renegade.

Bill King is almost the poster child for it. I know all stadiums and all teams have their traditions and quirks, but you hear players talk about Oakland when they leave. I get the sense that people are really heartbroken because it's so unique, even though there aren't a lot of fans at all times. Everyone gets it who is in there. It's blue-collar. I know it's changed, but it's still got that vibe. That's what harnesses the A's. Being a kid and seeing that and feeling that, it fueled a lot of things for me.

What is your personal connection with the A's fan base like?

It's awesome because it's quirky and it's unique. There are a thousand characters who pop into my head. We used to sit out in the left-field bleachers back in high school in the '80s. I recognized the guy with the net who would somehow get every foul ball or batting-practice ball. After a while, people just let him do it. Nobody cared, but you just know that guy.

Everyone that's a real A's fan really gets it. I'm not in right field and in a weird way, I wouldn't even go out there with those guys, because that's their spot. But I love them, and I feel part of it.

When Scott Hatteberg hit the home run, my dad and I were there, and without a doubt, that's the greatest sports moment I've experienced live in my life. Why it was cool, as a fan sitting upstairs: When that happened, it was a good 10 minutes of bedlam. No one wanted to leave. It was like a war had ended. I was hugging people I'd never known or seen. I watched my dad hug this big dude. When does that happen? It was like we had all somehow won that game together. It was also so redemptive, and I think that's why the movie and book are so great. That was the greatest night... people were crying and stuff. It was awesome.

How do you view the generational aspect of baseball?

I don't mean for this to sound so corny, but it was one of the great joys of my life, being able to walk in there with my family when I started making enough money to afford tickets.

After working at Pixar for a few years, I was finally able to get in on some season tickets. It was probably 1998 or so when we started getting the 20ish-game package. My dad and I have been doing that ever since. That's our thing now.

We usually pick the quieter games. I don't pick the Giants and Yankees, I like going when it's a little more mellow. Now I try to bring one of the kids to every game and they love it. They're small, but my daughters love it, too. They're starting to put the game together. To be able to sit there with my dad and my kids is pretty cool. I savor that. We have our routines, and we know where to go. We know where we sit.

I had met [Ken's broadcast partner] Vince Cotroneo through someone here at Pixar. One day, he said, "Come on up." When we got in the elevator and walked down the cinderblock hallway, we were freaking out. In our heads, there was this romance of going back there. It still feels like that whenever I get to pop up to the press level. People do that here at Pixar now, and that gave me a little perspective on why people get excited seeing all of this stuff. I remember walking on the field for the first time and thinking, "I have literally spent my life looking at this."

What was it like watching the star-packed teams in the '80s?

They were larger than life. They were like movie stars. That whole era, I loved it because I was in high school. That's one thing I do miss a little bit in today's game. I love all of the players, but those guys were giants. When you saw Jose Canseco on deck, that's the closest thing I ever felt to Casey at the Bat.

The Bash Brothers, back in the day. (AP Photo/Al Behrman)

It was insane. The color and personality on that team in that window is in my mind unrivaled. It feels like how I imagine the 1927 Yankees or something. It was cool. People jumping on the field to go see Hendu. It was so unique.

I was at the Stewart-Clemens game in the playoffs when Clemens got tossed a minute into the second inning. It just felt larger than life.

I get a little nervous about the moving thing. I want a new stadium. Everyone does, but I also look at the Coliseum and think there's so much history for me and my family in that place. There's something about that off-ramp and pulling in right there.

Have you talked to Tom Hanks about working at the Coliseum?

He's a great guy to talk to. He's a big A's fan. The HBO documentary, *Rebels of Oakland*, was a really great example... whoever did that, they got it. Hell's Angels, Raiders, A's, fights. When I watched it, I went, "Yep, that's it." And Tom is so great in that film!

How do you cope with the disappointment that comes with being an A's fan?

We've had some real hurt. It's hard to even organize them, to be honest. The 2014 wild-card game took me longer to recover from than most of them. That one still stings and I had to really work to regroup after that night.

It's hard to be an A's fan, and there's truth to that. Like most A's fans, I have a little bit of a love-hate relationship with the "Moneyball" thinking. We talk about this at Pixar, too. There's a certain part of it where you just have to turn off the logic and go "Does this feel right? Is this team the right dynamic to make this movie? Are we honoring the right things?" Otherwise, you can math it to death.

If we had done market research, we wouldn't have made *Inside Out*, because the studio would've said, "Well, it's not a princess girl. Is that going to fit in licensing molds?" We kept saying well, we don't know, we hope all of that stuff works, but this is our gut. Bob Iger, to his credit, said, "I like it. Let's try it." We could not prove it in the analytics of movie marketing or distribution that it was going to make any money, and luckily enough, I work for a company that's cool with that.

That's the part of it that I like, when you can balance it. You don't want to make something that's going to not make money or field a team that isn't going to win, but at a certain point, that's why there are coaches. That's why there are producers. That's why there are directors and story artists, because you're trying to get something that people are going to respond to.

I've got to think there's a parallel in a baseball team. Billy Beane would probably laugh in my face, but there is a voodoo and a magic to connections and people and history. There is. In that aggregate comes the fabric of a team.

We don't always guess right. Anyone would be wrong to spike it 100 percent one way. I feel in the modern era, the dial has been set too far over to the logic and math of it, but you'll always lose that argument because it's technically wrong.

I think it's really smart to look at things like pitches per at bat and all of the things that probably did need to be amplified, but when that becomes the rule as opposed to the philosophy…. That's been hard as a fan because you can't sit in Section 212 and say, "Well, we're smarter technically." It's just lame.

When I think about Disneyland, it reminds me of how I felt when I was a kid. When I'm part of these movies, my business is I want to try to create that vibe of going to Disneyland and that feeling that's cemented in me so deeply that I made a career out of it. And when I think about going to the Coliseum and watching the A's play, that's such a part of me. I would be doing everything I could to echo that. What is that? It's not just winning. The championships are part of it, but it's deeper.

I was thinking about sports movies: Every sports movie is about an underdog. The greatest sports movies are about the team who shouldn't win. The movie audience flocks to those and loves those, but yet, in sports, they do the opposite and I've always wondered why. They bandwagon onto the team they know that's going to win. I think that's so dramatically cheap. That's like pulling for Apollo Creed in *Rocky*. You don't do that when you go to the movies. I feel like people are confused. If they thought about the movies they like, that would lead them to all be A's fans.

What was the feeling like to accept the Oscar for *Inside Out*?

It's pretty neat. It's hard to describe the feeling. Growing up loving movies, it's something you never really dream could happen. Then it happens, and it happens fast. You're standing out there and then they rush you offstage. Pete Docter and I are looking at each other like, "What just happened?" We're standing in this hallway backstage with statues in our hands, before they take us to the press room, and the walls are filled with photos of past Oscar winners. It's Scorsese and Shirley Temple. It was surreal.

You get the Oscar without your name on it. They have all the nameplates at the Governors' Ball where the people from the foundry that make them attach the nameplates.

It says *Inside Out*, my name and Pete's name, then it's supposed to say the studio. But ours said "Walt Disney." They said they were going to make us another one because it should say Pixar. But it has my name next to Walt Disney, so I was like, "No, I'm going to keep this one."

CHAPTER 18
KEN KORACH: BROADCAST TIDBITS

You don't spend as much time as I have on the air without messing up plenty of times. I've called home runs that were doubles off the wall and let words slip into a broadcast that were better off not said.

There are two specific instances that stand out. Well, almost three, and I'll get to that a little later.

On Saturday night, July 10, 1993, I was at Camden Yards in Baltimore, working the White Sox broadcast with Ed Farmer, and John Rooney was there, too, for CBS Radio. I never did play-by-play in the fifth inning; I always turned things over to Ed to start the fourth, and he did the fourth and fifth. Only on this day, CBS Radio also was broadcasting the game, and CBS called the fifth its "Hometown Inning." They'd ask the local announcers to join their broadcast, so Ed, representing the visiting team, would do the top half of the fifth, which we discussed before the game.

Parenthetically, the CBS Hometown Inning was legendary in play-by-play circles for its brevity. It was uncanny: This was your big chance on the network, and it was guaranteed that it would be about eight pitches and three minutes and you were done. Mention the CBS inning to any play-by-play person and they'll know exactly what you're talking about. Even today, after a particularly fast inning on an A's broadcast, I'll get a text from our producer emeritus John Trinidad: "CBS!"

So I'm in Baltimore and the top of the fourth ends, and doing the fifth inning was the last thing on my mind. I *never* did the fifth. I decided to take a little walk between innings. I went downstairs to where the writers worked, then I went to the restroom. Totally oblivious.

Upstairs, Ed had walked down to the CBS booth and when the top of the fifth began, the Chicago White Sox Radio Network—30 stations in the Midwest—was a rudderless ship. The only people in the booth were our engineer, Frank Sorentino, and Sox general manager Ron Schueler, who was watching the game from the back of the booth.

Several pitches were thrown and I'm sure to those listening at home and especially to the brass at WMAQ, our flagship station, the dead air seemed like about 10 minutes. It was probably about two minutes before

Rooney, looking over from his booth and noticing the empty chairs, raced over from the CBS booth and picked up the play-by-play. Meanwhile, Sorentino was racing frantically down the hallways of the Camden Yards press box looking for me. I was blissfully ignorant of what was going on, until Frank found me wandering my way back toward the booth.

The first person I saw was Schueler. Ron's a mountain of a man, about 6'4", 250 pounds. On game days, especially, he was strictly business, and this was reflected in his attire: dark blue suit, white shirt, dark blue tie. He only said six words: "Don't ever let that happen again."

I wiped the egg off my face, took back my seat from Rooney, and sheepishly resumed the rest of the inning.

The fallout? I got a call that Monday from Jim Frank of WMAQ. He wasn't upset that I had spaced out. He said those things happen. He was upset that I hadn't called to tell him what had happened. "Mistakes happen," he said. "But you should have called with an explanation, so I would have an answer ready if I got a call from one of the newspapers." Point well taken. Truth is, I didn't call because I figured everybody knew what had happened. But it never hurts to pick up the phone, no matter how embarrassing it might be.

* * *

One game stands out from my basketball days. UNLV played a road game at Cal Poly San Luis Obispo on January 2, 1999, and the Mustangs played at tiny Mott Gym, where a telecast was a rare occurrence. Our TV crew came from all over California that day, and at least one key member of the crew was late. Things were getting frenetic in the production truck as game time approached, and I was bracing for a tough night. Those are the kinds of games where you put your head down and try to tune out the chaos.

We had planned to tape the on-camera open about 15 minutes before the top of the hour. The game was scheduled for a 7:05 tip and airtime was at 7:00 PM. But 6:45 came and went and I wasn't getting much in the way of instruction from the truck, because they were scrambling to get the technology to work. A telecast requires a tremendous amount of coordination because of all the equipment and personnel involved. I was just hoping we'd get the game on the air.

Now it's almost 7:00, and I hear our producer, Vaughn Kilgore, in my headset telling me that we're about to do the open. I recall the clock in the gym saying 6:57.

We start the open, and we're about 30 seconds in when I stumbled over a couple of words, and I said to my broadcast partner, Glen Gondrezick, "I didn't like that, let's do it again." I'm thinking, of course, that we're recording the open. Instead I hear: "[Expletives deleted!] Ken, we're live!" Now, what do I do? All I could do was look into the camera, tell our audience "I'm sorry," and pick up where we left off with the open, which was now becoming the worst open of all time.

I drove home and when I walked in the front door the next morning, our daughter, Emilee, was waiting. "Dad, that was kind of funny what you did last night," she said. At least she thought so!

The moral of the story: Always assume that the open is live even if you think it isn't, and never trust the clock in a gym.

* * *

My first encounter with Mark McGwire came before a spring training game in Phoenix in 1996. It was my first year with the A's and I hadn't spent any time with Big Mac before he hurt his foot running the bases early in the Cactus League schedule during a game in Mesa.

I was working on radio with Bill and Ray, and part of my routine was to head down to the A's clubhouse during the middle of the game to record an interview for the postgame show. Teams normally open their clubhouses to the press around the fifth inning and make that day's starting pitcher available.

On this day, as I walked in I heard a voice yelling at me from across the room. It was McGwire. Now I'm getting nervous because the last thing a rookie announcer needs is to have a problem with the star of the team.

It was clear that McGwire was going to begin the season on the disabled list, and we had speculated on the broadcast, based on information from the A's medical staff, how long Mac might be out of the lineup.

He wasn't happy with that. After he called me over, he said he was pissed at what I said. I said that I was just repeating what we had been told, and he then went into a long explanation about why he hated stuff like that: At this point in McGwire's career the injuries were mounting, and he was tired of the questions and rumors about what was going on.

He told me: "I hate the speculation for a few reasons. If I don't come back when you say I'm supposed to, then people are going to think several things. Number one, they'll say I wasn't trying hard enough to come back. Or they'll say I wasn't being a good teammate and didn't care enough about trying to win or that I'm not tough enough. Putting a timetable on it isn't fair."

I asked him, if he was me, what would he say: "Just say I'll be back when I'm back."

I thought he was being fair and it was a lesson well learned. Today, it bothers me when I hear an announcer say that a player tore his hamstring and he'll be back in three weeks. Every injury is different, every player is different, and the timetables are nebulous. Now I'll hedge by saying, "In the best-case scenario, he might be back in three or four weeks." How many times have you read that a player is supposed to be back in a month and it turns out to be two? Those are times when a little ambivalence is the best approach.

So the 1996 season gets underway and McGwire is on the DL. He came back to the A's in late April and, prickly from what he felt was unfair treatment, he announced that he was not talking to the press.

He found his stride in mid-May and had a huge game in Baltimore on May 25. The A's won 6–3 and McGwire went 2-for-3, homered off David Wells, walked, and drove in two runs. I decided I was going to try and get him for our postgame show. I left our booth—the same one where I had forgotten to do the fifth inning three years earlier—and stopped by the A's TV booth on my way down to the field to check with Ray Fosse. Ray gave me some great advice: "Don't ask McGwire about himself. He hates that. Ask him about the team."

When the game ended, I approached McGwire in front of the A's dugout as he was walking off the field. I asked him if he might have a minute for an interview. He didn't say anything. No facial expression at all. But he walked over to the dugout and sat down about 10 feet from me. I tried to make some small talk and I had a minute or two to try and warm him up since I recorded the interviews and then ran them up to the booth for playback after Bill finished the first segment of the show.

No response from McGwire. I tried to make a little conversation and nothing. He was stone faced. Now my career is passing before my eyes. This is going to be a disaster. If he's going to do the interview, I'm going to get one-word answers. What do I do? Just ask as many questions as I can to fill four minutes?

But I figured I might as well start. I opened the interview with kind of a generic comment about how it was a great win for the A's and he had a great game, but when I turned to McGwire with my microphone, there was nothing. Dead silence that seemed to last for an eternity. Then McGwire broke into a big grin and starting laughing: "It's about time you asked me to come on your damn show!"

I guess it was one of those "rookie, welcome to the team" moments and the rest of the interview was golden. He was expansive and talked glowingly about manager Art Howe and his teammates and how he was having the time of his life with the 1996 A's.

In fact, the interview was so positive that A's owner Steve Schott wanted to cut it up into a commercial. They didn't do that, thank goodness, because I didn't want McGwire to feel exploited, and if I was developing a good working relationship with him, I wanted to keep it going.

McGwire was traded by the A's to the Cardinals in the next summer, which signaled a changing of the guard in several ways. After making the trade, Sandy Alderson turned the reins of the A's over to Billy Beane. It wasn't the best trade the A's ever made, but Sandy had taken a bullet, in a way, for Billy. Billy didn't have to deal with the fallout from dealing McGwire and now he could move on as the team's architect.

Jason Giambi moved to first base, the A's drafted a third baseman named Eric Chavez, and even though it took three seasons after the McGwire trade, they began a run of four straight postseason appearances in 2000.

CHAPTER 19

ALLAN PONT: THE DOCTOR IN THE HOUSE

Dr. Allan Pont is a nationally recognized endocrinologist who was the chairman and chief medical officer of the Department of Medicine at California Pacific Medical Center in San Francisco and who also served as Chief Medical officer. He previously taught at Stanford. Pont, who studied medicine at McGill University in Canada and at Harvard, has been the A's primary team physician for 35 years. Pont chatted with Ken and Susan in the dugout at Hohokam Stadium in Mesa, Arizona, in March 2018.

How did you become a team doctor?

It's somewhat complicated. When I was in Montreal, where I went to medical school, the Expos' doctor was Bob Broderick, one of my mentors, and he asked me to handle games for the Expos in about 1974 when I was still a resident. That was kind of fun, very unofficial.

I left Montreal, and I went to Harvard for three years. After teaching at Stanford for five years, I went to San Francisco, and the Haas family had just bought the A's.

At the time, Charley Finley had 13 doctors covering the team, but Roy Eisenhardt, the new team president, decided the best doctor he could get would be an internal medicine doctor who would then be able to pick all the other specialists.

Roy hired a consultant who happened to know me. He said, "I'd like you to do it," and I said, "Excuse me, I'm a Harvard-trained endocrinologist. I don't know anything about sports medicine."

He said, "Go learn it," and I took the job in 1984. I showed up and met with Sandy Alderson. We agreed that he had no right to be a general manager and I had no right to be a baseball doctor—so we would try it. I've been there ever since. I've probably covered 2,500 games.

Sandy and I had a really good relationship. I think Sandy is one of the smartest people I've ever worked with at many levels. I was always prepared to explain why I was making the decisions I made. I wanted to be questioned. In the old days, I had a closer relationship with the ownership and the manager. Now a lot of that communication goes through the trainers. I used to be able to talk to the press, which I thought was appropriate. Now we can't really do that; I used to enjoy that because I thought there was a right to know in aspects of health.

What do your duties involve?

It was a little bit more time-consuming in the past than it is now. I would go down to Arizona during spring training and do the physicals. I have always been responsible for the major-league players and their families, but I don't do pediatrics. I take care of anyone in the A's employ who wants to be cared for. I did not know the Haas family before I took the job, but I became doctor to many members of the Haas family. And if anyone in the minor leagues was very sick, anything non-orthopedic, I would see them.

My job is to cover the game and/or provide a physician for the game. At the time, we only had one doctor covering the team. We did that for the first 29 years: I would be there for the whole game or I would have someone covering for me.

I accepted the resignation of the 13 doctors that were there. I selected the doctors for our team while understanding that many of the players, for specific orthopedic stuff, would also visit some nationally known experts.

I never pretended to be an orthopedist, I know enough to get by, but I always call the orthopedist if needed during a game. I was taught some very good rules: If it's broken today, it will still be broken tomorrow.

In baseball, the decision of whether you'll go back in the game is really not difficult. If you're too sick to play, you're too sick to play. It wasn't a matter of making instant decisions of whether you had to play or not.

Some people didn't know if I do internal medicine or orthopedics, especially the players. Now it's a little clearer because we have orthopedists there all the time. In the old days, people would say I was the doctor, so they would come to me for everything because I was the only person there.

You show up an hour or half hour before the game. There's a list of people you have to see. You see them and stay through the game. If someone gets a concussion, you're there. You stay for a half-hour after the game to make sure everybody is okay.

How would you describe your duties as an endocrinologist, your day job away from the field before retiring in 2017?

I had a very fun career because I did a lot of things. I did a lot of hospital administration. I developed drugs. I did a lot of science too. I never just practiced endocrinology. Many people who practice endocrinology only see people with diabetes, thyroid disease, etc. I've always had patients with general internal medicine problems. I've always had a group of patients who were my friends or were related to me. I've always had a relatively decent practice in internal medicine.

Because I was the head of a department of medicine at a hospital prior to becoming the chief physician, I had to know medicine—I had to be in charge of the quality of the medicine delivered at that hospital. I spent a huge amount of time trying to make sure I kept up.

My wife, Joan, is a doctor, and we would go to meetings and conferences every year, quiz each other, talk to each other, and discuss medicine. We discussed it enough that my kid never went into medicine.

I developed a drug that treats prostate cancer, Ketoconazole, but I didn't patent it. It was never licensed to treat prostate cancer, but it's still used all the time. Now there's "son of Ketoconazole," which is a derivative and took 20 years to develop. It's pretty effective. The drug was on the market for other purposes, but I discovered a side effect of the drug which we could utilize to treat prostate cancer.

What are some of the more unusual cases you've had with the A's?

We've had several cases of testicular cancer. We've had a case of sarcoidosis, many cases of thyroid disease, a couple of thyroid cancers, a Wolff-Parkinson White, that is a disorder of a heart rhythm.

We've had some issues there. I reviewed all of the cardiograms for the first 34 years, and we would discover problems and send people off to be fixed.

There was a ruptured kidney, which occurred during the 1990 World Series. That was one of my better diagnoses. That wasn't easy: Someone ran into [Eric Davis]. It's very rare, but he got hit. It was in a weird place, and I had him urinate, and there was blood.

We've had people who have been hit in very private parts by baseballs. We've had a case of systemic lupus. [Tim Raines] wasn't feeling good, one thing led to another and we did a lupus exam.

The testicular cancer we discover during physicals as a general rule. The other diseases come up because someone isn't feeling well.

Many of our coaches have had some wild stuff. We've had some cases of acute diverticulitis. We've had cases of acute appendicitis. In 35 years, I think I've seen virtually every disease in the world. We had a heart attack in the clubhouse. I've had a serious case of heart disease in a coach from another team who I had to transfer to a hospital.

We have people examined for skin cancer once a year by a dermatologist. That's very difficult. I'm not a dermatologist. I treat most rashes. If it goes away with simple measures, it's fine. If not, what you learn is to send it someone who can. During the physicals, I look at people's skin. If it's something ugly, I recommend a dermatological follow-up. I examine everyone's mouth, but I'm not a ears-nose-and-throat guy. In reality, oral cancer is a pretty rare disease.

How coordinated is the medical care around the majors?

The league is moving more and more toward that right now. In baseball, we have the doctors' association, which is a very good group. It meets once a year, and there are some pretty heavy hitters, many guys are the heads of various parts of various hospitals or universities.

Gary Green is a very smart guy, and he is the medical director for Major League Baseball. He's a very academic guy. We're doing some new stuff: We obviously have protocols, as they relate to concussions, that have evolved dramatically.

In reality, what the trainers and I do with concussions has really not changed. We've always been very careful. Now, the league and the Players' Association have to be involved.

This year for the first time, they mandated that a cardiologist has to read the cardiograms. We have discussed whether every player needs an echocardiogram, and we have everyone evaluated by a cardiologist. In reality, your chance of finding a cardiac abnormality in a high-level athlete is relatively small, but we look. If anyone has anything that suggests rhythm problems or chest pain, we have an EKG in the clubhouse, we have protocols for resuscitation. The league mandates that we practice once a year at least to be ready.

The most frightening medical issue in recent A's history was in 2012, when Brandon McCarthy was struck in the head by a line drive. What are your recollections of that?

I wasn't at that game because for the first 32 years, I couldn't go to any day games, except on the weekend. When McCarthy got hurt, the doctor who was there called me and I had Brandon transferred to a hospital where I knew the neurosurgeon.

I then arranged to have the right anesthesiologist and the right neurosurgeon. I arranged for a room for the patient. I arranged for the nurse. I arranged for his wife to have a place to sleep in the ICU.

During the procedure, I was called by someone in the room to say that Brandon probably wouldn't make it. There was a lot of damage. People in the room were really, really nervous that he wasn't going to make it. I was not feeling good. I think I had chest pain.

McCarthy's complete recovery was amazing.

I've had other pretty bad injuries on the field. I think Rickey ran into Jason McDonald once. I was stabilizing his head on the field.

We've had some pretty bad concussions. We've had some guys talk to the press while they've had concussions and I've worried that they probably shouldn't.

What's your background with baseball?

Having come from Montreal, where the Montreal Royals played, when I was seven years old, I would take a bus for 12 miles to go watch them play. I even got to watch Jackie Robinson play when he was with the Dodgers in an exhibition game.

I've always been a baseball fan, but I was a Dodger fan. When the A's hired me, I believe you love the one who pays you: I'm a complete

Bob Melvin, trainers, umps, and players surround Brandon McCarthy after he was hit in the head by a line drive off the bat of Angels shortstop Erick Aybar (not pictured) during the fourth inning of a game at the Oakland Coliseum on September 5, 2012.
(Kelley L Cox/USA TODAY Sports)

fanatic. I look at the box score of every game. I create my own All-Star teams throughout the year on my Excel spreadsheets. Every pitch means something to me on a team level.

As a rule, I don't get that close to individuals. I have people I like because they're nice people, but I care about everybody's hits. I do some teaching in other countries now, and last year I was teaching in Fiji and I was able to bring up MLB-TV in Fiji and I was watching MLB on the beach. Literally, I watch every game.

What have been some of the biggest challenges of the job?

The most interesting one was during the steroid era. I was a representative for Major League Baseball to the Olympic Committee because I was the only endocrinologist in all of baseball, so I know a lot about anabolic steroids.

Endocrinology includes hypogonadism, which is men who have low male hormone levels. I have some expertise in that. Because many of the players on the A's were involved or claimed to have been involved, people thought I must be involved in providing these anabolic steroids. I testified before the Mitchell commission for several hours.

It was one of the highlights of my career because I walked in a room and there were eight lawyers. They said, "Now, who's representing you?"

I said, "Nobody, because I have nothing to hide."

I told them what went on, and I pointed out that I could tell who was on steroids. It wasn't that complicated. I think my dog could tell, to be truthful, though I could tell in a more scientific way.

We were not allowed to measure steroids, so I pointed out that I could say to a player that I thought was on steroids, "I have some expertise in this area. I'm more than happy to go through the risks and benefits."

There were obviously some benefits in terms of the ability to play well, although the medical literature said it wasn't proven. It clearly worked: It made players stronger. There also were some dangers.

One hundred percent of the players with whom I spoke, even those with whom I was close, said, "I've never done them." One hundred percent of them denied it.

The Mitchell Commission realized that there was no one involved in medicine in Major League Baseball that had anything to do with the steroids. It was entirely related to outside sources.

What are the responsibilities if a player or team employee is doing or taking something that might have an adverse health effect?

If you thought guys were using some stuff that was dangerous, you really couldn't do much about it. We had one guy who was very depressed and we tried to work with him. We always have had a psychologist. There's a general rule that they don't use the team physician as the person to discuss their home relationships with. My practice is sort of like that too: Except for friends, most people don't sit down to discuss their home life with me.

The steroid testing is administered by the league. We're only involved in the sense that we helped develop the policy. Gary Green is an expert on drug testing. We're not involved in the least.

There was an issue early on when people stopped using amphetamines and they would come in and say they had an attention deficit disorder, and some team physicians would help order ADHD medicine for them.

I said, "We should get the docs out of this. If you say yes, you're a good guy. If you say no, you're a bad guy."

Now we don't even make those decisions. We have experts who make those decisions. I believe doctors should not be judged on patient satisfaction. They should be judged on if the patient gets better. My job is not to make you love me. My job is to help you.

CHAPTER 20

BASEBALL TRAVEL: GOING, GOING, (ALWAYS) GONE

Ken Korach

Anyone who travels with a major league team and complains about the flights and hotels should have their head examined. But that doesn't mean the summertime thunderstorms in the Midwest are saying, "It's the A's charter, we're going to back off now."

That's the only thing I dread. I can handle delays and long flights, but the white-knucklers? I've said many times that there will come a time, after a particularly wild ride, that I'll get off the plane and say, "That's it, I'm done. This is the last year."

Thankfully, that hasn't happened yet, although it's safe to say that on the same day Bob Melvin was hired in 2011, I experienced the worst day of travel in A's history: a brutal, rocking and rolling flight from Baltimore to Chicago that never made it to Chicago. The weather was so bad, we wound up spending the late night and early morning hours on the plane in the calmer conditions of Springfield, Illinois. From there, we were supposed to fly into Midway Airport but were redirected to O'Hare. Director of team travel Mickey Morabito managed to get our buses to O'Hare, but we wound up stuck in morning rush-hour traffic on the Kennedy Expressway.

I was sick as a dog and had lost my voice in Baltimore. Sleep deprivation didn't make it any better, and when I walked into Melvin's office at Comiskey Park (I think they were calling it US Cellular Field back then, but it's always Comiskey to me) and croaked my way into an introduction and told him we had a manager's show to record, I imagine he was thinking: "This guy hosts my radio show?"

The reality is 99 percent of the flights have been great. We travel in style on Mark Cuban's 757 that is outfitted with first-class seats from front to back. We share the plane with the Dallas Mavericks, which works out great since the seasons only overlap early in baseball season, especially if the Mavs don't have a postseason run. Mickey always has options and can find us a backup plane if there is a scheduling conflict.

The plane is our second home. I sit in the back, affectionately known as the "media slum." That's where the radio and TV announcers sit, along with the TV production crew and the A's PR folks. We have the same flight attendants and pilots for every flight, which is a comforting feeling and, unless we're flying home and driving upon landing, there's a glass of Cabernet waiting at my seat when we board.

There are hors d'oeuvres ready when we board, like quesadillas or chicken tenders and cheese and fruit. A printed menu is placed on each seat with the choices for a full meal. There's no shortage of food—you can spend the whole flight eating if you want—and the meals are generally quite tasty.

I'm a great example of how much food is available since my waistline normally expands in proportion to how many games have been played.

The 757 has a compartment up front with a big table between four seats that face each other where the coaches can work on scouting reports for an upcoming opponent.

There are some larger seats in the middle that were designed for the basketball players and Mickey awards them to A's players based on seniority. A second table —just before our section of the place—is home to a nonstop card game.

The short flights are more convenient than the long ones, of course, but short flights are hard to find for the A's. The American League West isn't really a Western division, when you consider that the Rangers and Astros are there. We flew around 55,000 miles in 2017, but the long flights don't bother me much and I've come around to Ernie Harwell's mantra that I've got a good book (or a TV show to watch or a podcast to listen to) and I'm not going to fight it. The flights are some of the most relaxing times during the season, since the phone isn't going to ring and there's no place you need to be.

I've done a lot of writing on the flights. At least half of *Holy Toledo* was written at 35,000 feet.

Unless we're in Toronto going through customs, we never see an airport terminal. The team buses normally leave the park after a road game about 50 minutes after the last pitch and drive right to the plane. Then we have buses waiting at the charter terminal to take us to the hotel after we land.

Most of the time, we'll begin a road trip by flying out immediately after the last home game, even if there is a day off the next day. The A's have the most convenient set-up in baseball. The Oakland Airport is five minutes from the Coliseum and we park our cars right next to the plane. It's one of the things about working for the A's that I've never taken for granted. So many teams have long drives to the airport in their home towns or leave their cars at their ballpark and bus to the airport and then back after a road trip. That can be a major ordeal, but our bags are sitting on the tarmac by the time we de-board and I'm home 20 minutes later.

We stay at first-class hotels and we're spoiled, there's no doubt. I've spent 27 years in the American League, so I've got my favorite spots, and, as Susan mentions, museums and sightseeing are important diversions during the grind of the season. I love walking in most of the cities. I'll substitute a trip to the gym with a long walk, especially once the weather warms up.

The only time the travel gets to me is when I'm not feeling well. Ordinarily, I can work—and have—25 days in a row, but when I'm sick and it's coupled with a bunch of days in a row and long flights and early morning arrivals and maybe an extra-inning game or two—that's when it gets to me. There have been times when I've been absolutely dead tired and wondering why I'm doing this after all these years. But, thank goodness, the rhythm of the season comes back around in my favor and I catch up on sleep and bounce back.

My favorite part of travel is the dinners. There is nothing I enjoy more than a nice dinner after a travel day or day game. Bill King was the greatest dinner companion of all time. You got a glass or two of wine in Bill and the stories started flowing. Those of us who grew up listening to him were enthralled as his memories took us back to our youth and the seasons Bill traveled with Wilt Chamberlain, Rick Barry, Ken Stabler, John Madden, and Co.

Susan and I have had tons of dinners and Mickey and Steve Vucinich are always up for a nice dinner as well. Take Mick to an Italian place with Sinatra playing and white tablecloths and he's in heaven.

The season starts in the Valley of the Sun for spring training. We normally broadcast just the weekend games and I wind up spending around 20 to 22 days every spring in Arizona. It's back and forth for the first couple of weekends, and then I always spend about 10 days to two weeks at the end when it's time to gear up. I've been driving lately from Vegas to Arizona in the spring. The drive through the desert seems to match the relaxed pace of the Cactus League and I'm on board with all the metaphors of how the saguaros bloom like the upcoming season.

We live in Pleasanton—about 20 minutes from the Coliseum—during the season and I've been spending six weeks to two months in the Bay Area in the off-season as well. Denise and I have deep roots in the Bay Area, so it's like being home for us, and I feel a responsibility to the A's to be available if needs arise like speaking at a function or taking part in an A's charity activity during the winter.

My favorite park? I have to say it's Safeco Field in Seattle. First, I love the city. Seattle might be the best walking city in the AL, and there's plenty of stuff to do. Plus, Safeco represents a bit of architectural genius. The retractable roof means there's never a rainout, but the roof is more like a carport that is open on the sides, so you don't feel like you're indoors. You don't get that sterile feeling you had with its predecessor, the Kingdome.

It used to be a huge thrill doing games at Yankee Stadium and the A's have had three postseasons there during my time, including the poignancy of opening the ALDS there only a month removed from 9/11. That was an incredibly emotional and difficult time and baseball provided a needed diversion. The fact the A's won the first two games meant they were on the doorstep of advancing, but Derek Jeter... well, you know that story. The new Yankee Stadium has all the bells and whistles, but the vibe of the old place is missing.

I still love going to Fenway Park. It's the one place left in the league where you can soak in the history and walk the same steps that Ted Williams and so many other legends walked.

Although I've spent almost 35 years on the road, I've been very fortunate to have taken to the travel. Like I said, it's hard to complain when you have people like Mickey and Vuc to make it all run like clockwork.

Susan Slusser

When writers and scouts get together, the bulk of their time is talking baseball, sure. The second most-discussed topic is travel. Scouts, writers, broadcasters, players—we all spend six-plus months of the year on the road, away from home at least half that time. We spend as much time with our luggage as our loved ones.

We're all constantly sharing hotel information and flight tips, finding better rates and smarter routes. Points programs are our great obsessions, lifetime and million-mile status the Holy Grail. If you want restaurant reviews or need a gym recommendation for just about anywhere in the country, ask a baseball scout. Most worked their way up through the organization and they've seen most of the major towns in nearly every state.

It takes a tough constitution to travel more than 50,000 miles a year on commercial airlines. Cancellations, delays, occasional poor or rude service, crowded airports, long lines—it's not for everyone. My husband hated the travel when he covered the Giants, and he got on the beat after spending several years working as an editor. When he was an editor, Dan said, he used to look at a writer's schedule and see "travel day" listed and think, "Oh, it's just a travel day, I can probably get them to also do X, Y, and Z."

Once he became a beat writer, Dan said he realized a travel day can be the worst work day of the week for a writer. (He'll re-attest to that after flight cancellations and bad weather meant he got back eight hours later than he was supposed to following the Warriors' Game 4 win at Cleveland in 2018.) After three years on the Giants, Dan decided he'd had enough. He mostly covered the NFL the next decade and a half, and he likes to say that covering football is like "Club Med compared to baseball." NFL travel is usually four days a month, max, and the workday week can be very short indeed—something that never happens in a sport that has games almost every single day. There are no bye weeks in baseball.

Having covered the NBA for two years, I can say I actually prefer baseball travel, even though there are more games and a longer season. NBA travel is during the winter, flights are cancelled and delayed much more often, half the passengers are sick, and teams are in and out of a city in one day, two at the most. There's often no time to unpack or see friends. It's rush, rush, rush to get to the next flight, the next city, the next shoot-around, and the next game.

At least in baseball, you can find a day in each city for lunch or dinner with friends, which is my favorite part of traveling. I love being able to catch up with loved ones once or twice a year or every six years if they're in an NL city. I know someone in every town the A's play in, from writers and former media members to high school and college friends and many, many cousins.

Like Ken, I also enjoy museums and historical exhibits and if we both have a free day, we'll head out to see some art and get a nice lunch while we're at it. I'd like to say I could pick a favorite, but there is so much to recommend the local art museums everywhere. Boston's Gardner Museum is wonderful, of course the Met and MOMA are spectacular, Chicago's Art Institute is mind-blowing but even the smaller galleries in various cities always have something interesting and different and nearly all have a nice dining experience of some sort. Kansas City's little Nelson-Atkins Museum usually has something unique and the restaurant features locally sourced food and a seasonal menu. Baltimore's American Visionary Art Museum has all sorts of funky folk art. If you're not into art, Baltimore of course has the Babe Ruth Birthplace and Museum, while Kansas City has the Negro Leagues Baseball Museum—both must-sees.

In the old days before Twitter and social media, when writers weren't on call 24/7, I'd occasionally see a movie before a night game, but it's just not possible these days, I'd spend the entire time worried a transaction might be just about to happen. Ken and I will try to attend a play on off nights in New York now and then—attending *Spamalot* on Broadway with Ken and stats expert David Feldman remains my favorite night of theater-going.

The best cities outside the Bay Area, in my opinion: New York, Toronto, Boston, Chicago, Pittsburgh. Best ballparks: Boston, Pittsburgh, Seattle, San Francisco, Minnesota. I won't tell you my least favorite cities, but one of them used to be Houston and since the Astros joined the AL West, it's really growing on me. The downtown is improving all the time, with much more to do and some really superb dining.

When I first became a full-time baseball writer, John Lowe, formerly of the *Detroit Free Press*, told me never to check a bag. I've followed that advice rigorously for 20 years—I'll do laundry in the middle of a three-city trip to avoid checking a large suitcase—and it's allowed me to switch flights at the last second or even change routes if I can fly into San Jose instead of San Francisco when a flight's been delayed or cancelled. I was the only beat writer to make it to Chicago when Bob Melvin was announced as the A's new manager in 2011 for just that reason: Bad weather in Baltimore created havoc with the flight schedules and because I had my carry-on with me, I was able to zip onto an alternate airline. No one else made it, including all the Japanese writers with the team that year covering Hideki Matsui. Melvin must have thought he was inheriting an extremely small press corps that first night.

There is much potential for frustration when you spend this much time traveling commercially. I missed a flight because my cab driver locked his keys in his trunk—with my suitcase. I missed another because I somehow forgot I'd need a passport for a Boston-Toronto trip; it didn't dawn on me until I was at Logan Airport trying to check in that Canada is a foreign destination. The good news: You can get a very pricey same-day passport in Boston in about three hours. I didn't miss the game, but I did get a lot of grief.

The dumbest thing I ever did, travel-wise, was return a car to the wrong airport. I flew into Dallas-Fort Worth, picked up a car there and then forgot I was actually flying *out* of Dallas' Love Field. Returning the car to DFW, walking into the rental-car facility and discovering there were no Southwest flights to Houston was a gut punch. A frantic cab ride to Love Field in rush-hour traffic was unsuccessful. I'm lucky it's a short trip, that Southwest is very cool about missed flights, and that there are flights to Houston every hour.

Susan and Dan at the Coliseum, 2015. (Luis Alberto Torres)

A fellow A's beat writer who will go unnamed to spare her embarrassment once had to pack a suitcase full of dirty laundry to *start* a trip after the team went home for just a weekend series and then hit the road again. She checked into the airport hotel the first night of the trip and did her laundry there. I took a photo as evidence.

A's fans often ask me if someone else books my travel, and the answer thankfully is no—I do everything myself. A local TV crew had a nightmare scenario during an A's playoff series one year when a higher-up at the station booked all the travel and got the dates wrong. They got to the airport and found they had no flights. At least if I make a mistake, and I have, I have no one to blame but myself.

I spend a lot of time checking and rechecking to make sure I'm getting the best rates possible; newspapers can't afford to travel lavishly, as had been common in the 1990s. When I worked at the *Dallas Morning News* in 1995–96, the paper sent more than 30 people to the 1996 Super Bowl. I was one of the few people who didn't go; I took vacation days to avoid having to scratch for the 30th most important story of the day. ("What does the backup long-snapper think about the halftime show?") One of the papers I worked at had an NFL writer who was famous for racking up enormous expenses, spending hundreds of dollars on dinner, ordering the best wine—when I filed expenses for the first time, I asked if there were daily limits and was told, "No, it's pretty much impossible to spend more than that [NFL] guy does." I even had editors back in the flush-with-cash '90s tell me I wasn't eating enough and needed to spend more.

Those days are gone, and I want to make sure the *Chronicle* stays as profitable as possible, so I'm careful about airfare and hotels. I'll stay with friends now and then if rates are outrageous, or I'll find a hotel in the suburbs or at the airport if need be; I stayed in Windsor, Ontario, when the A's played at Detroit in 2018 (a misfire—it's expensive and time-consuming to get over the bridge via cab or ride share before and after games). I try never to fly out the night before a series starts if I can help it—I'd rather have the extra night at home, and I'd prefer to save the paper an extra night of hotel expenses. So I wind up with a lot of 5:30 AM flights, which are truly as awful as you might think but which do have the advantage of rarely being late or cancelled.

I've flown on the A's team plane now and then—going to Japan and to Hermosillo, Mexico; escaping a hurricane one year; occasionally trying to get home a night early—and it's a nice way to travel. First-class seats, lots of food, free Wi-Fi, superb flight attendants.

(As a quick aside, here's another plug for seeing the A's play in Japan, which I also discussed in my book *100 Things A's Fans Need to Know and Do Before They Die.* Tokyo is spectacular, the people are among the best hosts in the world and the baseball experience is like no other—especially when the U.S. teams play Japanese teams in exhibition games. The fans wave flags and sing, women with pony kegs on their backs dispense beer, and the concessions choices are eye-popping. Do it! Also try to make a trip to the Dominican Republic sometime to see how the game is played there—it's a vibrant scene with wildly enthusiastic fans, rum sold in the stands, and delicious food. Colorful doesn't begin to describe Dominican baseball, and it also makes a great excuse to go to the Caribbean during the winter. Cuba is next on my wish list.)

Writers used to fly with the teams all the time; the demands of filing stories after games ended that, for the most part, in the 1980s and '90s, but Frank Blackman of the then-afternoon *San Francisco Examiner* was still flying with the A's in 1999–2000 because he could send in stories any time.

The comfy travel isn't worth it for most of us, though—the paper is still paying for flights, but there's no mileage program on Air Mickey. And we all keep our eyes firmly on that points-program prize.

CHAPTER 21

STEVE VUCINICH: HALF A CENTURY OF INSIDE DIRT

Steve Vucinich, who has been an A's employee since the team moved to Oakland in 1968, is the most celebrated equipment manager in the league because of his lengthy tenure and his friendships with many of the game's biggest figures over the past 50 years. Like so many of the key figures in A's history, Vucinich is an East Bay native, born and raised in Oakland—and the fact he went to St. Joseph High School in Alameda helped get him hired. When Vucinich was in the clubhouse interviewing to become a bat boy and clubhouse attendant, Hall of Famer Joe DiMaggio asked where he went to high school. Upon hearing the response, Joltin' Joe said, "A Catholic. Hire him." Vucinich chatted with Ken and Susan during a road trip at Chicago in June 2018.

What were your first impressions when you started working in the clubhouse in 1968?

I was probably mostly just in awe that the players were just normal, friendly people, guys like Jim Pagliaroni, Rick Monday, and of course Catfish Hunter. I got to know [*Oakland Tribune*] beat writer Ron Bergman because after my third day on the job, he had like four different stories in the *Tribune* about Catfish's perfect game. I got to know the longtime TV announcer Monte Moore—and in the Athletics' way, I learned you shouldn't talk to Charlie Finley unless he talks to you.

At the beginning of the second year, I wasn't sure I wanted to stay because they played a couple of exhibition games in the middle of March against the Cubs and I wasn't clicking with the new people who were working there. Then they changed the equipment manager, I stayed on past Opening Day, and my dad said, "Stick with it, give it a shot."

I did. I've been here ever since.

When did you begin to climb the ranks?

I was the assistant to the equipment manager, still making a paltry five dollars per day, when Frank Ciensczyk came over to the home side in 1969; he had been the visiting clubhouse manager in 1968. I became the visiting clubhouse manager in 1974, and I had to coordinate arrival times and truck times, delivery, unpacking equipment, hiring clubhouse staff, and coordinating meals—although the meal was really just a clubhouse snack at that time. There's responsibility, and if something goes wrong, then you're the guy.

What was your day like back then?

When I took over the visiting clubhouse, I came in at 10:00 AM. I would let the janitors in both clubhouses between 10:00 and noon and I would do the last load of laundry and pass out the uniforms that were back from the cleaners, then I went to lunch.

No players ever came in before 2:00 PM, so it's quite different now when you've got players walking in at 11:00 AM, 11:30 AM for a 7:00 PM game. And games were quicker then—they started at 7:30 or even 8:00 PM, but were only two hours, so I was out of the clubhouse by 11:00 PM, 11:30 at night.

Now that I have an able staff that can finish up, I really don't have any duties postgame other than to supervise everything. Once the last player or coach is gone, I can leave so it's still about a 12-hour day.

At that time, most of the teams landed in Oakland and stayed in Oakland. They'd have a truck pick up both the luggage and the equipment, and they would drop the luggage off at the hotel, which was usually one of the two on Hegenberger. Later, they went to the Hyatt Regency downtown.

The equipment would come in and we unloaded all of the bags first. The wet bags had all of the dirty laundry, uniforms, and so forth—*Get that wash started!* Then we'd wait for the players' individual bags to come down and unpack those. Batboys handled the shoes and made sure they were all clean, bottoms and tops, then we'd pass out the clean laundry and that would be the end of it.

When the team was leaving, the truck would pick up the luggage first, then the equipment after the game. It is so much more detailed now. We carry twice as much equipment, almost twice as many bodies.

What's different in the amount of gear that comes with you?

We used to take two bat bags with maybe two dozen in each bag. Now, every player has his own bat bag with about a half a dozen in it, plus two or three bats that come down to the dugout.

We also carry a lot more balls because guys throw them in the stands. Back in the '70s, if players did that, the coaches would charge them.

We carry more uniforms now. In the '70s, Charlie Finley actually had two road uniforms, but most teams only had one home and one road, both with wool sleeves.

Now, there is so much more, including performance-type wear, long sleeve, short sleeve, three-quarter sleeve, compression sleeves. I'm carrying 10 different types of undershirts around.

There's a lot more equipment. We carry extra helmets because we're moving guys all the time. We've got to have those guys' helmets.

The Royals were visiting one time in 1976, sometime in May, and they came back six weeks later and they had not made a roster change. That's unheard of today.

Between luggage and equipment, we're probably at 11,000 pounds. I would say the luggage is probably maybe 3,500 to 4,000. We provide a gross weight for our flights at the beginning of the season and we don't really need to adjust it much until September, when there are a bunch of call ups.

What are the toughest elements of the job?

The biggest challenge is to make sure you have everybody's uniform. The first thing I do in any series is I go through and make sure everybody has a green and gray jersey. I don't want to be caught off guard. I make sure everybody has their helmet. That's the immediate first-day challenge on the road.

The overall challenge is to get to know the players, get to know their personalities and their quirks, the nuances. Know what they like. Know when to stay away from them. Milton Bradley is an example—there were times to stay away, he could be so explosive. That's the biggest challenge, especially with the turnover of players, is knowing their personalities well enough to know if you can joke around with them.

How have the clubhouse meals changed?

When I started, we had a couple buckets of Kentucky Fried Chicken after the game, nothing before the game. We didn't have batting cages, we didn't have video, we didn't have TVs or stereos and video games in the clubhouse. Players would come in for a 7:30 PM game at 3:30 or 4:00 PM. They'd already had a full lunch. They didn't have anything between batting practice and the game because the visiting team would get through infield at 6:30 PM; they had to run inside, change their uniforms, and come back out.

Now you're required by the CBA to have a meal at noon at home, 1:00 PM on the road. You're required to have a different meal after batting practice, some hot food included. After the game, there's another meal. Because Red Bull is approved by the Players Association, you have to provide that. You have to provide juices.

A lot of the clubs won't allow the team to have soda in the locker room, the players have to bring their own. When I started, we didn't have soda at spring training because it was viewed as a bad thing for your stomach.

The whole nutrition aspect has changed dramatically over my 50 years, especially in the last 15 years, and it's only gotten better and better.

Beer is available on the road because nobody is driving. It's not provided at home, and with the alcohol awareness that's going on in the world now, it's probably a good thing. In the '80s and early '90s, we would put a bucket of beer on each table in the clubhouse and guys would sit around and talk baseball. It wasn't viewed as a bad thing back then, but now it can be so dangerous.

When I worked in the visiting clubhouse, some teams would come in and say no beer. I remember the Angels came in and said, "Two beers for each player," so 50 beers. There have been some abstract rules over the years.

How is the turnaround time between visiting teams coming in or when the A's are going into a city on the road?

A lot of credit goes to the clubhouse staffs whether it's us in Oakland or a visiting clubhouse staff on the road. They know how to get the stuff to the movers and out to the truck. We can direct them and give them times, truck arrival, bus arrival, whatever.

We've done it for so long, and it's important to have the same truck drivers, the same bus drivers. They know our nuances and our timing.

I liken it to a circus or a carnival coming to town. When I ran the visiting clubhouse, the staff would get off work at 3:30 AM after getting one team out, and the next team would just be coming in, so they'd come back at 7:00 AM to start their shift—the Yankees all moved out, the Red Sox all moved in. People always said it was amazing to see a whole team's stuff leave and another team come in overnight—that was us in the middle of that, doing everything.

What goes into postseason clinching celebrations and playoff series clinchers? When do you start setting up the clubhouse, since it has to be done while the game is still being played, and how often is the celebration all set up and not used?

That's one of the biggest headaches there is. We've done that—we had the champagne set up for two games in Oakland in 2001, one game in 2000. You have to be ready and you have to be able to tear it down fast if we don't use it.

Some people say it's a jinx, but you can't put all that plastic sheeting up in 90 seconds. Thankfully, the teams do stay on the field a little longer now if you need to re-set it.

In Kansas City in 2014, with a lead in the wild-card game, we had all the stuff up—so when the Royals came back and tied it, I said, "Let's leave it up there, because it doesn't take long to tear it down. It takes a lot longer to put it up." They scored the winning run and we were ripping it out of there.

The same thing happened the year before. Detroit had a 2–0 lead, but Sonny Gray was pitching a great game… Billy Beane is not like Bob Melvin in terms of superstitions but even Billy didn't want it up too early. Finally, I said, "Billy, we have to put it up." And he said, "Okay, but I don't want any cameras in there." All of a sudden, it showed on our monitors that the camera was on the clubhouse and Billy screamed, "Turn that camera off!" I got a call from Mark Mulder two minutes after that about what a great f-bomb that was on TV.

The best one was 2000 after the division clinch, because we didn't have to fly to Tampa for the extra game. That was the biggest celebration of all. That was bigger than all our World Series celebrations because there are more people involved nowadays, more front-office staff, more media, more personnel on staff. Those celebrations are bigger, but 2000 was the best.

The 2000 A's celebrate on the field after beating the Rangers to win the American League West. (AP Photo/Eric Risberg)

319

Every equipment manager has their list of favorite players, and your all-time Vuc team includes a lot of the game's biggest names. Who's at the top?

Catfish Hunter. Cal Ripken Jr. is on that team, Dwight "Dewey" Evans, Buddy Black, Dave Righetti, Mark Ellis. George Brett—had my wife given birth to a son, he'd have been named Brett Vucinich.

I used to say there are 10 guys on my list, but there are probably more like 25. Mark Kotsay. Ken Holtzman. Holtzman was a veteran with us, he saw how things worked and talked to everyone about things. Dusty Baker. Guys who treated everybody the same, big names who didn't act like it.

What are the biggest misperceptions about the job?

Maybe that we make as much money as the players do. "You work for a ballclub, you must make a ton of money." Don't I wish? But it is a job that once you get it, there are only 30 of them.

You have to like the game. You have to get along with everybody. You have to be open to making changes. There are some guys who refuse to make changes—and they've been changed.

What's the worst part of the job?

The entitlement of the players nowadays is killing me and driving people out, people across baseball. Coaches can be former big-league players who become minor-league instructors for two or three years and they come back to the big leagues and say, "What the hell happened to these players?" I hear it all the time. Their attitudes have changed.

And what's the best part of the job?

Being a part of a team when you're trying to win, that's everybody's goal. In baseball, only one team can win a championship. In business, IBM can be successful and Xerox, but they're not going head-to-head. In baseball, you've got one winner at the end. That's the challenge.

CHAPTER 22
AN IMPROBABLE 2018

Susan Slusser

Much as they did in 2012, the A's went into the 2018 season with no expectations. They'd finished in last place for three consecutive seasons. A .500 record was maybe the best hope for a young, rebuilding team.

And then Oakland began to lose starting pitchers. First, projected rotation member Jharel Cotton went down with a torn ulnar-collateral ligament and required Tommy John surgery. Next was top prospect A.J. Puk, who appeared a logical replacement for Cotton. He, too, needed a UCL repair. Before the A's even had left spring training, they were without two significant starters.

The trend continued throughout the season. Opening Day starter Kendall Graveman, never quite right all year, also wound up needing Tommy John surgery. Sean Manaea, whose no-hitter against Boston on April 21 was the first big highlight of the season, was the ace of the staff most of the year but in August he was shut down with shoulder discomfort. Amazingly, Manaea said he'd been pitching the whole way with a damaged shoulder—even including his no-hitter. He had surgery in September.

Andrew Triggs had surgery for thoracic-outlet syndrome after missing most of the season with nerve trouble in his right arm. Daniel Gossett needed Tommy John surgery. Paul Blackburn, such a promising young member of the rotation in 2017, was out nearly the entire way with forearm discomfort.

How was this team going even to make it to the .500 mark with no starting pitching? The national baseball media downgraded the A's to a likely last-place club again.

The team scrambled to piece together a rotation of available parts that included Trevor Cahill and Brett Anderson, back for their second go-arounds with Oakland; veteran Edwin Jackson, who tied Octavio Dotel's record by joining his 13th different major-league team; and Mike Fiers, who was acquired in a deal with Detroit on August 6.

And somehow, some way, the A's charged into contention.

Oakland's run began on June 16, and at first, few noticed. The A's were 34–36 when things kicked off with a 6–4 win over the Angels, then they began piling up series victory after series victory—including at Cleveland and Houston. It wasn't until the end of July that Oakland dropped a series, and after five weeks of sustained success, it was becoming clear the team might have something special despite the pitching woes.

"I felt like we always thought we were a good team, even at the beginning of the year, we just couldn't finish out some games or weren't getting the big hits when we needed it, but then we kind of started rolling a little bit and rolling and our confidence kept growing, and then we continued to play that way," third baseman Matt Chapman said. "We felt like we believed that was who we were, so it was just us coming out and finally playing the kind of baseball we knew we were capable of."

The A's went a major-league best 63–29 from June 16, two games better than the majors' winningest team, the Red Sox. And no one saw it coming, with the possible exception of shortstop Marcus Semien, who expressed strong belief in the team from the get-go, and manager Bob Melvin, who'd told vice president of baseball operations Billy Beane how much he liked the group assembled during spring training.

So was Oakland a year ahead of schedule with its rebuild?

"The baseball players here are a very talented group," Beane told the *Chronicle*. "We didn't necessarily see it early on that it would come together this quickly, but we played some other teams early in the year and we started hearing from people that thought we had a pretty good team. They'd say, 'This team is going to surprise people with how good they are.'

"I don't want to underestimate these guys, nothing they do surprises me anymore. I don't think they've ever stressed me out—every other team has stressed me out at some point. We didn't have any long losing streaks. We started the season 5–10 and when we took off, we were still around .500 and that seemed totally appropriate. Then they kept on winning and winning and winning, and of course there's a lot of joy there."

Astonishingly, the A's finished the season with 97 wins—their best showing since 2002, all the way back to the days of the Big Three and

Miguel Tejada and Eric Chavez. Their record was the fourth best in the majors, and they wrapped up the second wild-card spot with nearly a week to play.

"It's just been such a fun group," Melvin said. "We had similar results in 2012, where we weren't expected to do a whole lot. We ended up having a great second half, a great last month. So there's some similarities as far as '12 goes. But this group of guys, the mix of the veteran guys, the mix of the guys that Billy and [GM David Forst] brought in, especially the bullpen guys and some of the starters, meshed really well. It's a fun-personality team. We have guys in our organization that are really prideful in being Oakland A's. I think that's important.

"It's a group that literally plays for the guy next to him. I've had instances where I've pinch-hit for a guy, and the guy who's being pinch-hit for is walking off the field high-fiving the guy that's pinch-hitting for him. It's kind of a unique trait as far as the group and how they mesh together and how they support each other. In that respect, it's been as fun a year as I've had."

How did the A's sneak up on everyone? Oakland has always played its best when going under the radar, loves to have a chip on its shoulder, so there was some of that going on, certainly.

"What we were able to accomplish, with nobody believing in us but ourselves, makes it that much sweeter," Chapman said. "We're a real team and that's what real teams do, pick each other up. To everyone else, we're a surprise, but to us, we're not. Marcus reminded me that he told me during spring training, 'We're going to the playoffs,' and we believed him from Day 1. Pretty cool."

Along with that unshakeable self-confidence, Oakland had any number of key contributions, some of them expected (hi, Khris Davis' 40-plus homers and annual .247 average) and some wildly unanticipated. Some of the most surprising highlights:

- The A's had Bruce Maxwell pegged as their everyday catcher, but when Maxwell underperformed during spring training, Oakland decided to look elsewhere. In one of the most major strokes of luck the team enjoyed in 2018, Jonathan Lucroy, a former All-Star, was still available on the free-agent market—and in March. Lucroy became a rock for the pitching staff, especially as starters dropped out of the rotation. He calmly shepherded the staff through every change, always thoroughly prepared and enthusiastic. Despite a mediocre offensive season, Lucroy emerged as a team leader, his work behind the plate proving instrumental in the A's success.

• Ramon Laureano was called up on August 3, a transaction that went almost as unnoticed as the trade that had brought him to the A's the previous fall, a minor-league deal with the Astros after Laureano had a disappointing season at Double-A. Once he came up, Laureano quickly established himself as Oakland's center fielder the rest of the year and for the coming year, pushing highly regarded Dustin Fowler to a corner spot. In just 47 games, Laureano hit .288 with five homers and he led all rookies in outfield assists, with nine, including a tremendous throw at Anaheim on August 11, when he raced deep into the gap in left center for a flyball by Justin Upton,. Jr., then turned and fired to first to double off Eric Young, Jr., on the fly.

"To put it that far with that accuracy? To go 80 feet, to have his back turned, realize what he's got to do and put it on the money? That was next-level," said utility player Chad Pinder, who was in left field at the time.

• Another rookie outfielder made an equally surprising splash. Nick Martini came up for several stints and by September, he had the primary leadoff spot nailed down, showing an ability to put together super at-bats. Martini—signed as a six-year minor-league free agent after never making it up with the Cardinals' organization—hit .296 and contributed some key hits down the stretch, batting nearly .400 the final month. "I texted David one day and said, 'I really like this Martini kid,'" Beane said. "David texted me back, 'Yeah, me too!'"

- Oakland went 14–3 in Jackson's starts, as he gave up more than three runs just three times after joining the team in June. The 34-year-old also endeared himself to the team, like Lucroy, quickly turning into a team leader. "The energy here is outstanding, it's amazing," said Jackson, who enjoyed being with the A's every bit as much as they enjoyed having him.

    The less unexpected heroes of Oakland's season are no less deserving of mention.

- At the top of the list, without a doubt, is Blake Treinen, who had the most magnificent season by an Oakland closer since Dennis Eckersley won the Cy Young and MVP awards in 1992. Treinen's 0.78 ERA was the lowest in major-league history by a pitcher with a minimum of 80 innings and he was the first pitcher in history with 30 or more saves, an ERA below 1.00 and 100 or more strikeouts. Treinen, reacquired from the Nationals in the Sean Doolittle–Ryan Madson deal the previous year, made the All-Star team for the first time and he was the primary reason Oakland was 70–2 when leading after seven innings.

- The A's other All-Star: Jed Lowrie, who, at the age of 34 put together a career year—not just offensively, but in the field, where he was among the top second basemen in the game. He finished with a career high 26 homers and 99 RBIs, and his 4.8 WAR was second only to Chapman's among A's players.

- Chapman, in his first full season, took a step toward becoming one of the top players in the game. The 25-year-old's 8.4 WAR was the third-highest mark in the league, and his defensive numbers were eye-popping: He led the majors in defensive WAR, with a 3.5 mark, and his 29 defensive runs saved were *eight more* than the next man on the list, Andrelton Simmons of the Angels, and 22 more than the next third basemen. The previous year, in just 84 games, Chapman had 19 defensive runs saved, second most among all major-leaguers and just one behind his high-school teammate, Colorado third baseman Nolan Arenado. When the A's played the Rockies in

July, Arenado said of their days at El Toro High School in Orange County, California, "He was my backup shortstop—it's funny, he's probably better than me now."

- Then there is Davis, who quietly amassed the most homers in the game (133) during his first three seasons with Oakland and hit a major-league high 48 in 2018, driving in 123 runs, a career high and second most in the majors. Acquired from the Brewers in 2016 for minor-league catcher Jacob Nottingham and minor-league pitcher Bubba Derby, Davis never has made an All-Star team, but he hit nine more balls out of the park than Giancarlo Stanton over that three-year span. The only player in franchise history with three consecutive seasons with 40 or more homers and 100 RBIs or more? Hall of Famer Jimmie Foxx. Rangers shortstop Elvis Andrus called Davis "the best clutch power hitter in the game," and Texas catcher Robinson Chirinos told the *Chronicle*, "It's hard, man. It seems like we have a good game plan, we get him out a couple of times, and then he makes an adjustment. He's been unbelievable since he came to Oakland. Not just against us—against everyone."

For the fourth year in a row, Davis finished with a .247 average, the first time in major-league history a player has finished with the same average in four consecutive seasons. "I'm kind of speechless," he said. "I don't know, it's just weird.... I'm just kind of shocked. It was meant to be. That's all I got."

Two units stood out all season: The A's bullpen as a whole, with those lock-down numbers after seven innings, and the defense, which was dramatically improved. During Oakland's three years at the bottom of the AL West, the team's fielding was dreadful. In 2018, with Chapman at third full time and Matt Olson at first base for his first full big-league season, the A's shot up the defensive rankings, finishing third overall in FanGraph's assessment, which considers numerous metrics.

Olson's importance can't be overstated: He, too, topped most defensive rankings, and his 14 defensive runs saved were the most among big-league first baseman. The presence of the 6-foot-5 Olson at first certainly helped Lowrie and shortstop Marcus Semien, who both had career years in the field, finishing in the top five at their respective positions.

The combination of a solid bullpen and the top-notch defense—and the team's power, fueled by Davis—helped the A's overcome their rotation issues most of the season. But when Cahill missed time with a back-muscle strain, Anderson was out with forearm discomfort and Manaea was lost to his shoulder injury, the front office began to consider something dramatically different.

Earlier in the year, the A's had faced Tampa Bay when the Rays were using their unusual "bullpenning" pitching plan—scheduling a relief pitcher to work the first inning, then following the reliever with a more traditional starter to begin the second inning. Using this method several times a week, the Rays were climbing the AL East standings and they wound up giving Oakland a good run for the money down the stretch for the second wild-card spot.

Forst told *The Chronicle* in late August that the A's were pondering the same tactic, based on the gaps in the rotation and the fact that an "opener" could mean that the second pitcher in would face the top or middle of the order only two times rather than three times through.

In September, Oakland plunged into the new waters, using reliever Liam Hendriks to "open" eight games in the final month, with mixed results. The starters who followed Hendriks typically were uncomfortable at least the first time they did so, although Daniel Mengden took to the role well after a poor initial outing. The team went 4–5 using openers, including rookie Lou Trivino once when the A's wanted to make sure to get the reliever some work.

There's little doubt the bullpen was Oakland's strength, which only improved at the trade deadline and even beyond, as Beane and Forst and Co. added All-Star closers Jeurys Familia and Fernando Rodney and experienced right-hander Shawn Kelley. Rodney slotted into the seventh inning, Familia in the eighth and Treinen closed games, a wealth of riches for the back end of the bullpen.

So when it came down to the wild-card game against the Yankees on October 3, the A's decided to go with a full bullpen game. Mengden—who had pitched extremely well against New York in September, working 4⅔ scoreless innings and allowing only one hit—was not even on the roster for the game, despite his success entering games in the second inning.

"There's been some trial and error with this," Melvin said the day before the game. "But I think the reason that we started looking at this is because we've had so many injuries in our rotation, and we're just trying to do the best possible thing that we think for a particular day."

The decision was ripe for second-guessing when Hendriks gave up a two-run homer to Aaron Judge two batters into the game. Then, in the sixth, Rodney took over and allowed one run, and his wild pitch put a man at third. Treinen, so spectacular all year, came in—his earliest appearance of the season—with a 1–0 count to Giancarlo Stanton, and he walked Stanton after walking just 21 in 68 appearances during the year.

Luke Voit then put together a terrific at-bat against Treinen, fouling off three two-strike sinkers before lashing a two-run triple to right. In the eighth, Stanton hit a solo homer off Treinen, who'd allowed no more than one run in any of his regular-season outings.

Asked afterward about his unusual role, Treinen said, "We were all kind of prepared for anything. The situation itself wasn't ideal by any means, but we've been so good all year at picking each other up. I just didn't do a good job of executing pitches. I left mistakes up late, and I give them credit for fouling off some really good sinkers.

"More times than not, I think that's going to go in our favor, but Stanton and Voit really did a good job battling off pitches and extending the inning.... Kind of tough to swallow, coming this late in the year."

The A's absorbed criticism in the wake of the game, with bullpenning called into question, but really, the biggest issue in the wild-card game was Oakland's inability to score runs. Oakland didn't even record a hit off Luis Severino until the fifth inning. Both of the A's runs came on Davis' two-run homer in the eighth.

After playing so unexpectedly well for nearly four months, the A's season was over. With the accelerated success for the young core group of players, however, the quick exit did not squelch hopes for the future, only whetting the A's desire for more in the coming years.

"We were happy to be here but we wanted to win and we expected to win, so it is disappointing," Chapman said. "But coming into a season where no one expected us to do anything, what we achieved we should be proud of. I think it's just the beginning for us."

Ken Korach

After the dust settled and Susan and I realized we needed to add some writing about the A's remarkable 2018 season, I wondered if there was a game that best defined what the year was all about. The games tend to run together after you've played 162, but there was one that stood out. It was a game between the A's and the Yankees on September 5, and it's the best example of why the season was so meaningful.

The 2018 campaign marked the 50th anniversary of the A's in Oakland, and Dave Kaval and his staff were intent on making it a celebration. After all, the A's had been to the postseason 18 times and won four World Series in Oakland and the rich history of the team featured colorful characters like Charlie Finley and Billy Martin and some of the greatest players of all-time.

The A's honored their 50th anniversary team, as chosen by the fans, before the second game of the season and, as kind of a bookend, they inaugurated their first Hall of Fame class before that September 5 game against the Yankees.

I had always felt the A's were remiss in not having their own Hall of Fame. There should be a place where a team can honor its greats, even if most of them fall short of making it to Cooperstown. After all, Cooperstown is for the elite of the elite, but that doesn't mean that there aren't so many other people, in uniform or out, who deserve special recognition and a chance to be saluted by the fans.

In the case of the A's, they've had five players who although they also played elsewhere had deep roots with the team and are honored in Cooperstown: Dennis Eckersley, Rollie Fingers, Rickey Henderson, Jim "Catfish" Hunter, and Reggie Jackson. Those five would be part of the A's first class in addition to former owner Charlie Finley and 1989 World Series MVP—and Oakland icon—Dave Stewart.

One can only imagine how difficult the task will be in subsequent years. You can't induct everybody at once, but one would think that players like Campy Campaneris, Joe Rudi, and Vida Blue and managers like Tony La Russa and Dick Williams will be at or near the top of a long list. The A's are forming a committee that will be tasked with the responsibility of making the selections. That will be a tough job, especially because the entire history of the franchise dating back to the Philadelphia days will be considered.

I was honored when the A's asked me to emcee the pregame ceremony from the field at the Coliseum. Eck, Rollie, Rickey, Reggie, and Stew addressed the crowd. So did Helen Hunter, Jim's widow, and Paul Finley, who was there on behalf of his late father.

It was a moving ceremony, and I could sense the emotion swelling in the crowd, especially because the speeches were so genuine. Jackson, never shy about making a grand statement, said the honor meant more to him than his day at Cooperstown. It was a huge thrill to see such an exalted group on the field together, and it felt like a family reunion for the fans and inductees—especially for local guys like Eck, Rickey and Stew.

The game itself encapsulated everything that made the 2018 A's one of baseball's best stories.

- It was fitting that leadoff hitter Ramon Laureano scored the game's first run. For the previous two years, our listeners were probably tired of me talking about how the Houston Astros were running circles around the A's because of a disparity in athleticism. The A's changed that in 2018, and once Laureano was called up from Nashville, he changed things even more. It's hard to win without dynamic players who make an impact, and Laureano quickly emerged as one of those.

• Laureano's run was the first of four the A's scored in the bottom of the first against Yankees starter Luis Severino. The inning was a great example of how the A's were able to grind out at-bats and frustrate opposing pitchers. Jed Lowrie's disciplined approach set the tone all season, and his single drove in Laureano in the first.

The bottom of the first was also a lesson in why it's so instructive to have Ray Fosse in the radio booth when he's not on TV. The bottom of the first was a disaster for Severino and catcher Gary Sanchez, and it afforded Ray the perfect opportunity to break down why the New York battery combined for two passed balls and two wild pitchers. Ray was on fire as he described Sanchez's futile attempts. "The palm of his mitt was down instead of up. He wasn't moving his body laterally. He didn't get down low to block balls in the dirt. He was stabbing at pitches." It was a clinic by Ray.

• Stephen Piscotty's story was the most emotional of the year. A local kid who grew up 20 minutes from the Coliseum in Pleasanton, he had always been on the A's radar, back to his high school days and then to college at Stanford. He quickly became a centerpiece player for the Cardinals after they drafted him the first round in 2012. But his 2017 season was difficult because of injuries and because his mom, Gretchen, was back in the Bay Area battling ALS, also known as Lou Gehrig's Disease. The A's brought Stephen home before the '18 season. They traded some good, young talent to get him, but the Cards' magnanimity also helped to facilitate the deal.

Predictably, Piscotty got off to a tough start; he was hitting .227 at the end of May. His mom passed away early that month and Stephen stayed home with his family while the A's played a series at Yankee Stadium. Then, in a Hollywood scene, he homered in his first at-bat back with the team at Fenway Park. He placed his hand on his heart and glanced skyward as he neared home plate. That one was for his mom, and by the time the season had ended, a flood of homers and RBIs followed, including two RBIs in the September 5 game against the Yankees.

- Matt Chapman's defensive metrics were off the charts all season, and he also led the majors in doubles and the American League in runs and extra-base hits after the All-Star Break. His sixth-inning double keyed another A's rally and sent Laureano home with the A's eighth run.

- Chapman and Matt Olson gave the A's the best defense on the infield corners in the league. And as first-round draft choices playing their first seasons as regulars, the A's and their fans believe they'll be foundational players for years to come. Olson doubled home Khris Davis and scored on one of Severino's wild pitches.

- The A's easily won the game 8–2. Mike Fiers was the winning pitcher. Fiers had been acquired in a waiver deal from the Tigers in early August and quickly established himself as the A's best starter. He was 5–2 with a 3.74 ERA after the acquisition and helped a patchwork rotation exceed expectations.

- The A's record after the game stood at 84–57. More impressive, it was their 50th win after a 34–36 start. The bullpen worked three scoreless innings, which left the A's at 60–0 when leading after seven.

- The game marked the end of a grueling stretch in which the A's played 20 straight days. But despite their relative youth, the 2018 A's displayed a steady, determined professionalism. As Bob Melvin noted after the game in his meeting with the press: "Grinding through the 20 days, it's finally over, in the middle of August, against teams we were matched up against, pretty impressive. I told them that after the game. They play with the same pace every day."

The September 5 game and the entire season were ensemble efforts with so many heroes and, even after another postseason loss in the wild-card game in New York, I'll always look back on 2018 as a nearly perfect and fitting year. The A's celebrated their past, but the present was worth a celebration as well.

ACKNOWLEDGMENTS

Ken Korach

I told myself after writing *Holy Toledo* that it was going to be one and done. But I'm glad Susan approached me with this project, because it's been such a joy to work with her and examine our years with the A's.

It starts before that, of course, and I owe so much to my dad, who instilled the love of sports in me and is still the No. 1 inspiration in my life. To have a father who is 100 and is just as passionate about life as he's always been—it's been amazing, is all I can say.

Susan and I talked quite a bit before tackling the chapter about my mom and she never wavered in her belief that it was a story that should be told. It wasn't easy to write, but it was worth it if the message resonates, and, from my standpoint, there's catharsis every time I write or talk about her. She was an incredible mom—it was just a shorter time.

And, as far as that chapter is concerned, I owe a huge thanks to my first cousin, Susan Camarillo, who not only helped with fact-checking and her own reflections, but, like Susan Slusser, encouraged me to share my feelings and helped me tap into them.

The Oakland A's: I'm just a guy who grew up with Vin Scully and had a dream of becoming a broadcaster. To think I've had 23 years with the same team—I owe so much to them. Not only have they kept me employed all these years, but they've trusted me to tell their story and that trust has meant the world to me. I've never had to look over my shoulder wondering what they were thinking. Their support has been 100 percent. You can't quantify what that kind of freedom means.

I could go through an entire list of A's employees, both past and present, beginning with my broadcast partners Vince Cotroneo and Ray Fosse, but the list would take up too many pages. Suffice to say, it starts with Dave Kaval, Billy Beane, David Forst, the A's execs and owners, and is a mile long from there. On the broadcast side of things, Ken Pries, Warren Chu, Matt Perl, Mike Baird, Robert Buan, John Trinidad, Robert Costa, Scott Pastorino, Roxy Bernstein, Steve Bitker, Chris Townsend, and Marty Lurie and co. have kept things together and their support has been unyielding. And thanks to the A's PR staffs, past and present—thanks for all the info and assistance. Thanks to Kyle Skinner and the social media team for their help with the Twitter poll. And to David Feldman for the history lessons and to the great Lowell Cohn, for his encouragement and suggestions for the "approach" chapter. And to Dallas Braden, for reading much of the manuscript in its early stages and saying he was moved when he read about how his special day moved so many of us.

Thanks to Ted Enberg for being so forthcoming when we talked about his legendary father.

I've written plenty about Bill King, and by now I'm sure most of you know how I feel. He wasn't just a great broadcast partner and friend, but I've come around to the thinking that working with Bill was like playing in a band—where the vibe's energy lifts the music to levels you couldn't attain by yourself.

Dan Brown was an unbelievable editor. Dan is also a great writer and has a special sense of how to convey what good writing looks like to others. It wasn't an easy process trying to juggle two writers and several interviews and trying to coalesce everything into a book. There were times, in fact, where I think it was only Susan who had a feel for all of that. But Dan and I were on the same page throughout, and I assume Dan and Susan were as well. I mean, they're still married, at least last I checked or until Dan beats Susan on another story, which—I think—never, ever happens. The best story we're all going to share is when Susan goes into the Hall of Fame. Mark my word.

Speaking of marriage, Denise and I celebrated number 30 in August of 2018. She likes to say we've been married that long because, really, with all the time on the road it's only been half that time. But truth is, she's never wavered in her support and understanding that this is a little different, especially those years when life on the road meant over 100 days away from home every year. And to have an incredible daughter like Emilee, I'm the most fortunate person on earth. She never knew my mom, but there's a bunch of my mom in her.

Susan and I owe so much to everyone who agreed to be interviewed. We tried to keep the interviews to about a half-hour, but they were all so enthralling that we wound up looking at our watches after 45 minutes or so, wishing we had more time. This all made for a heavy workload for the amazing Allison Mast, who went to great lengths to transcribe everything. And a special nod goes to Bob Melvin, who's put up with me for over 1,000 "BoMel Shows" and is always forthcoming and insightful.

No way I'd still be working for the A's without the support of their fans. This book is for them, and I hope the stories bring back some memories. It's been a wonderful ride, and as Vin used to say, I'm honored that they've "pulled up a chair" to spend part of their summers with me.

Susan Slusser

The biggest round of applause for this project goes to Ken Korach for agreeing to take part just a few years after writing his own *Holy Toledo* book. Ken's knowledge of the A's and his gift for storytelling made him an ideal writing partner. There's a reason he's the best in the business, he's got that magic touch with words. Not many people finish writing a book and say, "Wow, that was fun!" I can—thanks to Ken Korach.

Also making this book possible: our transcription wizard, Allison Mast—thank you, Zak Basch, for recommending her!—and our editors at Triumph, especially Jesse Jordan.

My everlasting thanks to all the reporters, columnists, PR people, scouts, execs, agents and, especially, the players who have helped me over the ages. An enormous thanks in particular to those who contributed interviews for this book—Rickey Henderson, David Forst, Bob Melvin, Steve Vucinich, Mickey Morabito, Clay Wood, Dr. Allan Pont, Jonas Rivera—and to Dennis Eckersley for providing the foreword. Thanks, too, to the Oakland A's organization, especially the PR staff: Catherine Aker, Fernando Alcala, Mike Selleck, Mark Ling and Juan Dorado, and Major League Baseball, particularly Patrick Courtney, Mike Teevan, and John Blundell, as well as BBWAA secretary Jack O'Connell. David

Feldman, as always, earns a special mention for his all-encompassing A's (and pop-culture) knowledge.

I am indebted always to my colleagues past and present, especially *Chronicle* baseball writers John Shea and Henry Schulman and my editor, Janny Hu, *Chronicle* sports editor Al Saracevic and executive editor Audrey Cooper.

My love always to all my friends and relatives, especially the Rev. Michael Slusser, all my RLS and Berkhamsted folks, the Ellin family, the Pate-Zugelders, the Rosenberg-Neuberts, Tracy and Kevin Dennison, Lexi, all my Weller people—Sara Cody!—Curtis Bowden, Rod Searcey, Dean and Sherrie and all the Browns, Stephen St. Germain, my godsons, Michael Gerlach and Dugan Ellin, and my bestie, Christine Winge.

This book never would have been completed without Dan Brown's feedback, and the same holds true for the rest of my life, because Brownie is the one who holds down the fort, feeds the cats, provides numerous airport rides, and makes me laugh, usually intentionally. Thanks, Dan, for allowing the use of snippets of your articles, though the one I most wanted to include was "Manly Men Who Love Taylor Swift." Maybe next time.

31901065205124